Jade Ginty

Religion for Living

Revision Workbook

Connie Duffy

Alpha Press Ltd.

Toda Singh

Contents

(H) = Higher Level.

Section A - Communities of Faith

The *Syllabus Aims* in this section are:

◆ To explore the nature and pattern of human communities.

◆ To identify the characteristics of Communities of Faith/ Churches.

◆ To examine these characteristics as they occur in Communities of Faith/ Churches in local, national and international examples.

Key Concepts in Communities of Faith *(Section A)*

Communities

> **KEY CONCEPTS**
>
> **Community**: is a group of people who share common interests.
>
> **Sharing**: people dividing what they have with others.
>
> **Co-operation**: people's willingness to work together for the benefit of all.
>
> **Communication**: the exchange of information and ideas with other people.

Community

◆ A community is a group of people who share common interests. For example, it might be that they live together in the same place, or work together in the same job, or pray together in the same church.

◆ There are many types of communities,
e.g. a family community,
     a school community,
     a parish community.

Other communities include: a football team, a group of friends, a choir, a drama group, a neighbourhood, a fan club, a basketball team, a youth club, a town, the Catholic Church, the European Union, a religious order.

◆ People belong to a number of different communities at any one time.
To what communities do you belong? Make a list.

Sharing

◆ Sharing is a characteristic of communities.
People divide and share all kinds of things with one another,
e.g. their time,
     their talents,
     their ideas
     their possessions.

◆ The class is an example of a community where people share with each other. Each person in the class is unique and has their own ideas and their own range of gifts or talents.

◆ It is important to be aware of one's own talents. It is equally important to know and appreciate the talents of other people. When people share what they have and what they are good at, the whole community benefits.

Co-operation

◆ Co-operation is a characteristic of communities. When people co-operate they are choosing to work together for everyone's benefit.
Lack of co-operation is a refusal to work with others for selfish reasons.

◆ In a class or a team everyone has a part to play. People rely on each other to play their part to the best of their ability. When that happens, everyone benefits. This is called co-operation.

◆ When people make an effort to get along with each other and help each other out, at home and at school, they are behaving in a co-operative way.
Things get done when people are able to work together. Co-operation is at the heart of all communities including the family community, the school community and the church community.

Communication

◆ Communication is a characteristic of communities. Communication is the exchange of information and ideas that occurs when people talk, listen and pay attention to each other. During a conversation one person speaks, the other person listens. The speaker gives a message. The listener receives a message. Communication is always two-way.

◆ Good communication is essential in any community. When people communicate, they are able to share their ideas. This helps them to get on better with everyone else in the community. Good communication helps people to understand and respect each other better. Everyone benefits.

◆ Communication skills can be learned. People can learn to talk and listen to each other properly. Three communication skills that are easy to learn are:

a. Good body language.

b. Good eye contact.

c. Active listening.

Test Yourself

1. Name four different types of communities. _____

_____

_____

2. Why is sharing an important characteristic of community life? _____

_____

_____

_____

3. Provide examples of co-operative behaviour in a school community or a family community.

_____

_____

_____

_____

4. Why is communication important:

   a. at home? _____

   _____

   _____

   b. at school? _____

   _____

   _____

   c. in the parish? _____

   _____

   _____

   d. among friends? _____

   _____

   _____

Roles and Responsibilities

> **KEY CONCEPT**
>
> **Roles**: tasks that people are expected to perform in a community.

Roles

◆ **Roles** (including leadership roles) are another characteristic of communities. Roles are the special tasks that people are expected to perform as members of a community.

In human communities no one person has all the gifts or talents necessary for an entire community to work effectively. Everyone must co-operate. They must carry out their particular role for the benefit of the rest of the community.

◆ **A school** is an organisation for educating children. Everyone in a school has their own task or particular role to play.

a. List three roles that are vital to the smooth running of any school.

_____

_____

_____

b. What are the responsibilities of those who occupy each of these roles?

_____

_____

_____

_____

◆ **A family** is a small community of parents and children. Being a parent is an important role in any family.

a. What are the responsibilities of parents within the family?

_____

_____

_____

_____

◆ **A team** is a group of people who have skill and talent in a particular sport. Each member of the team has a role or a position and a special job to do. Everyone depends on him/her to do it right.

a. List three different roles/positions on a sports team of your choice.

_____

_____

_____

b. Outline the responsibilities of one person with a particular role on the team.

_____

_____

_____

_____

◆ **A parish** is a community of Christian people who gather together to pray and worship God in their local church. Members have different roles and work together as a team, generously sharing their various talents for the benefit of all.

a. Identify three roles that are important for the celebration of Sunday Mass in a Catholic church.

_____

_____

_____

b. What are the responsibilities of those who occupy these roles at Sunday Mass?

_____

_____

_____

_____

_____

Community Breakdown

> **KEY CONCEPT**
>
> **Community breakdown**: disruption in a group due to poor communication, lack of co-operation and failure to carry out roles responsibly.

Community Breakdown

◆ **The family is an example of a community.** Each family member has certain responsibilities according to his/her age and level of maturity.

◆ Relationships within a family community can sometimes break down. Parents, for example, might want to protect their teenage children by not allowing them to do certain things. Teenagers may think they don't need that kind of protection any more.

◆ This difference of opinion can cause tension in the family. It can result in a temporary breakdown in communication within the family.

◆ All families have their ups and downs. Disagreements arise when parents and teenagers do not see eye to eye on certain matters.

◆ Family relationships can break down due to:
  - poor communication,
  - lack of co-operation, or a
  - failure to carry out roles and duties responsibly.

◆ The mature way of dealing with disagreements is to communicate. Parents and their teenage children can learn to meet each other half way. This is called compromise. Good communication is at the heart of compromise.

◆ Compromise means working together to find an answer to a problem, an answer which is fair to everyone. Solving problems is not easy; it takes time. It means talking and listening to each other. It means trying hard to understand the other person's point of view.

Test Yourself

1. What might be a source of tension:

   ● Within families?_____

   ● Among friends? _____

   ● Among team mates? _____

2. What happens when a breakdown occurs in the relationship between family members, friends or team mates?

   _____

   _____

   _____

3. What steps can be taken to resolve matters when relationships within a community break down?

   _____

   _____

   _____

Exam Questions

---

1. This is a photograph of people sharing in a community of faith. ....2009(O)

    A. Pick **one** thing from this photograph which shows sharing among the people in this community of faith.

    B. Give **one** other example of a way in which sharing can be seen in a community of faith.

    C. State **one** reason why sharing is important for members of a community of faith.

RexFeatures/SIPA

---

2.   Communication ☐   Co-operation ☐   ....2009(H)

    Tick ✓ **one** of the above and explain why it is important for a community of faith.

---

3. A. a. Communication is a characteristic of communities of faith. .... 2003(H), 2011(O)

        True ☐   False ☐   (Tick ✓ the correct box)

    b.   ● CO-OPERATION   ● MISSION   ● SHARING

        Choose **two** of the above and explain a reason why each is important for the members of a community of faith.

    B. a. In all communities people take on different responsibilities.
        Name **two** roles people can have in a community of faith.

        b. Describe what is involved in **each** of the roles in a community of faith that you have named above.

---

4. This is a photograph of an enclosed religious order launching its website. ....2005(H)

    A. Pick **one** thing from the photograph which shows that communication is important for this community of faith.

    B. Give **two** reasons why communication is important for a community of faith.

    C. Give **one** other example of how a community of faith can encourage communication.

The Irish Times

---

5. A. a. A parish is an example of a community. (Tick ✓ the correct box) ....2013(O)

        True ☐   False ☐

    b. ● COMMITMENT   ● COMMUNICATION   ● CO-OPERATION

       Describe the role that **two** of the qualities listed above have within a community of faith.

    B. a. Community breakdown is caused by _____

       b. Describe **two** consequences that community breakdown can have for a community of faith.

Serving Others

KEY CONCEPTS

Service: work carried out to meet the needs of a person or a community.

Commitment: the decision to spend time and energy doing something on behalf of others.

Service

◆ Abraham Maslow has shown that human beings everywhere have the same needs. These needs can be listed in a certain order.

People need...

To feel they are developing their full potential. → **Self Actualisation needs.**

To feel self-confident and respected by others. → **Esteem needs.**

To feel loved and wanted. → **Social needs.**

To feel safe and protected. → **Safety needs.**

To have food, water, clothing, sleep, shelter. → **Physical needs.**

◆ People's human needs are met in the communities to which they belong. Each community provides a unique service for its members. The role of the family community, for example, is to love and care for children and to help them grow up to be responsible adults.

Commitment

◆ Parents show great commitment in caring for their children. They love all of them equally. They spend time, money and effort meeting their children's physical, safety and social needs, as well as their needs for self-esteem and self-actualisation.

◆ The family does a lot for its members, but it cannot do everything. Other communities such as the school, the parish, various organisations and friends support the work of the family.

◆ Many voluntary organisations actively support individuals and families at home and abroad.

  ▸ The Society of St. Vincent de Paul, L'Arche and the Hospice Movement are examples of organisations that provide a service to local communties throughout Ireland.

  ▸ Trocaire and Christian Aid are examples of organisations that assist individuals and families abroad in developing countries.

Test Yourself

1. **a.** What is the role of the family in society? _____

   b. How do parents show their commitment to their family?

   _____

   _____

2. Name one voluntary organisation active in your area: _____

   What service does it provide for the community?

   _____

3. Identify one local, one national and one international organisation.
   What services do these agencies provide for people at home or abroad?

   _____

   _____

   _____

Society of St. Vincent de Paul (SVP)

KEY CONCEPTS

Service: work carried out to meet the needs of a person or a community.

Vision: a vivid dream or mental image of something important.

Leadership: the task of a leader in guiding a group or organisation.

Commitment: the decision to spend time and energy doing something on behalf of others.

OBJECTIVE:
Know the variety of roles within SVP, and the vision that inspires the work of SVP today.

Service

◆ The **Society of St. Vincent de Paul** is an example of a community of faith. It is a Christian organisation that offers friendship and help to people in need.

◆ SVP provides an essential **service** to help people in need in local communities through:

- Home visits.
- Hospital visits.
- Prison visits.
- Holiday breaks.
- Money management.
- Homework clubs.
- Thrift shops.
- Meals on wheels.

Vision

◆ **Frederic Ozanam** founded the SVP in France over 170 years ago. He firmly believed in Jesus' teaching to "love God and love your neighbour as yourself". His **vision** was to actively help people in need like Jesus did.

Leadership

◆ **Leadership** is a characteristic of communities. The role of the leader or director of SVP is to guide the organisation in following the vision of its founder.

◆ The local leader and the members plan and organise the work that needs to be done. SVP volunteers have different roles in the organisation according to their interests and talents. For example, some assist families to budget and manage their money, others organise after-school clubs, while others prepare food for people who are housebound.

Commitment

◆ Today SVP is an international organisation helping people in need in over 100 countries world-wide.

◆ Adults and young people join SVP because they want to put their Christian belief into action. Members make a **commitment** to spend at least one afternoon or evening each week helping the less well off in their community.

Test Yourself

1. What service does SVP provide in the community?

   _____

2. What vision inspired the founder of SVP? _____

   _____

3. What roles do members have in SVP?_____

   _____

   _____

4. What commitment do people make when they join SVP?

   _____

   _____

L'Arche

KEY CONCEPTS

Service: work carried out to meet the needs of a person or a community.

Vision: a vivid dream or mental image of something important.

Leadership: the task of a leader in guiding a group or organisation.

Commitment: the decision to spend time and energy doing something on behalf of others.

Service

◆ **L'Arche** is an example of a community of faith. L'Arche provides an important service to people with intellectual disabilities.

◆ In L'Arche, people with an intellectual disability (the core members), and their assistants, live together in a spirit of friendship.

Vision

◆ **Jean Vanier**, a Catholic layman, is the founder of L'Arche. He believes deeply in Jesus' teaching 'to love God and love one's neighbour as oneself.'

◆ Jean Vanier's vision was to build a community where people could live as Jesus did. He founded the first L'Arche community in Trosly in France in 1964. Today there are over one hundred communities in different parts of the world.

Leadership

◆ **Leadership** is a characteristic of communities. Each L'Arche community has its own leader. The role of the leader is to guide the day-to-day running of the community in following the vision of the founder.

◆ Assistants volunteer to serve in L'Arche. Their role is to live and work alongside the core members in the house, in the garden and in the workshops.

Commitment

◆ Jean Vanier has worked tirelessly establishing L'Arche communities throughout the world.

◆ Assistants make a commitment to live and work in L'Arche for a year, sometimes longer. They join L'Arche because it is a community where Christian values are put into practice on a daily basis.

Test Yourself

1. What service does L'Arche provide for the community?

_____

_____

2. What vision inspired the founder of L'Arche?

_____

_____

3. What roles do members have in L'Arche?

_____

_____

4. What commitment do people make when they join L'Arche?

_____

Hospice Care

KEY CONCEPTS

Service: work carried out to meet the needs of a person or a community.

Vision: a vivid dream or mental image of something important.

Leadership: the task of a leader in guiding a group or organisation.

Commitment: the decision to spend time and energy doing something on behalf of others.

Service

◆ A **hospice** is a place where special care is given to people who have a terminal illness.

◆ The hospice provides a special type of service for people who are terminally ill. The hospice is run more like a home than a hospital. The environment is bright and cheerful. Patients receive pain relief and counselling, and are given relaxing therapies.

Vision

◆ **Dr. Cicely Saunders**, a member of the Church of England, is the founder of the Modern Hospice Movement. Her vision was to help people to die with dignity. She wanted each person to be treated with love and kindness so they would feel at peace near the end.

Leadership

◆ Leadership is a characteristic of communities. The Director is the leader of a hospice community. His/her role is to ensure that the hospice runs smoothly on a day to day basis, and that it operates according to the vision of the founder.

◆ Doctors, nurses, counsellors, chaplains, therapists and volunteers have important roles in the organisation. All offer care and respect to every patient.

Commitment

◆ Hospice staff work hard to provide a high level of patient care. They make a commitment to:

  ▶ create a homely atmosphere in the hospice.

  ▶ treat everyone with love and respect.

  ▶ help each person to die with dignity.

Test Yourself

1. What service does the hospice provide for the community?

_____

_____

2. What vision inspired Dr. Cicely Saunders to develop hospice care for the dying?

_____

_____

3. What roles exist for patient care in a hospice?

_____

_____

4. What is the level of commitment to patient care in a hospice?

_____

Section A - Communities at Work

Exam Questions

1. Communities of faith work locally and nationally. ....2006(O)

    A. a. Name **one** community of faith that you have studied which works either locally or nationally.

        b. Outline the work done by the community of faith you have named above.

    B. Explain **one** way in which the needs of people are being served in the work done by a community of faith.

    C. Explain how any **one** idea of the founder / earliest followers can be seen in the work of a community of faith.

---

2. Read the following notice about a community of faith and answer the questions that follow. ....2004(O)

THE INTERNATIONAL GOSPEL CHOIR

We are a group of people from all over the world who meet for worship every week.
We sing, dance, praise the Lord, and try to follow the example of Jesus in our daily lives.

Choir leader: Ben Neilson
Lead singer: Johanna Colby
Lead musician: Jake Harpur
Chaplain: Helena Corscadden

Next Event: *Charity Concert in aid of the homeless*
                Sunday 27th June 2004
Venue: See local press for details

    A. Briefly outline the inspiration for this community of faith.

    B. There are many roles within this community of faith, name two roles.

    C. Describe how the work done by this community of faith might affect people who are not members of it.

---

3. Fill in the following information for a Church or religious organisation or order associated ....2004(O)
with a world religion you have studied.

    A. Name of Church or religious organisation or order.

    B. Inspiring vision.

    C. Work.

    D. Roles.

---

4. a.   COMMITMENT ☐   RESPECT ☐   ....2010(O)

        Tick ✓ **one** of the words listed above and outline what it means in a religious tradition.

    b. Describe **one** example of how *either* commitment *or* respect can be seen in the work of a community of faith that you have studied.

5. Imagine that you are writing a piece for a school magazine about the way in which .... 2011(H)
a community of faith is organised. Outline what you would write about the
organisation of a community of faith under the following headings:

i. COMMUNICATION

ii. VISION.

NOTE: *This is an essay question.*

---

6. This is a photograph of a religious sister serving the needs of others. .... 2007(O)

Veritas

A. Pick **one** thing from the photograph which shows that this religious sister
is serving the needs of others.

B. Name **one** example of a community.

C. Suggest **one** reason why people need to be part of a community.

---

7. Outline how a community of faith you have studied shows a sense of:. ....2007(H)

i   Commitment.

ii Vision.

NOTE: *This is an essay question.*

World Religions

KEY CONCEPT

Religions: organisations that express belief in God or gods through prayer, worship and a way of life.

Religions

◆ Five major world **religions** that express a belief in and worship God or gods are: Hinduism, Judaism, Buddhism, Christianity and Islam.

◆ Each religion is also referred to as a community of faith.

Hinduism

- Began 4,500 years ago.
- There were many Gurus (teachers) but the exact founder is unknown.
- The Vedas is the sacred text.
- The mandir is the Hindu place of worship.

Judaism

- Began 4,000 years ago.
- Abraham and Moses are the founders of Judaism.
- The Tanakh is the sacred text.
- The synagogue is the Jewish place of worship.

Buddhism

- Began 2,500 years ago.
- Siddhartha Gautama, later known as the Buddha, is the founder of Buddhism.
- The Tipitaka is the sacred text.
- The temple is the Buddhist place of worship.

Christianity

- Began 2,000 years ago.
- Jesus Christ is the founder of Christianity.
- The Bible is the sacred text.
- The church is the Christian place of worship.

Islam

- Began 1,500 years ago.
- The prophet Muhammad is the founder of Islam.
- The Qur'an is the sacred text.
- The mosque is the Muslim place of worship.

Test Yourself

1. Link the **founder** to the religion:

Jesus ○	○ Hinduism
Buddha ○	○ Judaism
Prophet Muhammad ○	○ Buddhism
Abraham and Moses ○	○ Christianity
Founder unknown ○	○ Islam

2. Link the **sacred text** to the religion:

The Tipitaka ○	○ Hinduism
The Bible ○	○ Judaism
The Qur'an ○	○ Buddhism
The Vedas ○	○ Christianity
The Tenakh ○	○ Islam

3. Link the **place of worship** to the religion:

Church ○	○ Hinduism
Synagogue ○	○ Judaism
Mandir ○	○ Buddhism
Mosque ○	○ Christianity
Temple ○	○ Islam

4. Link the **founding date** to the religion:

1,500 years ago ○	○ Hinduism
2,000 years ago ○	○ Judaism
2,500 years ago ○	○ Buddhism
4,000 years ago ○	○ Christianity
4,500 years ago ○	○ Islam

Christianity

OBJECTIVE:

Retell the story of the founder and earliest followers of Christianity.

KEY CONCEPTS

Founder: the person who established a community or an organisation for a special purpose.

Inspiring vision: a dream or idea so powerful it motivates people to act on it.

Sacred text: a book of holy or sacred writings of a community of faith.

Gospel: the Good News of the life, death and resurrection of Jesus Christ in the New Testament.

Revelation: the way in which God chose to make himself known to human beings.

Founder

◆ **Jesus of Nazareth** is the founder of Christianity. Jesus lived about 2,000 years ago.

◆ Jesus' mother Mary was a young Jewish girl who lived in the village of Nazareth. An angel told her she would have a baby, and would name him Jesus. Her child would be the Son of God.

Inspiring Vision

◆ When he was thirty years old, Jesus went to be baptised by John the Baptist in the River Jordan. There Jesus had a vision of God's great love for the world. He felt called to go and tell everyone about it.

◆ Jesus became a travelling teacher. For almost three years he went from place to place preaching, teaching and working miracles. A small group joined him and became his disciples.

◆ In the last week of his life Jesus and his disciples shared **The Last Supper**, their final meal together.

On **Good Friday**, Jesus was crucified and died on the cross. His body was placed in a tomb.

On **Easter Sunday** morning his friends went to the tomb and found it empty. Jesus appeared to them. God had raised Jesus from the dead. This is called the resurrection.

Sacred Text/ Gospel/ Revelation

◆ **The Bible** is the Word of God. It is the sacred text of Christianity.

◆ The story of Jesus is written in the first four books of the New Testament. This is the Gospel, it means 'good news'. The Gospel tells the Good News of the life, death and resurrection of Jesus Christ.

◆ The Gospel is an account of revelation, the special way in which Jesus himself shows or reveals to us what God is like.

Test Yourself

1. What do you know about the founder of Christianity?

_____

_____

_____

2. What inspired Jesus to become a travelling teacher?

_____

3. Why do you think Christians have such a high regard for their sacred text?

_____

_____

Judaism

KEY CONCEPTS

Founder: the person who established a community or an organisation for a special purpose.

Inspiring vision: a dream or idea so powerful it motivates people to act on it.

Sacred text: a book of holy or sacred writings of a community of faith.

Revelation: the way in which God chose to make himself known to human beings.

Founder

◆ **Abraham** is one of the founders of Judaism. He lived about 4,000 years ago and is called the patriarch or 'Father of Judaism'.

◆ Abraham and his wife Sarah lived in the city of Ur, they had no children. Although people at that time worshipped many different gods, Abraham worshipped one God.

Inspiring Vision

◆ Abraham had a vision, he felt God was calling him to leave everything and go on a long journey. Abraham, a man of great faith, travelled all the way from Ur in the east to the land of Canaan in the the west. God promised him land and many descendents and guided him safely to the 'Promised Land'.

◆ God made a **covenant**, a sacred promise, with Abraham. God promised to look after Abraham and his descendants forever. In return, Abraham promised that his people would worship God and obey God's laws.

◆ God kept his promise and in their old age Abraham and Sarah had a baby boy, named Isaac. They had many descendants. Abraham's descendants settled in Canaan and worshipped one God.

Sacred Text / Revelation

◆ The story of Abraham's journey of faith is told in a sacred text called the **Torah**, which is part of the **Tenakh**, Judaism's sacred text. The Torah is written on scrolls in the Hebrew language.

◆ Today the Torah is read aloud at Jewish religious services. The Torah is an account of revelation, the special way in which God made himself known to the Jewish people.

Test Yourself

1. What do you know about the founder of Judaism?

_____

_____

_____

_____

2. What inspired Abraham to go on a long journey to an unknown land?

_____

_____

3. In which sacred text would you find the story of God's revelation to the Jewish people?

_____

Islam

KEY CONCEPTS

Founder: the person who established a community or an organisation for a special purpose.

Inspiring vision: a dream or idea so powerful it motivates people to act on it.

Sacred text: a book of holy or sacred writings of a community of faith.

Revelation: the way in which God chose to make himself known to human beings.

Founder

◆ The religion of Islam began 1,500 years ago. **The prophet Muhammad** is the founder of Islam.

◆ Muhammad grew up in Arabia in the Middle East. He was a successful businessman in the city of Mecca, but became troubled by the corruption and injustice that existed there.

Inspiring Vision

◆ Muhammad went alone to pray and fast in a cave in the hills outside Mecca. One day, something special happened, he had a vision - an angel of God spoke to him. The angel told him that there is one God, Allah, and Muhammad is his prophet.

◆ The angel's words to the prophet were later written down in a sacred text called the Qur'an.

◆ Muhammad began to preach in the streets of Mecca. He told everyone to believe in one God, Allah, and to be honest and live good lives.

◆ Muhammad was eventually forced to leave Mecca, so he travelled to Medina. This journey, called the Hijra, marks the beginning of Islam. Muhammad later returned to Mecca and established a shrine to Allah in the centre of the city. Mecca then became the holy city of Islam.

Sacred Text / Revelation

◆ The story of the prophet and the Word of Allah are written in the **Qur'an**, the sacred text of Islam.

The most important event in the story of Islam is the revelation of the Word of Allah to Muhammad through the messages of the angel.

Test Yourself

1. What do you know about the founder of Islam?

_____

_____

_____

2. Describe the vision that inspired Muhammad to change his life.

_____

_____

3. Name the sacred text of Islam and say why it is treated with reverence by the Muslim community.

_____

_____

Christian Communities of Faith

◆ A **community of faith** is a group of people who share the same religious beliefs and practices. Christianity is an example of a community of faith.

Denomination

◆ Christianity consists of a number of different denominations, each having its own leaders and a distinctive set of beliefs and practices. Each denomination is referred to as a community of faith.

◆ The main divisions within Christianity are:
  ▶ The Roman Catholic Church.
  ▶ The Protestant Churches.
  ▶ The Orthodox Churches.

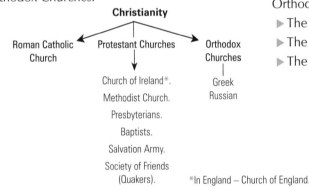

Christianity

Roman Catholic Church — Protestant Churches — Orthodox Churches

Church of Ireland*.
Methodist Church.
Presbyterians.
Baptists.
Salvation Army.
Society of Friends
(Quakers).

Greek
Russian

*In England – Church of England.

Faith/Belief

◆ Christianity is one of the great world religions.
  ▶ Jesus Christ is the founder of Christianity.
  ▶ The religion of Christianity is based on the life, death and resurrection of Jesus.
  ▶ The Bible is the sacred text of Christianity.

◆ All Christians share the same basic faith/belief. They:
  ▶ Believe in God.
  ▶ Follow the teachings of Jesus.
  ▶ Accept the Bible as the Word of God.

◆ However, Roman Catholic, Protestant and Orthodox Christians have different beliefs about:
  ▶ The leadership of the Church.
  ▶ The number of sacraments.
  ▶ The meaning of the Eucharist.

Test Yourself

1. Explain the meaning of the term 'denomination'.

2. What are the three main parts or divisions within Christianity?

3. What religious beliefs are shared by all Christian people?

Divisions in Christianity

KEY CONCEPTS

Church: a community of Christian people.

Identity: the distinct characteristics by which an individual or group is recognised.

Church

After Jesus' death and resurrection, the apostles spread the Good News, and the Christian Church grew and expanded for over 1,000 years. Then difficulties arose that resulted in two major divisions within Christianity and the emergence of:

1. The Orthodox Churches.
2. The Protestant Churches.

The Great Schism

◆ In the 11th century a dispute about Church leadership took place that divided Christianity in half. It was called 'The Great Schism'.

◆ In the West the **Catholic Church** followed the leadership of the Pope in Rome.

In the East the **Orthodox Churches** followed the guidance of the Patriarch of Constantinople.

The Reformation

◆ In the 16th century, Christianity divided again. **Martin Luther** protested about corrupt practices that had developed in the Catholic Church and called for change. He also rejected Church teaching on the sacraments and the authority of the Pope. This was The Reformation, and the beginning of the **Protestant Churches**.

◆ In England, people separated from the Catholic Church and formed the Church of England. Luther's ideas spread and other groups took the protest even further. They formed the Presbyterian Churches, Baptist Churches, the Society of Friends (also called Quakers), the Methodist Church, the Salvation Army and many others.

Identity

◆ Each Christian Church has a unique identity, or distinct characteristics, by which it is recognised.

◆ A Church's identity is expressed in:
   ✣ The way it is organised; its form of **leadership**.
   ✳ Its style of **worship**.

Some Christian Churches

The Roman Catholic Church

✣ The Pope is the leader of the Catholic Church and has authority over the Catholic Church throughout the world.

The archbishop, bishops and priests lead the Catholic community.

✳ Catholics attend Mass and receive Holy Communion every Sunday.

The Orthodox Churches

✣ The Patriarch of Constantinople is the most senior bishop but does not have full authority over individual Orthodox Churches.

A Patriarch, bishops and priests lead the Orthodox community.

✳ Orthodox Christians attend Divine Liturgy and receive Holy Communion every Sunday.

The Church of Ireland

✣ The Archbishop of Canterbury is the senior bishop in the Anglican Communion but does not exercise overall authority.

The Archbishop, bishops, priests and deacons lead the Church of Ireland community.

✳ Members of the Church of Ireland attend church on Sunday where Holy Communion is celebrated in most parish churches.

The Methodist Church

✛ The Methodist Church in Ireland is part of the World Methodist Council. There is no overall leader.

There are no bishops or archbishops. Ministers and lay preachers serve the Methodist community.

✳ Methodists attend church on Sunday where the Bible, the preacher's sermon and hymn singing is the focus of worship.

The Society of Friends (Quakers)

✛ The Society of Friends has no overall leader. There are no bishops, priests or ministers, and there are no sacred buildings.

✳ Friends attend a meeting house on Sunday. Sitting together in silence until someone feels God wants them to speak, is the main form of worship.

Test Yourself

1. What was the outcome of:

   a. The Great Schism? _____

   _____

   b. The Reformation? _____

   _____

   _____

   _____

2. What form of leadership exists in:

   a. The Catholic Church? _____

   _____

   b. The Orthodox Churches? _____

   _____

   c. The Church of Ireland? _____

   _____

   d. The Methodist Church? _____

   _____

   e. The Society of Friends? _____

   _____

3. What is the main form of Sunday worship in:

   a. The Catholic Church? _____

   b. The Orthodox Churches? _____

   c. The Church of Ireland? _____

   d. The Methodist Church? _____

   e. The Society of Friends? _____

The Catholic Church

OBJECTIVES:

State the titles and names of leaders in the Catholic Church.

Explain how Roman Catholics express their religious commitment.

KEY CONCEPTS

Church: a community of Christian people.

Inspiring vision: a dream or idea so powerful it motivates people to act on it.

Religious commitment: the decision to make a sincere effort to put one's religious beliefs into practice.

Preaching: to speak out and explain a religious truth and urge people to act on it.

Church/Inspiring Vision

◆ The Catholic **Church** is a community of Christian people who share the same faith in Jesus Christ. The person and preaching of Jesus is the **inspiring vision** that motivates the work of the Church today.

◆ Leadership roles in the Catholic Church:

▶ The **Pope** is the leader of the Catholic Church throughout the world. Catholics believe he is the representative of Jesus Christ on Earth. The Pope is the bishop of Rome and lives in the Vatican.

▶ **Cardinals** are chosen by the Pope. They give advice to the Pope on important Church issues.

▶ An **Archbishop** is a very senior bishop. The Archbishop of Armagh is the leader of the Catholic Church in Ireland.

▶ A **Bishop** is the leader of the Catholic Church in a diocese. The role of the bishop is to preach and teach the Catholic faith in the diocese.

▶ **Priests** are men ordained by the bishop to work in parishes. The parish priest is the leader of the Catholic community in a parish. His role is to celebrate Mass and the sacraments and to preach the message of Jesus.

▶ **Lay people** are baptised Catholics who are not ordained. Some serve in the parish church as Ministers of the Word or Ministers of the Eucharist.

Religious Commitment

◆ Catholics show their **religious commitment** and put their beliefs into practice by attending Mass on Sunday, celebrating the sacraments and living good Christian lives.

◆ Confirmation is the sacrament through which Catholic teenagers make a religious commitment to put their Christian faith into practice.

Preaching

◆ An important part of the role of the bishop and the priest is to **preach** the Word of God in the diocese and the parish. They speak out and explain the teachings of Jesus and the Church and urge Catholics to act on it.

Test Yourself

1. What are the titles and names of a local, national and international leader in the Catholic Church today?

Title: _____ Name: _____

Title: _____ Name: _____

Title: _____ Name: _____

2. What is the role of a bishop in the Catholic Church?

_____

3. How do Catholic lay people show their religious commitment?

_____

_____

The Orthodox Churches

KEY CONCEPTS

Church: a community of Christian people.

Inspiring vision: a dream or idea so powerful it motivates people to act on it.

Religious commitment: the decision to make a sincere effort to put one's religious beliefs into practice.

Church/Inspiring Vision

◆ The Orthodox Churches are communities of Christian people who share the same faith in Jesus Christ.

◆ The life and teaching of Jesus is the inspiring vision that motivates the work of each Church.

◆ Leadership roles in Orthodox Churches:

▶ **Patriarchs** are the leaders of the Orthodox Churches; there is one for each country. The Patriarch of Constantinople is the most senior although he does not have full authority.

▶ **Bishop** - a bishop leads the Orthodox community in a diocese.

▶ **Priest** - a priest is ordained to lead the Orthodox comunity in a parish.

▶ **Deacon** - deacons assist the priest in a parish.

Religious Commitment

◆ Orthodox Christians show their religious commitment, and put their beliefs into practice by attending Divine Liturgy on Sunday, celebrating the sacraments and living good Christian lives.

◆ Every child in an Orthodox Church receives three sacraments when he/she is eight days old. At the Christening the baby is Baptised, is Confirmed and receives Holy Communion.

◆ Inside an Orthodox church, the altar is behind a large screen decorated with icons. An icon is a picture of Jesus, Mary or the saints. On Sunday, at Divine Liturgy, the doors of the icon screen are opened and the priest celebrates the mystery of the Eucharist at the altar.

Test Yourself

1. What is the title of the leader of an Orthodox Church   (i) in each country.   (ii) in each parish.

   _____

   _____

2. How do Orthodox Christians show commitment to their religious beliefs

   _____

   _____

   _____

3. What is distinctive about the interior of an Orthodox church?

   _____

   _____

The Church of Ireland

OBJECTIVES:

State the titles and names of leaders in the Church of Ireland.

Explain how its members express their religious commitment.

KEY CONCEPTS

Church: a community of Christian people.

Inspiring vision: a dream or idea so powerful it motivates people to act on it.

Preaching: to speak out and explain a religious truth and urge people to act on it.

Religious commitment: the decision to make a sincere effort and put one's religious beliefs into practice.

Church/Inspiring Vision

◆ The Anglican Communion is the Church of England spread throughout the world. It is a community of Christian people who share the same faith in Jesus Christ.

◆ Anglicans in Ireland belong to the Church of Ireland. The life and teaching of Jesus is the inspiring vision that motivates the work of the Church.

◆ Leadership in the Church of Ireland.

▶ The **Archbishop of Canterbury** is based in England. He is the senior bishop in the Anglican Communion world-wide, but does not exercise overall authority.

▶ The **Archbishop of Armagh** is a leader of the Church of Ireland. Although the Church of Ireland is part of the Anglican Communion, it is self governing.

▶ A **bishop** is the religious leader of a diocese. Bishops preach the Word of God and manage religious affairs in the diocese.

▶ A **priest** ordained in the Church of Ireland is called a rector. His/her role is to celebrate Holy Communion, preach from the Bible and look after the religious life of members of the parish.

▶ A **deacon** is a person who is training to be a priest. He/she assists in the parish.

▶ A **lay reader** is trained to preach sermons and lead religious services such as Morning and Evening Prayer.

Preaching

◆ An important part of the role of the bishop and the rector is to preach the Word of God. Bishops and priests speak out and explain the teaching of Jesus and urge people to act on it.

Religious Commitment

◆ Members of the Church of Ireland show their religious commitment and put their beliefs into practice by attending church services, celebrating the sacraments and special occasions, and living good Christian lives.

◆ Confirmation is a special occasion when Anglican teenagers express their commitment to the faith, and become grown up members of their Church.

Test Yourself

1. What is the title and the name of the senior bishop in the world-wide Anglican Communion?

   Title: _____ Name: _____

2. What is the title and the name of a national leader in the Church of Ireland?

   Title: _____ Name: _____

3. How do members of the Church of Ireland show their religious commitment?

   _____

   _____

   _____

The Methodist Church

OBJECTIVES:

State the titles and names of leaders in the Methodist Church.

Explain how its members express their religious commitment.

KEY CONCEPTS

Church: a community of Christian people.

Inspiring vision: a dream or idea so powerful it motivates people to act on it.

Preaching: to speak out and explain a religious truth and urge people to act on it.

Religious commitment: the decision to make a sincere effort to put one's religious beliefs into practice.

Church/Inspiring Vision

◆ The Methodist Church is a community of Christian people who share the same faith in Jesus Christ. The life and teaching of Jesus is the inspiring vision that motivates the work of the Church.

◆ Leadership in the Methodist Church.
There is no single leader and there are no bishops in the Methodist Church.

  ▶ **President** - A new President is elected every year at a meeting called the Annual Conference. The President guides the Methodist community in Ireland for that year.

  ▶ **Ministers** - Men and women are ordained in the Methodist Church. Their role is to preach, celebrate the sacraments and guide people in their faith.

  ▶ **Lay Preachers** - some lay people are trained to preach and to lead Sunday worship. They do not celebrate the sacraments.

Preaching

◆ An important part of the roles of the minister and the lay preacher is to preach the Word of God. Ministers and lay preachers speak out and explain the teaching of Jesus and urge people to act on it.

◆ There is also great respect for the sermons of John Wesley, the founder of Methodism.

Religious Commitment

◆ Members of the Methodist Church show their religious commitment and put their beliefs into practice by attending church services, celebrating sacraments and special occasions, and living good Christian lives.

◆ Confirmation is a special occasion when Methodist teenagers express their commitment to the faith and become adult members of their Church.

Test Yourself

1. What is the title of the leader of the Methodist Church in Ireland?

   _____

2. What is the role of either a minister or a lay preacher in the Methodist Church?

   _____

   _____

3. How do members of the Methodist Church show their religious commitment?

   _____

   _____

   _____

Religious Orders

OBJECTIVE:
Explain what a vocation is, and identify the vision that inspires the life and work of one religious order.

KEY CONCEPTS

Founder: the person who establishes a community or an organisation for a special purpose.

Vocation: a feeling of being called by God to serve others.

Inspiring vision: a dream or idea so powerful it motivates people to act on it.

Mission: the specific work carried out by members of a faith community.

Founder

◆ The Missionaries of Charity is a religious order founded by **Mother Teresa**. It is a community of faith that works at local, national and international level.

Vocation

◆ As a young woman Mother Teresa felt she had a religious vocation. She felt God was calling her to serve others in a special way, so she became a Catholic nun. She went to live in India where she saw the suffering of the poor at first hand.

Inspiring Vision

◆ Mother Teresa had a dream, a vision. She wanted to follow Jesus and his teaching by serving the poorest of the poor.

◆ In 1950 she became the founder and the leader of the **Missionaries of Charity**.

Mission

◆ Mother Teresa's mission began among homeless people in the city of Calcutta. The work of the Missionaries of Charity was to search the city streets and find people who were sick and destitute. The sisters cared for them in their 'Home for the Dying'. They also set up health centres and started classes for children and adults.

◆ The Missionaries of Charity live as a community. They take vows of poverty, chastity and obedience and work among the poorest of the poor in cities throughout the world.

◆ Those who join the order are inspired by the life of Mother Teresa, the founder, and the way she followed the example and the teaching of Jesus.

Test Yourself

1. What inspired Mother Teresa to found the Missionaries of Charity?

   _____

   _____

   _____

2. What kind of work is undertaken by the Missionaries of Charity?

   _____

   _____

3. How does the work of the Missionaries of Charity benefit people in the community?

   _____

   _____

Exam Questions

---

1. A. Tick ✓ **one** of the following major world religions you have studied: .... 2008(O)

    Buddhism ☐   Christianity ☐   Hinduism ☐   Islam ☐   Judaism ☐

    a. Name the founder/earliest followers of the world religion you have ticked above.

    b. Outline a story from the life of *either* the founder *or* earliest followers of a world religion you have studied.

B.   ▲ Commitment   ▲ Communication   ▲ Co-operation

    a. Choose **two** of the above and give an example of how each can be seen in a community of faith today.

    b. Explain why **one** of the above is important for a community of faith today.

---

2. A. a. Dr. Yaakov Pearlman is the name of a leader associated with a .... 2012(H) community of faith in Ireland. Name **another** leader associated with a community of faith in Ireland.

    b. Being a leader is one part that a person can play within a community of faith. Describe what is involved in **two** other roles that people can have within a community of faith.

    c. Explain **one** reason why having a variety of roles within a community of faith is of benefit to its members.

B. a. In religious traditions the term 'revelation' refers to the will of the divine/God/gods becoming known. (Tick ✓ the correct box)

        True ☐   False ☐

    b. Outline an example of how revelation can be seen in the story of **one** of the following major world religions:

        BUDDHISM   CHRISTIANITY   HINDUISM   ISLAM   JUDAISM

---

3. A. Describe the work being done today locally or nationally by a church, religious organisation, ...2004(H) or order associated with a world religion.

B. Outline **one** way in which the work described above helps people to live as a community.

C. Outline **one** way in which the work described above reflects the founding story of the world religion you have selected.

---

4. This is a photograph of some leaders of communities of faith in Ireland. .... 2003(O), 2005(O)

    A. Give the titles of any **two** leaders associated with communities of faith in Ireland

    B. Imagine you are the leader of a community of faith in Ireland. Briefly describe your role.

The Irish Times

5. A. a. An Archbishop is a religious leader associated with the Church of Ireland. ....2012(O)
   (Tick ✓ the correct box)

   True ☐   False ☐

   b. Describe what is involved in the work done by a leader in a community of faith.

B. a. Explain **two** reasons why leadership is important for a community of faith.

   b. ☐ INSPIRING VISION   ☐ RELIGIOUS COMMITMENT

   Tick ✓ **one** of the above and outline an example of how it can be seen in the work done by the members of a community of faith today.

---

6. A. a. Name **one** religious leader associated with a community of faith in Ireland. ....2010(H)
   b. Describe **one** example of the work done by a religious leader in a community of faith in Ireland.

B. a. ● COMMITMENT ● PREACHING

   Describe what is meant by each of the above terms in a community of faith.

   b. Explain **two** reasons why *either* commitment *or* preaching is important for the members of a community of faith.

---

7. This is a photograph of a person preaching during a religious service. ....2013(O)

A. Pick **one** thing from this photograph which suggests that the person is preaching during a religious service.

B. A pulpit is a place associated with preaching. (Tick ✓ the correct box)

    True ☐   False ☐

C. State **one** purpose that preaching can have within a community of faith.

(Source:www.anglicantaonga.org.nz)

---

8. a. Name **one** community of faith that exists in Ireland today. ....2009(O)

   b. Explain **two** reasons why belonging to a community of faith could be important for a person.

---

9. A. Name a Church or a religious organisation or a religious order found in present day Ireland, ...2006(H) and outline two ways in which its beliefs influence the way of life of its members.

B. a. Outline **one** challenge that a Church **or** a religious organisation **or** a religious order faces in Ireland today.

   b. Briefly outline how the beliefs of the church **or** the religious organisation or the religious order you have named above could help its members to deal with this challenge.

---

10. Profile **one** community of faith in Ireland today that you have studied using the following headings: .2009(H)

   i. Inspiring Vision.

   ii. Ministry.

   NOTE: *This is an essay question.*

11. A. A vocation can be described as a calling to serve in a community of faith. ....2009(O)
(Tick ✓ the correct box)

        True ☐   False ☐

B. Outline what is involved in **one** example of a vocation in a community of faith that you have studied.

---

12. A a. In religious traditions what does the term 'vocation' mean? .... 2008(H)

    b. Outline **two** ways in which people live out their vocation in a community of faith you have studied.

B. a. Describe **two** things that inspire the religious commitment of members in a community of faith you have studied.

    b. Explain why **one** of the above is important for a community of faith today.

---

13. This is a photograph of a religious sister comforting a death-row prisoner. .... 2003(H)

A. State **one** thing from the photograph which suggests that the sister is comforting the prisoner.

B. Give **two** reasons why a religious person would work with prisoners in this way.

C. Suggest **one** positive effect this work could have on the prisoner.

Saint Mary's Press

---

14. This is a photograph of a person living out a religious vocation. .... 2013(O)

(Source:theinnerkingdom. wordpress.com)

A. Pick **one** thing from this photograph which suggests that the person has a religious vocation.

B. A religious vocation can be described as a calling to serve God and others. (Tick ✓ the correct box)

        True ☐   False ☐

C. State **one** way that a religious person can live out his/her vocation other than the way shown in the photograph.

---

15. A. a. The name of a Christian denomination found in Ireland today is _____ .... 2014(O)

    b. Describe **one** example of how religious commitment is shown today by the members of the Christian denomination that you have named above.

B. a. The Augustinians are an example of a religious order found in Ireland today. (Tick ✓ the correct box)

       True ☐   False ☐

    b. RELIGIOUS ORDER ☐   RELIGIOUS ORGANISATION ☐

    Tick ✓ **one** of the above and outline an example of how its members are dealing with a challenge that it faces in Ireland today.

Sectarianism

OBJECTIVE:

Outline the implications of sectarianism in Ireland and elsewhere, and explain the meaning of tolerance.

KEY CONCEPTS

Sectarianism: hatred of people because they belong to a different religious group.

Religious conflict: a clash or struggle between different religious groups.

Tolerance: allowing everyone to have their own religious beliefs and practices.

Sectarianism/Religious Conflict

◆ When people in an area belong to a different religious group they can become a target for verbal and physical abuse. This behaviour is called sectarianism. Hatred of people's religious beliefs fuels sectarianism.

◆ Sectarianism can result in acts of violence that cause great suffering. In **Northern Ireland**, for example, over three and a half thousand people were killed since 'The Troubles' began in 1969.

◆ A breakdown in the relationship between different communities of faith has led to religious conflict in many parts of the world. Such a clash, or struggle has taken place in:

  ▶ Northern Ireland: between Catholics and Protestants.
  ▶ Israel: between Jews and Muslims.
  ▶ India: between Hindus and Muslims.
  ▶ Chad: between Muslims and Christians.
  ▶ Former Yugoslavia: between Christians and Muslims.

◆ The cause of sectarian conflict in any country is deep and complex. However the consequences are the same everywhere; there is hatred, tension and divided communities.

Tolerance

◆ Tolerance is the key to solving sectarianism. The problem of sectarianism needs to be addressed not by violence but through:

  ▶ Communication: begin to talk, listen and have respect for other people's point of view.
  ▶ Education: learn about other people's beliefs and way of life in order to understand them better.
  ▶ Government: make laws to stop unequal treatment of different groups.

◆ Tolerance is about respect and allowing people to have their own religious beliefs and practices without interference from others.

In Ireland, the **Glencree Centre for Reconciliation** in Co. Wicklow was set up to build bridges between the Protestant and Catholic communities in Ireland, North and South.

In Northern Ireland, the **Corrymeela Community** in Co. Antrim was set up to promote tolerance between the two faith communities in the North.

Test Yourself

1. What is sectarianism?

_____

2. What are the consequences of sectarianism and religious conflict?

_____

_____

3. What is religious tolerance and how is it cultivated?

_____

_____

Ecumenism

KEY CONCEPT

Ecumenism: a movement to help the Christian Churches become more united.

Ecumenism

◆ All Roman Catholic, Protestant and Orthodox Christians have faith in God, follow the teaching of Jesus and believe the Bible is the Word of God. However, they have different beliefs about Church leadership, the sacraments and the meaning of the Eucharist.

◆ Ecumenism is a movement to help the Christian Churches become more united. It helps Christians to focus more on what unites them, instead of what divides them.

◆ Ecumenism aims to:
promote respect, understanding and co-operation between all the Christian Churches.

Activities that promote Christian unity

◆ Christians from all Churches now co-operate more with each other, they:

▶ Pray together, e.g. during the Week of Prayer for Christian Unity in January.

▶ Join together to raise awareness about justice issues, e.g. during Lent.

▶ Fundraise together for charity.

▶ Share each other's church buildings when the need arises.

▶ Attend ecumenical services on different occasions. An ecumenical service is a joint act of worship that Catholics, Protestants and Orthodox Christians attend together.

Places that promote Christian unity

◆ **Corrymeela** is an ecumenical community in Northern Ireland. It was founded by Rev. Ray Davey to help members of the Protestant and Catholic communities to meet and understand each other better.

◆ **Taize** is an ecumenical community in France. It was founded by Brother Roger Schultz as a place for Christians of all traditions, Catholics, Protestants and Orthodox to meet and pray together.

Organisations that promote Christian unity

◆ **The World Council of Churches** is an international organisation set up to promote unity among Christians. In Ireland inter-Church meetings are held to increase understanding and respect among members of different Christian Churches.

Test Yourself

1. What is ecumenism? _____

2. Is Christian unity a good idea? Explain your answer.

_____

_____

_____

3. Describe an example of ecumenism in action.

_____

_____

_____

_____

_____

Inter-Faith Dialogue

OBJECTIVE:
Explain the meaning of
inter-faith dialogue.

KEY CONCEPT

Inter-faith dialogue: open and honest discussions between the major world religions.

Inter-Faith Dialogue

◆ The five great world religions are:
  ▶ Christianity ▶ Judaism ▶ Islam
  ▶ Hinduism ▶ Buddhism.

  Each religion is a community of faith.

◆ Inter-faith dialogue involves leaders and members of the different world religions meeting and talking about their religion. Partners respect their own beliefs, and learn to understand and respect the beliefs of others.

◆ Inter-faith dialogue aims to:
  ▶ Promote contact between the major world religions.
  ▶ Build trust between people of different faiths.
  ▶ Develop respect and tolerance for different points of view.
  ▶ Prevent religious conflict.

Activities that promote inter-faith dialogue

◆ **World Day of Peace**
  In 1986, 1993 and 2002, Pope John Paul II invited leaders from the religions of Christianity, Judaism, Islam, Hinduism and Buddhism to meet together for a day of prayer for world peace.

◆ **Inter-faith Services**
  Inter-faith services take place in schools and local communities. On special occasions Christians, Jews, Muslims, Hindus and Buddhists gather together to pray, each in their own way.

Organisations that promote inter-faith dialogue

◆ **The Council of Christians and Jews** was set up in Britain and Ireland to promote good relations between Christians and Jews.

◆ **The Three Faiths Forum** was set up to establish links between Christians, Jews and Muslims in Ireland. Dialogue is also being developed with the Hindu and Buddhist communities.

Test Yourself

1. What is meant by inter-faith dialogue?

   _____

2. What is the difference between inter-faith dialogue and ecumenism?

   _____

   _____

   _____

3. Describe an example of inter-faith dialogue in action.

   _____

   _____

   _____

   _____

Exam Questions

1. A. (i) Hatred of another person because of his/her religion is (Tick ✓ the correct box.) ....2007(O)

Ecumenism ☐   Humanism ☐   Sectarianism ☐

(ii) Describe **one** example of people being in conflict because of their religion.

B. (i) Describe **one** example of people working to build respect for the beliefs of others.

(ii) Give **two** reasons why people work to build respect for the beliefs of others.

---

2. a. In religious traditions the term 'sectarianism' refers to _____ .... 2005(H), 2013(H)

b. Examine **two** ways that the lives of people can be affected by sectarianism.

c. Describe **one** example of how unity between Christians is being encouraged in Ireland today.

---

3. A. a.   ● COMMITMENT   ● COMMUNICATION   ● SHARING ....2008(H), 2010(O), 2014(H)

Choose two of the above and describe how each can be seen in a community of faith today.

b.   COMMUNITY BREAKDOWN ☐   LACK OF CO-OPERATION ☐

Tick ✓ **one** of the above and explain why this would be a challenge for the members of a community of faith.

B. a. 'The Pope' is one example of a title that is given to a leader in a community of faith in Ireland today.

Name **another** title that is given to a leader in a community of faith in Ireland today.

b.   ● COMMUNITY BREAKDOWN   ● LACK OF CO-OPERATION

Suggest how the leader of a community of faith could address the challenge posed by **one** of the above.

---

4. This photograph is from a newspaper article describing how people from different Christian ....2005(O) denominations in Westport, Co. Mayo, are using the same church building for religious services.

A. Explain how sharing the same church building as described above is a good example of community life.

B. a. What is ecumenism?

b. In what way is the sharing of the same church building as described above an example of ecumenism?

C. Outline **one** other example of ecumenism.

Irish Independent

---

5. A. a. In religious traditions the term 'ecumenism' refers to _____ ....2011(H)

b. Describe **one** example of ecumenism that you have studied.

c. Explain **two** reasons why ecumenism is important for members of a community of faith.

B. a. Within a religious organisation or denomination the term 'community breakdown' refers to _____

b. Outline **two** ways in which community breakdown could be prevented within a religious organisation or denomination.

6. This is a photograph of religious leaders at an ecumenical service. .... 2006(O), 2008(H)

   A. Pick **one** thing from the photograph which shows that this is an example of ecumenism.

   B. Give **one** other example of ecumenism.

   C. State **two** reasons why people work for ecumenism.

www.comece.org

7. This is a photograph of people gathering for inter-faith dialogue.. .... 2004(H), 2006(H), 2011(O)

www.santegidio.org

   A. Pick **one** thing from this photograph which suggests that it is an example of an inter-faith gathering.

   B. Give **another** example of inter-faith dialogue.

   C. State **one** reason why the members of a community of faith take part in inter-faith dialogue.

8. Examine the work being done by a community of faith found in Ireland today to promote .... 2014(H) dialogue between different major world religions using **each** of the following headings:

   i. The inspiration for the work.

   ii. The impact of the work.

   NOTE: *This is an essay question.*

9. The principal of a local primary school has asked you to talk to the 6th class pupils .... 2010(H) about the importance of inter-faith dialogue for communities of faith. Outline the points that you could develop in the talk you would give using the following headings:

   i. The benefits of inter-faith dialogue.

   ii. The challenges associated with inter-faith dialogue.

   NOTE: *This is an essay question.*

10. Examine what is involved in **two** ways of promoting dialogue between different .... 2013(H) major world religions in Ireland today.

   NOTE: *This is an essay question.*

11. A. Briefly describe **two** ways members of communities of faith in Ireland .... 2003(O) could try to work for ecumenism or inter-faith dialogue.

   B. Give **one** reason why working for ecumenism or inter-faith dialogue is important.

Catholic Church Leadership

OBJECTIVES:
Identify different styles of leadership in human communities.

Recognise the connection between leadership and authority in the Roman Catholic Church.

KEY CONCEPTS

Leadership: the task of a leader in guiding a group or organisation.

Authority: the power given to an individual or group to make important decisions.

Ministry: special duties performed by priests, ministers and lay people to serve God and the Church.

Service: work carried out to meet the needs of a person or a community.

Leadership

◆ **Leadership** is a characteristic of communities. There are three basic styles of leadership in human communities.

▶ **Authoritarian**
The leader decides everything and tells the group what to do, without asking their opinion.

▶ **Enabling**
The leader motivates and helps the group to make its own decisions.

▶ **Consultative/ Democratic**
The leader brings an idea to the group and seeks their opinion on it. The leader listens to their suggestions, then he/she makes a final decision.

Leadership in the Catholic Church

◆ The Catholic Church is a community of faith that believes in Jesus Christ and follows his teaching. Its leaders guide the Church at local, national and international level.

The Pope - Is the leader of the Catholic Church throughout the world.
- Is the direct successor of St. Peter the first leader of the Church.
- Has full authority over the Catholic Church.

Cardinals - Are the most senior bishops in the Catholic Church.
- Elect a new Pope.
- Are chief advisers to the Pope.

Archbishops - An archbishop is the senior bishop of the Catholic Church in a country. The Archbishop of Armagh is the Primate of all Ireland. (Primate means senior bishop.)

Bishops - A bishop is the leader of the Catholic Church in a diocese. There are twenty seven diocese in Ireland, each with its own bishop.
- The bishop's role is to preach and spread the Catholic faith in the diocese.

Priests - Are ordained by a bishop to lead the Catholic community in a parish.
- Celebrate Mass and the sacraments.
- Preach sermons on the Gospel and explain Church teachings.

Lay people - Are baptised persons who are not ordained.
- Some are Ministers of the Word, and Ministers of the Eucharist at Mass.
- All serve God at home, at work and in the community.

The Pope
Cardinals
Archbishops
Bishops
Priests
Lay People

Structure of Leadership in the Roman Catholic Church.

Authority

◆ Authority is the power given to an individual or group to make important decisions that affect the lives of others. The Pope and the bishops have the power to make important decisions that affect the lives of Roman Catholics.

◆ **The Magisterium** is the teaching authority of the Church. It consists of the Pope and the bishops who have the authority to guide the faith and morality of Catholics.

  ▶ The teachings of the Catholic Church are written in:
  - The Papal Encyclicals.
  - The Catechism of the Catholic Church.
  - The Documents of Vatican II.

Ministry/Service

◆ Priests follow the example of Jesus in their daily ministry by guiding the Christian community in the parish, and bringing them to God.

◆ The priest serves the needs of the parish community in Jesus' name. It is his role to:

  ▶ Celebrate Mass.

  ▶ Celebrate the other sacraments.

  ▶ Give witness to the love of God.

  ▶ Work with the parish council.

Test Yourself

1. Identify the following leaders in the Roman Catholic Church:

   ○ Our parish priest - _____

   Name the parish: _____

   ○ Our bishop - _____

   Name the diocese _____

   ○ The Archbishop - _____

   ○ A Cardinal - _____

   ○ The Pope - _____

2. Describe the structure of leadership in the Roman Catholic Church?

   _____

   _____

   _____

   _____

3. What kind of authority do the Pope and bishops have in the Catholic Church?

   _____

   _____

   _____

4. What style of leadership do you associate with the Catholic Church?

   _____

5. What is the role of the Catholic priest in a parish?

   _____

   _____

Protestant Church Leadership

KEY CONCEPTS

Leadership: the task of a leader in guiding a group or organisation.

Authority: the power given to an individual or group to make important decisions.

Leadership

◆ Leadership is a characteristic of communities. The Church of Ireland and the Methodist Church are communities of faith in the Protestant tradition.

The Church of Ireland

◆ Members of the Church of Ireland believe in Jesus Christ and follow his teaching. Its leaders guide the Church at local and national level.

▶ **Archbishops** The Anglican archbishops of Armagh and Dublin are the leaders of the Church of Ireland.

▶ **Bishops** There are twelve diocese in the Church of Ireland; each diocese is guided by a bishop.

▶ **Priests** Men and women are ordained to serve the spiritual needs of the parish community by:
- Preaching and leading Sunday worship.
- Baptising new members, and being present at significant moments in people's lives.

▶ **Deacons** - assist in the parish as part of their training to be ordained ministers.

▶ **Lay readers** - are appointed to lead certain forms of worship such as Morning and Evening Prayer.

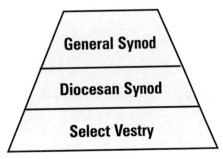

Structure of leadership in the Church of Ireland

Authority

◆ Authority is the power given to an individual or group to make important decisions that affect the lives of others.

◆ The General Synod is the ruling body of the Church of Ireland. It comprises bishops, ministers and lay people. It meets once a year to make important decisions about issues of concern to the Church.

The Methodist Church

◆ Members of the Methodist Church believe in Jesus Christ and follow his teaching. The Methodist Church has a democratic style of leadership at all levels.

Society: The local congregation is called a society.

Lay preachers are trained to preach and lead worship at morning prayer on Sunday.

Circuit: Several societies link together to form a circuit.

An ordained minister looks after the churches in a circuit. He/she will preach and celebrate Holy Communion in every church once a month.

District: A district is a number of circuits joined together. In Ireland there are eight districts. A district superintendent is elected to oversee the work of a district.

Annual Conference: The Conference is the governing body of the Methodist Church in Ireland. Ministers and lay people attend representing all the circuits in the country.

A new president is elected each year. He/she acts as spokesperson for the Methodist Church in this country.

- ◆ **Authority** is the power given to an individual or group to make important decisions that affect the lives of others.

- ◆ The Bible is the only source of authority for the Methodist community.

- ◆ The Methodist Church is non-episcopal. There are no bishops in authority and no one person has overall authority.

- ◆ Decisions about Church matters are made at the Annual Conference where ministers and lay people work together in partnership, and elect a new president every year.

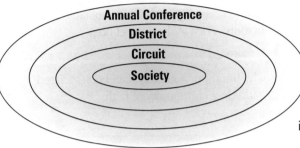

Structure of leadership in the Methodist Church.

Test Yourself

1. Outline the structure of leadership in either the Church of Ireland or the Methodist Church.

_____

_____

_____

_____

_____

_____

2. What style of leadership and authority do you associate with either the Church of Ireland or the Methodist Church? Provide evidence to support your opinion.

_____

_____

_____

_____

_____

_____

_____

_____

_____

_____

Exam Questions (HIGHER LEVEL)

1. This is a photograph of a person who is a religious leader. .... 2014(H)

A. Pick **one** thing from the photograph which suggests that this person is a religious leader.

B. Pope Francis is the name of a religious leader associated with a Christian denomination. (Tick ✓ the correct box)

True ☐   False ☐

C. State **two** reasons why the term 'authority' can be associated with the role of a leader in a community of faith.

(Source:http://news.yahoo.com)

2. A. Giving direction is one way a person can lead a community. .... 2007(H)
Outline what is involved in **two** other ways of leading a community that could be used by a leader.

B. Explain how the way in which a community is led can have an effect on its members.

C. Being a leader is one role a person can have within a community.
Describe **another** role a person can have within a community.

3. Outline **two** styles of leadership found in a community of faith. .... 2005(H)

NOTE: *This is an essay question.*

4. a. In religious traditions the term 'ministry' refers to the service a person performs .... 2013(H)
in a community of faith. (Tick ✓ the correct box.)

True ☐   False ☐

b. Outline what is involved in **one** example of a ministry in a community of faith that you have studied.

5. Briefly outline the role of a religious leader in a community of faith you have studied. .... 2005(H)

6. Profile **one** community of faith that you have studied under the following headings: ....2003(H), 2012(H)

i. LEADERSHIP STRUCTURE.

ii. CHALLENGES TO LEADERSHIP.

NOTE: *This is an essay question.*

7. Outline the way in which leadership within a community of faith involves: .... 2008(H)

(i) Authority.

(ii) Service.

NOTE: *This is an essay question.*

Section B - Foundations of Religion: Christianity

The *Syllabus Aims* in this section are:

◆ To explore the context into which Jesus was born.

◆ To identify the Gospels as the main source of knowledge about Jesus.

◆ To examine the meaning of the life, death and resurrection of Jesus for his followers, then and now.

Key Concepts in Christianity (Section B)

The Holy Land

KEY CONCEPT

The Holy Land: a name for Palestine, the country where Jesus was born.

The Holy Land

◆ Jesus lived all his life in Palestine, a small country beside the Mediterranean Sea. Palestine is also known as the Holy Land.

◆ Palestine is divided into three political regions or provinces:

- *Galilee* in the north.
- *Samaria* in the middle.
- *Judaea* in the south.

◆ The main geographical features of Palestine are:

▶ Two lakes - the Sea of Galilee and the Dead Sea.

▶ The main river is the River Jordan.

▶ The capital city is Jerusalem.

▶ Some small towns are:
- Nazareth, Cana and Capernaum in the north.
- Bethlehem, Jericho and Bethany in the south.

◆ Jesus grew up in Galilee in northern Palestine. His public ministry began after his baptism in the River Jordan.

Jesus:	Bible Refs.
✴ Was born in Bethlehem.	- Luke 2: 5-7
✴ Grew up in Nazareth.	- Luke 2: 39-40
✴ Was baptised in the river Jordan.	- Matt 3: 13-17
✴ Performed his first miracle in Cana.	- John 2: 1-11
✴ Met his first disciples at the Sea of Galilee.	- Matt 4: 18-22
✴ Taught people in Capernaum.	- Mark 2: 1-2
✴ Healed people in Jericho.	- Mark 10: 46-52
✴ Visited friends in Bethany.	- John 11: 1-3
✴ Was crucified outside Jerusalem.	- Luke 23: 26-28

Test Yourself

1. In Palestine, name: **a.** two political regions. **b.** one river and two lakes. **c.** one city and four towns.

_____

_____

_____

2. Select one place in the Holy Land associated with the life of Jesus.
   a. What occurred there? **b.** What did Jesus say or do? **c.** How did people respond to Jesus?

_____

_____

_____

_____

The Roman Empire

KEY CONCEPT

The Roman Empire: the lands ruled by ancient Rome.

The Roman Empire

◆ The Romans came from Rome in Italy.
The Emperor was the head of the Roman Empire.

◆ The Roman Empire included the lands bordering the Mediterranean Sea. When Jesus was born, Palestine was ruled by the Romans.

◆ Palestine was located in a strategic position at the crossroads of three continents, Europe, Africa and Asia. Whoever controlled Palestine controlled the great trade routes in and out of those areas.

Roman Rule

◆ The Romans invaded Palestine in 63BCE* and put their own governors in charge to rule the people.
At the time of Jesus' public ministry:
  ▶ Galilee was ruled by **Herod Antipas** (a son of King Herod).
  ▶ Samaria and Judea were both ruled by **Pontius Pilate** (a Roman Governor).

(***BCE** = Before Common Era)

◆ Each governor ensured that the Jewish people of Palestine obeyed Roman laws and paid Roman taxes. In return the Jews were allowed to follow their own customs and practice their own religion.

◆ The Jews did not accept Roman rule, they believed they were God's 'chosen people' to be ruled by God and no one else.

Tax Collectors

◆ Jews had to pay taxes for the upkeep of the Roman army based in Palestine. The money was collected by some Jewish people called tax collectors.

◆ Most Jews hated the tax collectors because they worked for the Romans. Tax collectors were regarded as traitors and cheats. They were allowed to keep part of the money they collected, but some took more.

◆ Tax collectors were shunned as social outcasts by the Jewish population in Palestine.

Test Yourself

1. What was the role of the Roman Governor in Palestine?

_____

2. Why did Jews resent the Roman presence in Palestine?

_____

_____

3. Why did Jewish people despise tax collectors?

_____

_____

_____

_____

Homelife in Palestine

KEY CONCEPT

The Holy Land : a name for Palestine, the country where Jesus was born.

The Holy Land

◆ Jesus' family home in Nazareth would have been typical of the homes of ordinary people in first century Palestine.

◆ In the Holy Land where Jesus was born, the village houses were small one roomed buildings with one window and a door. The walls were built of clay bricks and stone, and whitewashed to reflect the heat of the sun. Upstairs flat roofs were used as extra space to dry fruit and grain, hang out clothes to dry, and sit out for meals in the cool of the evening.

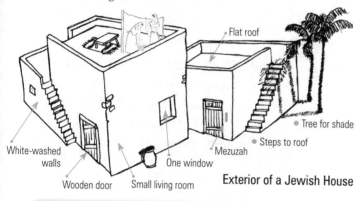

White-washed walls

Wooden door

Small living room

One window

Mezuzah

Steps to roof

Tree for shade

Flat roof

Exterior of a Jewish House

◆ A **mezuzah** was a small wooden or leather box containing a tiny scroll on which the words of the Shema (Deut 6:4) was written. It was fixed to the doorframe of all Jewish homes, and was touched prayerfully by Jews entering and leaving the house.

◆ Village houses were dark and cool inside and were divided into two levels.
  ▶ The family lived on the upper level.
  ▶ The lower level was a stable for their animals.

◆ Each house had:
  ▶ An oil lamp – that burned day and night.
  ▶ Jars – to store water and oil.
  ▶ A chest – for scrolls and special belongings.
  ▶ Mats – for sleeping, rolled up during the day.
  ▶ Dishes – for cooking.
  ▶ Hooks – to hang up clothes and wineskins.
  ▶ A broom – for sweeping the earthen floor.
  ▶ A manger – to hold animal feed.

Test Yourself

1. Describe the houses in which ordinary people lived in first century Palestine.

_____

_____

_____

_____

2. What factors do you think influenced the type of houses built for ordinary people in Palestine in Jesus' time?

_____

_____

_____

3. What feature would suggest that a house was occupied by a Jewish family?

_____

Worklife in Palestine

OBJECTIVE

Describe the lifestyles and occupations of ordinary people in Palestine at the time of Jesus.

KEY CONCEPT

The Holy Land : a name for Palestine, the country where Jesus was born.

The Holy Land

◆ Jesus' education and choice of occupation would have been typical of boys his age in first century Palestine.

◆ In the Holy Land Jewish boys went to school in the synagogue. The rabbi, a teacher in the synagogue, taught them the sacred writings of the Jewish people. The boys learned to read and write Aramaic (their own local language) and Hebrew (the ancient language of the Jewish people).

◆ At thirteen years of age, boys left school to learn their father's trade. Jesus became a carpenter and builder like Joseph, his foster father.

◆ Girls in Palestine were taught at home by their mothers. They learned home-making and child-rearing skills, and the way to carry out religious duties in the home.

◆ Jesus grew up in Galilee in the north of Palestine where ordinary people earned their living as:

▶ **Fishermen** catching fish with nets and boats on Lake Galilee.

▶ **Shepherds** minding sheep on the hillsides outside their towns and villages.

▶ **Farmers** growing crops such as grapes, olives and corn on the thin soil in the valleys.

▶ **Tradesmen**:

Builders - putting up houses, digging wells.

Carpenters - making chests, doors and shelves.

Potters - making jugs, oil lamps and dishes.

Leatherworkers - making sandals and leather goods.

Merchants - buying and selling goods in the markets.

Inn Keepers - providing food and shelter for foreign traders passing through the region.

Test Yourself

1. What was the aim of the education offered to boys and girls in first century Palestine?

_____

_____

2. How did the geography of the region affect the way people earned their living in Galilee in Jesus' time?

_____

_____

_____

3. Do you think daily life in Palestine was easy or difficult for ordinary men and women in Palestine 2,000 years ago? Explain.

_____

_____

Jewish History

KEY CONCEPT

Ancient Judaism: the history and culture of the Jewish people at the time of Jesus.

Ancient Judaism

The history and culture of Ancient Judaism at the time of Jesus had evolved over a period of almost 2,000 years.

1. **Abraham** is the father of Judaism. God makes a covenant (a sacred agreement) with Abraham. His descendants become God's 'chosen people'. Abraham's family settle in the 'Promised Land' of Canaan and worship one God.

2. **Slavery in Egypt** - A famine breaks out in Canaan. Abraham's grandson Jacob moves the family to Egypt. They are forced into slavery for 300 years.

3. **Moses** - God calls Moses to lead the people out of slavery, back to the Promised Land. This is called the Exodus. At Mount Sinai, God gives Moses the Law and the Ten Commandments.

4. **Return to Canaan** - Led by Joshua, the people return to Canaan and fight battles to regain control of the land. The kingdom of Israel is established.

5. **David** - David becomes King of Israel. He wins many battles against the enemies of Israel and makes Jerusalem his capital city. His son Solomon builds the Temple in Jerusalem.

6. **The Prophets** - The Jews fall into wicked ways and fail to keep God's Law. God sends prophets, holy men such as Ezekiel and Jeremiah, to warn them of the dangers. They refuse to listen.

7. **Jerusalem Destroyed** - The country is invaded and the Temple and the city of Jerusalem are destroyed. The people are taken away to Babylon.

8. **The Exile** - The people work like slaves in Babylon. Too late they realise they had deliberately turned away from God. They now turn back to God and begin to write down the laws and beliefs of their faith. This will become the Torah, part of the sacred text of Judaism.

9. **Return from Exile** - The Jews are set free and return to Jerusalem where they rebuild the Temple. They make a fresh start and begin to practice their faith in a sincere way.

10. **Foreign Rulers** - The Jews pray in their local synagogues on the Sabbath and try their best to obey God's Law. Over the next 400 years, one foreign power after another invades the country. The Romans invade Palestine in 63BCE.

11. **The Messiah** - The Jews long for a leader, a Messiah, to set them free. They want someone powerful like King David of old who will make their country a great Jewish Kingdom once more.

Judaism Timeline

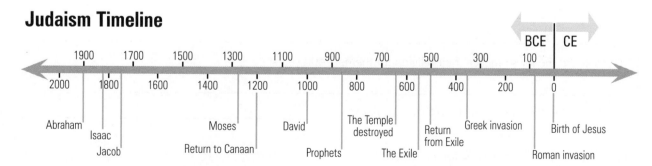

NOTE: ❖ BCE = Before common era. CE = Common era.
    ❖ No one knows the <u>exact</u> dates when some of these events took place.

Test Yourself

1. Who was Abraham?

_____

_____

2. What is the covenant?

_____

_____

3. How did God help the 'chosen people' through Moses?

_____

_____

4. What happened when the 'chosen people' returned to Canaan?

_____

_____

5. What was special about David?

_____

_____

6. Who were the prophets? What was their role?

_____

_____

7. What disaster took place in Jerusalem?

_____

_____

8. What important lesson did the people learn during the Exile?

_____

_____

9. What did the Jews do on their return from Exile?

_____

_____

10. How did the Jews practice their religion for the next 400 years?

_____

11. Who ruled Palestine at the time Jesus was born? _____

12. Why were the Jews waiting for a Messiah?

_____

_____

Jewish Religion

> **KEY CONCEPT**
>
> Ancient Judaism: the history and culture of the Jewish people at the time of Jesus.

Ancient Judaism

- At the time of Jesus, Jews had two kinds of religious buildings in which to worship God.
  - ▶ The Temple in the city of Jerusalem.
  - ▶ The synagogues in each town and village.

- **The Temple** in Jerusalem was a sacred building. Jews believed it was the dwelling place of God. The Ark of the Covenant (the chest containing the Ten Commandments) was originally kept there.

- Jewish pilgrims went to the Temple once a year at Passover to pray and offer sacrifice to God.

- The Temple was a very large ornate building.

  In the *Court of Gentiles* money changers changed the pilgrims' Roman coins into temple currency. Stall holders sold birds and animals for sacrifice.

  In the *Court of Priests* the temple priests sacrificed the pilgrims' offerings on the altar.

The *Holy of Holies* was the most sacred part of the Temple. The High Priest entered it once a year to offer sacrifice and pray for forgiveness for all.

- **The synagogue** was the focal point for the Jewish community in villages throughout Palestine.

- Jews attended the synagogue on the Sabbath to pray to God and listen to the scriptures. The rabbi read from a scroll and gave a talk about the readings.

- Each synagogue featured:
  - ▶ An Ark, a special cupboard for storing scrolls.
  - ▶ A curtain in front of the Ark and a light burning beside it.
  - ▶ A desk facing the Ark for reading the scrolls of sacred scripture.
  - ▶ Seating for men downstairs.
  - ▶ A gallery for women upstairs.

Test Yourself

1. Why was the Temple important to the Jews?

   _____

   _____

   _____

2. Describe what took place in the Temple during Passover.

   _____

   _____

   _____

   _____

3. How important was the synagogue in Jewish life?

   _____

   _____

Religious Groups

> **KEY CONCEPT**
>
> **Ancient Judaism:** the history and culture of the Jewish people at the time of Jesus.

Ancient Judaism

Jews reacted in different ways to the Roman occupation of Palestine. Some Jews accepted the Romans, others rejected them, each group had its own followers.

◆ **The Sadducees** accepted Roman rule and co-operated with the Romans.

  ▶ They were mainly priests and were the religious leaders in the Temple in Jerusalem.

  ▶ They controlled the **Sanhedrin**, a court of law based in the Temple. The Sanhedrin passed judgement on Jews who broke religious laws.

  ▶ The Sadducees were wealthy and powerful. They co-operated with the Romans to keep their position in the Temple.

◆ **The Pharisees** rejected Roman rule. They ignored the Romans and focused instead on practicing their religion.

  ▶ They were educated laymen who were the religious leaders in the synagogues.

  ▶ The Pharisees taught Jewish scripture, and were strict with the Jews about keeping God's Law.

◆ **The Zealots** rejected Roman rule. They refused to co-operate with the Romans.

  ▶ The were religious Jews who hated the Romans and used violence against them. They wanted to force the Romans out of Palestine at all costs.

  ▶ The Zealots were a revolutionary group. They refused to pay taxes and caused unrest among ordinary Jewish people.

◆ **The Essenes** rejected Roman rule. They refused to co-operate with the Romans or with Jewish leaders whom they saw as weak and corrupt.

  ▶ They were a community of monks who went to live in remote desert places near the Dead Sea.

  ▶ The Essenes lived a simple prayerful life and followed God's Law.

Test Yourself

1. Which Jewish group:

   ● Was willing to use violence to free Palestine from Roman rule? _____

   ● Ignored the Romans and strictly observed Jewish law? _____

   ● Withdrew to remote places to live simply and follow God's Law? _____

   ● Co-operated with the Romans and controlled the Jewish Court of Law? _____

2. What was the function of the Sanhedrin? _____

   _____

3. Why do you think Jews in Palestine had different attitudes toward the Roman occupation?

   _____

   _____

   _____

   _____

Awaiting the Messiah

KEY CONCEPT

Messianic expectation: the hope of the Jewish people that a new leader, a Messiah, would bring them to freedom.

Messianic Expectation

◆ The Jews believed God spoke to them through the prophets. Prophets were holy men and women who carried messages from God.

◆ The **prophets** told of God's promise to send a great leader to guide and rule the Jewish people.

◆ A leader sent by God was called a Messiah. The Jews waited expectantly for the Messiah.

◆ The word **'Messiah'** means 'anointed one'. All great leaders were anointed or blessed with oil as a sign that they were chosen by God for an important task. David, Israel's greatest King, was anointed or blessed with oil at the start of his reign.

◆ Jewish people in every generation looked forward with great expectation to the coming of the Messiah. Messianic expectation is the hope expressed by Jews in Jesus' time that God would send a Messiah, a great leader, to free them from Roman rule.

◆ By the first century, Jews in Palestine believed the Messiah:

▶ Would be a powerful king-like figure.

▶ Would free them from foreign rulers.

▶ Would bring God's peace and justice to all.

Test Yourself

1. What does the word 'Messiah' mean?

_____

_____

2. In Judaism what did it mean for a person to be anointed with holy oil?

_____

_____

_____

3. What were the Jews' expectations of the Messiah at the time of Jesus?

_____

_____

_____

_____

1. A. Tick ✓ the correct location of Palestine in **one** box on the map. ....2004(O)

B. Listed below are places and provinces in Palestine at the time of Jesus.

Tick the box which matches each place to its province.
One place has been matched as an example for you.

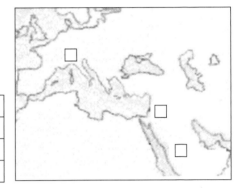

Places in Palestine at the time of Jesus:

	Cana	Jerusalem	Nazareth	The Dead Sea
Province of Galilee	✓			
Province of Judea / Judaea				
Province of Samaria				

2. a. In the spaces marked on the map of Palestine write: ....2006(H)

● The name of the city shown at a)

● The names of the seas shown at b) and c).

b. Name an important event in the life of Jesus which happened in one of the places you have named above.

Name of place: _____

Name of event: _____

c. Briefly outline what happened in the event you have named.

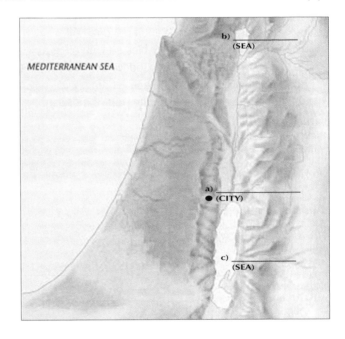

3. Profile what life in Palestine was like for people living at the time of Jesus ....2014(H)
using **each** of the following headings:

i. Geography.

ii. Religion.

NOTE: *This is an essay question.*

4. a. Each of the different religious groups described below lived in Palestine at the time of Jesus. .... 2008(H)

Tick ✓ the box that most correctly matches each description to the name of a religious group given below. The first description has been correctly matched as an example for you.

Religious Group 1	Religious Group 2	Religious Group 3
We are wealthy aristocrats and have strong links with the Temple in Jerusalem. We accept Roman rule and have power in Palestine.	We reject Roman rule in Palestine and are ready to fight the Romans.	We do not co-operate with the Romans. We run the local synagogues and are strict about keeping all the laws of Judaism.
Pharisees ❏ Sadducees ☑ Zealots ❏	Pharisees ❏ Sadducees ❏ Zealots ❏	Pharisees ❏ Sadducees ❏ Zealots ❏

b. ● Pharisees. ● Sadducees. ● Romans.
Choose two of the above groups and explain why each came into conflict with Jesus.

---

5. a. The people who held political power in Palestine at the time of Jesus were the .... 2011(O)
(Tick ✓ the correct box.)

BABYLONIANS ❏   EGYPTIANS ❏   ROMANS ❏

b. Outline how **one** of the following religious groups reacted to those who held political power in Palestine at the time of Jesus:

● PHARISEES   ● SADDUCEES   ● ZEALOTS

---

6. a. Galilee is the name of one province that existed in Palestine .... 2012(H)
at the time of Jesus.

Name **another** province in Palestine at the time of Jesus.

b. Explain **two** reasons why there was conflict between the Roman and Jewish leaders in Palestine at the time of Jesus.

c. Outline **two** expectations that the Jewish people had about the Kingdom of God at the time of Jesus.

---

7. a. Outline what the Jewish people expected .... 2006(H)
the Messiah to be like at the time of Jesus.

b. Outline **one** way in which Jesus was like the Messiah that the Jewish people were expecting at the time.

c. Outline **one** way in which Jesus was not like the Messiah that the Jewish people were expecting at the time.

---

8. Describe life in Palestine at the time of Jesus referring to each of the following: .... 2009(H)

i. The political structures.

ii. The religious structures.

NOTE: *This is an essay question.*

OBJECTIVE

Explain the purpose of the four evangelists in writing the Gospels.

The New Testament

Gospel

◆ The word 'Gospel' means 'good news'. The Good News is that Jesus is the Son of God. This is the message of the first four books in the New Testament.

◆ There are four Gospels in the New Testament in the Bible.
  ▶ The Gospel of Mark.
  ▶ The Gospel of Matthew.
  ▶ The Gospel of Luke.
  ▶ The Gospel of John.

◆ The Gospels explain the purpose of Jesus' life on Earth.

Witness

◆ The authors of the four Gospels:
  ▶ Firmly believed that Jesus is God.
  ▶ Felt compelled to tell the Good News to other people. They gave witness, or publicly proclaimed their faith, through their writings.
  ▶ They wrote the Gospels:
    - To spread the Good News of Jesus.
    - To enable others to have faith in Jesus too.

Evangelist

◆ The evangelists were the authors of the four Gospels. They were men of great faith who wrote the Gospels to spread the Good News of Jesus Christ.

◆ The four evangelists are:
  ▶ **Mark**.
  ▶ **Matthew**.
  ▶ **Luke** .
  ▶ **John**.

◆ Their writings set out to show that Jesus is the Son of God, the Messiah, the Saviour of all. To achieve this aim the evangelists focused on the events in the final three years of Jesus' adult life.

  In the New Testament the Gospels focus mainly on Jesus'
  ▶ teaching.
  ▶ miracles.
  ▶ death.
  ▶ resurrection.

◆ The four Gospels were written for Christians in the Roman Empire in the first century CE. Each community had its own problems. The evangelists emphasised certain aspects of Jesus' life and teaching to meet the needs of each community.

Gospel	Evangelist	Date	Written for.....	Main points
★ Mark	❑ Mark was a Jew before he became a Christian. ❑ He knew Peter, who was Jesus' closest disciple. Mark listened carefully to Peter and wrote down all the stories Peter told him about Jesus.	❑ Around 70CE. The first Gospel to be written.	❑ New Christians in the city of Rome who were suffering terrible persecution at the hands of the Romans.	★ Jesus is the Son of God. ★ Jesus had feelings like everyone else. He suffered a lot. He was crucified and died on the cross.
✦ Matthew	❑ Matthew was a Jew before he became a Christian. ❑ He may have been a rabbi (a teacher) who taught Jewish scripture in the synagogue.	❑ Around 85CE. Written fifteen years after Mark's Gospel.	❑ New Christians in the city of Antioch who had been Jews until they realised that Jesus is the Messiah. It changed their lives.	✦ Jesus is the Messiah. ✦ Jesus knew a lot of Jewish scripture. He taught his followers a new way of living.
◉ Luke	❑ Luke was a Gentile (a non-Jew) before he became a Christian. ❑ He was a doctor. Luke was impressed by the healing work of Jesus.	❑ Around 85CE. Written around the same time as Matthew's Gospel.	❑ New Christians in the city of Corinth who had been Gentiles (non-Jews) before they heard about Jesus. The Good News changed their lives.	◉ Jesus is the Saviour of all people. ◉ Jesus was a friend to everyone: he cared for rich and poor, Jew and Gentile, sinners and sick people....
☆ John	❑ John was a Jew before he became a Christian. ❑ He may have been a follower of the youngest disciple of Jesus, who was also called John.	❑ Around 95CE. The last Gospel to be written.	❑ Mature Christians in the city of Ephesus who had been Christians for many years.	☆ Jesus is the Messiah, the Son of God. ☆ Jesus had a spiritual nature and thought deeply about things. Have faith in him.

Test Yourself

1. Explain the meaning of the word 'Gospel'.

_____

_____

2. Who were the Evangelists?

_____

_____

_____

_____

3. What aspects of Jesus' life did the Evangelists focus on in the Gospels?

_____

_____

_____

_____

4. How did the Evangelists bear witness to their faith in Jesus Christ?

_____

_____

_____

Three Gospel Stages

KEY CONCEPT

Evidence from oral and written traditions: the way information about Jesus passed from the spoken to the written word.

Evidence from oral and written traditions

◆ The evangelists believed in Jesus and wrote about him in their Gospels. Yet none of them actually met Jesus when he was alive. The evangelists wrote the Gospels more than forty years after Jesus' death and resurrection.

◆ The Gospel came together in three separate stages:

Stage 1 - The Life Stage (30 – 33CE)

The words, actions, death and resurrection of Jesus convince the disciples that Jesus is the Messiah

▶ Jesus teaches and performs miracles in the last three years of his life.

▶ Jesus is crucified and dies on the cross.

▶ Jesus is raised from the dead after three days, and appears to his disciples.

Stage 2 - The Oral Stage (33 – 70CE)

The oral tradition - a period when the apostles travel all over the Roman Empire to **TELL** the Good News of Jesus Christ.

Stage 3 - The Written Stage (70 – 95CE)

The written tradition - a period when the evangelists, Mark, Matthew, Luke and John, **WRITE** the story of Jesus in the four Gospels.

◆ The apostles' account of Jesus is gathered together and written down by the evangelists. It was important to do this before the main witnesses of all Jesus had said and done grew too old or died.

◆ A written Gospel would help new Christians at that time and in the future to know Jesus and follow his teachings.

Test Yourself

1. On the Gospel timeline, mark in the following: ● Jesus' private life.   ● Jesus' public life.
   ● Jesus' death and resurrection. ● The oral stage of the Gospel.   ● The written stage of the Gospel.

10	1	5	10	15	20	25	30	35	40	45	50	55	60	65	70	75	80	85	90	95	100

BCE   CE

2. Why did the early Christians want a written account of the life and teaching of Jesus?

_____

_____

3. What is the difference between the contribution of the apostles and the evangelists to the formation of the Gospels?

_____

_____

_____

_____

OBJECTIVE:
Identify the characteristics
of the Synoptic Gospels.

The Synoptic Gospels

Synoptic

◆ The Gospels of Mark, Matthew and Luke are very similar, they are known as Synoptic Gospels. When seen together it is clear that these three Gospels agree on:

▶ The main events in Jesus' life.

▶ The order in which those events occurred.

▶ Jesus' words on those occasions.

◆ Similarities in the Synoptic Gospels are due to:

▶ Mark's Gospel being written first.

▶ Matthew and Luke's Gospels, written twenty years later, rely a lot on Mark's account of Jesus' life.

◆ Differences in the Synoptic Gospels are due to:

▶ Matthew and Luke using other sources in addition to Mark's Gospel.

- The **Q** document (a collection of Jesus' sayings written down at an earlier time).
- **M**: eye witness accounts unique to Matthew.
- **L**: eye witness accounts unique to Luke.

The Fourth Gospel.

◆ John's Gospel is not one of the Synoptic Gospels. It was written last and used other sources to tell the story of Jesus.

◆ John's Gospel focuses more on explaining who Jesus is, rather than describing what he says and does.

◆ The writing style in John's Gospel is poetic and abstract with no reference to Jesus' parables and few references to his miracles.

Test Yourself

1. Why are the Gospels of Mark, Matthew and Luke known as Synoptic Gospels?

_____

_____

_____

2. In what ways are the Synoptic Gospels alike or similar to each other?

_____

_____

_____

_____

3. How is John's Gospel different from the Synoptic Gospels?

_____

_____

_____

_____

Documents of Faith and History

Evidence

Sources of information about Jesus from **Christian** sources

◆ **Documents of faith** provide evidence that Jesus is God.

◆ The Gospels of Mark, Matthew, Luke and John are the main source of evidence about Jesus. They were written by men of faith for a special purpose - to show that Jesus is the Messiah, the Son of God.

◆ The four **evangelists** focused only on the last three years of Jesus' life. They looked at all the facts and examined eye witness reports of Jesus':

● Teaching. ● Miracles. ● Death. ● Resurrection.

◆ The Gospel writers then explained the meaning and importance of these facts. For the evangelists, Jesus' words and actions were the evidence, the proof, that Jesus is the Son of God.

◆ The Gospels are documents of faith that tell important facts about Jesus. They invite the reader to believe that Jesus is the Son of God.

Sources of information about Jesus from **non-Christian** sources

◆ **Historical documents** provide evidence that Jesus did exist.

◆ Most of what we know about Jesus comes from the New Testament. Other information comes from historical documents of the first century CE written by:

● Josephus, a Jew. ● Tacitus, a Roman.

◆ **Josephus** and **Tacitus** were non-Christian historians who wrote about people and events in the Roman Empire. Both historians mention Jesus in their writing. They report the facts that:

▶ Jesus lived in Palestine.

▶ A group of people known as Christians were his followers.

▶ Jesus was sentenced to death by Pontius Pilate, governor of Palestine.

Test Yourself

1. Why are the Gospels called documents of faith?

_____

_____

_____

2. What do first century historical documents add to our knowledge of Jesus Christ?

_____

_____

_____

3. Explain the difference between a document of faith and a document of history?

_____

_____

_____

_____

Exam Questions

---

1. A. a. Below you will find a list of the stages in the development of the Gospels. ....2006(O)

Number these stages giving number 1 to the first stage, number 2 to the second, and number 3 to the third.

Number	Stages in the development of the Gospels
	The writing down of the Gospels.
	The events that took place.
	The disciples preaching about these events.

b. Describe **one** of the stages in the development of the Gospels.

B. The people who wrote the Gospels are known as the evangelists. Tick ✓ **one** of the evangelists listed below:

John ❑   Luke ❑   Mark ❑   Matthew ❑

Give **two** reasons why the evangelist you have ticked above can be described as a person of faith.

---

2. THE GOSPEL ❑   THE GOSPEL ❑   THE GOSPEL ❑   THE GOSPEL ❑ ....2014(O)
OF JOHN   OF LUKE   OF MARK   OF MATTHEW

Tick ✓ **one** of the Gospels listed above and describe what was involved in two different stages of its development.

---

3. Imagine you have been asked to give a talk at a bible meeting explaining the stages ....2004(H)
involved in the development of the Gospels from the oral tradition to the written word.

Outline the talk you would give making reference to the importance of the Gospels in the Christian community of faith.

NOTE: *This is an essay question.*

---

4. a. Outline **one** reason why the Gospels were important for the Early Christian communities. ....2013(O)

b. Explain why the Gospels of Matthew, Mark and Luke are known as the Synoptic Gospels.

---

5. a. The writings of Josephus are an example of historical evidence about Jesus ....2013(O)
of Nazareth. (Tick ✓ the correct box)

True ❑   False ❑

b. Describe an example of what **one** historical document has to say about Jesus of Nazareth.

---

6. Outline **two** historical sources of information about the life of Jesus of Nazareth ....2007(H)
and discuss the ways in which they are similar to what the Gospels say about his life and death.

---

7. a. Explain **two** reasons why the Gospels are described as documents of faith. ....2009(H)

b. Outline what was involved in **three** different stages in the development of the Gospels.

The Kingdom of God

OBJECTIVE:
Outline what Jesus meant
by the Kingdom of God.

KEY CONCEPT

Kingdom of God: Jesus' vision of a way of life that loves God and does good
to other people.

Kingdom of God

◆ Jesus' baptism in the river Jordan was important as it marked the beginning of his public life. He spent the next three years as a teacher travelling around Palestine, telling people about the Kingdom of God.

◆ The Kingdom of God is the central idea in all Jesus' teaching, it is mentioned over a hundred times in the Gospels. The Kingdom of God is Jesus' dream or vision of a way of life that loves God and does good to other people.

◆ The Kingdom of God is people everywhere living as God wants them to live - in peace, love, justice and truth.

◆ The Kingdom of God is not a place that can be found on a map. It is found in people, in the goodness of their hearts.

◆ Jesus used words and actions to help people understand what he meant by the Kingdom of God.

▶ He told **parables** to teach people about the love of God.

▶ He performed **miracles** to show people the love of God.

▶ He shared meals and **table-fellowship** to help all people experience the love of God.

▶ He called people to **discipleship** so that they could learn from him and follow a way of life based on the love of God.

◆ Jesus' words and actions were the first sign that the Kingdom of God had arrived.

Test Yourself

1. How important is the Kingdom of God in the New Testament?

_____

_____

_____

2. What is the Kingdom of God?

_____

_____

_____

_____

3. How did Jesus explain what he meant by the Kingdom of God?

_____

_____

_____

_____

Parables

> **KEY CONCEPT**
>
> **Kingdom of God**: Jesus' vision of a way of life that loves God and does good to other people.
>
> **Parable**: a short story told by Jesus to teach people about the Kingdom of God.

Kingdom of God in Parable

◆ At the time of Jesus, telling parables or short stories about familiar events was a common way of teaching new ideas.

◆ Jesus told parables or stories to teach people about the Kingdom of God.

◆ Each parable is a simple story with an underlying message. Jesus invited people to work out the meaning of each parable and then apply its message to their own lives.

◆ The parables in the New Testament are about ordinary things such as: farming, minding sheep, housework, leaving home, family celebrations, and going on journeys.

◆ Jesus' parables showed God's love at work in real everyday situations that everyone knew about. Jesus' parables were therefore easy to understand, and easy to remember.

◆ About fifty of Jesus' parables are recorded in the Gospels. A selection of Jesus' well known parables are presented in the table below.

Parables of Jesus

Bible Reference	Parable	Characteristics of the Kingdom of God
Mark 4:30-32	**The Mustard Seed.** It's about planting a small seed that becomes a tall plant.	Shows that God's love is a gift planted in people's hearts where it can grow and mature.
Luke 15:4-9	**The Lost Sheep. The Lost Coin.** It's about a farmer and a householder searching for something precious.	Shows that in the Kingdom of God, God loves every single person without exception.
Matt 13:3-8, 13:18-23	**The Sower** It's about a farmer sowing seeds on different types of soil.	Shows that people respond in different ways to Jesus' message about the Kingdom of God. Those who accept it try to build the kind of world that God wants for everybody.
Luke 10:25-37	**The Good Samaritan.** It's about a person in need being cared for by a stranger.	Shows that loving one's neighbour is essential in the Kingdom of God.
Luke 15:11-32	**The Prodigal Son** It's about a person who regrets leaving home and wants to return.	Shows that in the Kingdom of God, God will always forgive the sinner who is truly sorry.

Test Yourself

1. What is a parable?

_____

_____

_____

2. Name some of Jesus' parables.

_____

_____

_____

_____

_____

_____

3. Why did Jesus tell parables?

_____

_____

_____

_____

_____

4. Select one parable and explain its meaning:
   a. for Jesus' followers in first century Palestine.   **b.** for Christians in this country today.

_____

_____

_____

_____

_____

_____

_____

_____

_____

_____

_____

_____

_____

Miracles

> **KEY CONCEPT**
>
> **Kingdom of God**: Jesus' vision of a way of life that loves God and does good to other people.
>
> **Miracle**: an amazing cure or deed performed by Jesus to show the power and love of God.

Kingdom of God in Miracle

◆ Jesus performed miracles to show people the Kingdom of God at work in the world.

◆ Jesus performed different types of miracles:

1. **Healing miracles**
   He healed people who were sick or disabled.

2. **Nature miracles**
   He changed something in nature such as calming a storm, or turning water into wine.

3. **Expelling miracles**
   He got rid of evil spirits from people's lives.

4. **Raising to life miracles**
   He raised the dead to life.

◆ In the Gospels, the evangelists regard the miracles as a sign that Jesus is the Messiah. Jesus fulfills Old Testament prophesies about the promised Messiah when he made:

▶ Blind people see.
▶ Deaf people hear.
▶ Lame people walk.

Jesus heals a man born blind.

Reasons why Jesus worked miracles

◆ Jesus worked miracles in order to:

▶ Show God's love.
▶ Show God's power.
▶ Strengthen people's faith in God.

◆ The miracles help people to **see God's love**.
Jesus wanted those who were sick or sad or disabled or poor to know that God loves and cares for them.

◆ The miracles help people to **see God's power**.
Jesus made it known that his ability to perform miracles came directly from God. Through God the Father, Jesus has power:

▶ over disease.   ▶ over evil.
▶ over nature.   ▶ over death.

◆ The miracles help to **strengthen people's faith**.
Jesus did not perform miracles to show off, or to amaze people. He worked miracles only for those who had faith in God's presence.

◆ The miracles of Jesus were signs that the Kingdom of God was present and at work in the world.

◆ The Evangelists record thirty five of Jesus' miracles in the Gospels.

A selection of Jesus' well-known miracles are presented below.

Miracles of Jesus

1. Healing Miracles	3. Expelling Miracles
● Healing a blind man called Bartimaeus in Jericho. (Mark 10:46-52) ● Healing a person with leprosy in Galilee. (Mark 1:39-45)	● Expelling an evil spirit from a man in Capernaum. (Mark 1:21-28) ● Expelling an evil spirit from a man in Gerasa. (Mark 5:1-20)
2. Nature Miracles	4. Raising to Life Miracles
● Calming a storm on Lake Galilee. (Mark 4:35-41) ● Turning water into wine at a wedding feast in Cana. (John 2:1-12)	● Raising Jairus' daughter to life in Galilee. (Mark 5:21-42) ● Raising Lazarus to life in Bethany. (John 11:38-44)

Test Yourself

1. What type of miracles are described in the Gospels?

_____

_____

_____

_____

2. Why did Jesus perform miracles?

_____

_____

_____

3. Describe one miracle Jesus performed and explain what it teaches about the Kingdom of God.

_____

_____

_____

_____

_____

_____

_____

_____

Table-fellowship

OBJECTIVE:
Identify characteristics of
the Kingdom of God
in table-fellowship.

KEY CONCEPT

Kingdom of God: Jesus' vision of a way of life that loves God and does good to other people.

Table-fellowship: the way Jesus shared meals with everyone to show the Kingdom of God is open to all.

Kingdom of God in Table-fellowship

◆ In Jewish life breaking bread and sharing a meal with someone was a sign of closeness and friendship. Jews generally shared meals only with their family and friends.

◆ Jesus shared meals with everyone, including those outside his social group such as sinners, tax collectors and other outcasts.

◆ For Jesus this was table-fellowship. Sharing meals with all kinds of people was a way of showing that the Kingdom of God is open to all.

◆ The Kingdom of God is open to anyone who:
  ▶ Turns toward the love of God.
  ▶ Turns away from sin and wrongdoing.

◆ Jesus was criticised for being a friend to sinners, tax collectors and other social outcasts.

'When the Pharisees saw Jesus eating with sinners and tax collectors they said to his disciples, "Why does he eat with such people?". On hearing this Jesus said, "people who are healthy do not need the doctor, only those who are sick. I did not come to call respectable people, but sinners." '
(Adapted from Mark 2:15-17)

◆ Jesus set out to show that God is loving and forgiving. Jesus wants his followers to be like that too.

Table-fellowship in the Gospels

▶ Jesus and Zacchaeus. (Luke 19:1-10)

▶ Jesus and Levi. (Luke 5:27-32)

▶ Jesus at the home of Simon the Pharisee. (Luke 7:36-50)

Test Yourself

1. What did Jesus mean by table-fellowship?

_____

_____

_____

2. How did Jewish leaders react to the way Jesus mixed with social outcasts?

_____

_____

3. Why did Jesus share meals with sinners and tax collectors?

_____

_____

_____

_____

Discipleship

KEY CONCEPT

Kingdom of God: Jesus' vision of a way of life that loves God and does good to other people.

Discipleship: following Jesus and his teaching.

Kingdom of God in Discipleship

◆ Jesus had many followers. He chose twelve of them to be his disciples.
A disciple is someone who learns from a teacher (a rabbi). Jesus wanted his disciples to learn from him and to follow his example.

◆ The call to **discipleship** is a big step. It means following Jesus and his teaching. In the **Kingdom of God** a follower of Jesus is one who puts God and other people first before him or herself.

◆ Jesus' disciples were twelve ordinary men from all walks of life. They were:
- fishermen,
- tradesmen,
- a tax collector,
- one was a Zealot.

◆ Jesus needed the disciples to help him establish the Kingdom of God on Earth.
The disciples learned:
▶ To open up their hearts to God.
▶ To love their neighbour as themselves.

◆ The twelve travelled with Jesus all over Palestine. After Pentecost they would continue Jesus' work: teaching, healing and forgiving members of a new community of faith, Christianity.

Discipleship in the Gospels

▶ Jesus calls his first disciples. (Mark 1:16-20)

▶ Jesus calls the twelve disciples. (Matt 10:1-4)

▶ Jesus calls Levi. (Mark 2:13-17)

Test Yourself

1. Who were Jesus' disciples?

_____

_____

_____

2. What was challenging about a call to discipleship?

_____

_____

_____

_____

3. Why did Jesus need disciples to help him with his work?

_____

_____

_____

The Beatitudes

> **KEY CONCEPT**
>
> **Discipleship**: following Jesus and his teaching.

Discipleship

◆ Jesus spent his public life teaching about the Kingdom of God. He used parables, miracles and table-fellowship to get his message across. Jesus also spoke directly to people through sermons.

◆ In the *Sermon on the Mount-*, Jesus began by teaching the Beatitudes. This is a list of the qualities that Jesus' followers must have in order to be part of the Kingdom of God.

◆ **Discipleship** means following Jesus and his teaching, and through good example passing his message on to others.

The Beatitudes (Matt 5:1-10)

Jesus says "Happy are..."	these are people who...	Be-Attitudes
1. The poor in spirit.	have faith and depend on God.	- *Be prayerful.*
2. The mournful.	are sorry for their sins and want to start over again.	- *Be repentant.*
3. The gentle.	treat others with kindness, and show care for the Earth.	- *Be gentle.*
4. Those who hunger and thirst for what is right.	try to do what is right and just.	- *Be fair.*
5. The merciful.	forgive those who hurt them and let them down.	- *Be forgiving.*
6. The pure of heart.	are respectful and won't take advantage of others.	- *Be respectful.*
7. The peacemakers.	work for peace and an end to conflict.	- *Be a peacemaker.*
8. Those persecuted for doing what is right.	can get into trouble because they stand up for what is right.	- *Be brave and have integrity.*

Test Yourself

1. What are the Beatitudes?

_____

2. What qualities did Jesus say are necessary for building the Kingdom of God on Earth?

_____

_____

_____

3. Can you identify a person, a group of people or an organisation that could be associated with one of these Beatitudes today?

_____

_____

_____

Discipleship Today

KEY CONCEPTS

Discipleship: following Jesus and his teaching.

Vocation: a feeling of being called by God to serve others.

Mission: the specific work carried out by members of a Christian community.

Discipleship/Vocation

◆ In the beginning Jesus called twelve people to follow him and be his disciples. Today, Jesus continues to call people to discipleship and to follow his teaching.

◆ The Christian way of life involves following the teaching of Jesus "to love God and love one's neighbour as oneself".

◆ A vocation is a person's sense of being called by God to serve others in a certain way. Catholics, for example, can fulfil their vocation and follow Jesus either:

　▶ As lay people, single or married.

　▶ As a nun or a brother in a religious community.

　▶ As an ordained priest.

Mission

◆ All Christians lay and religious, male and female, young and old, answer the call of Jesus in different ways. Each one has a mission, or specific work to do as a member of the Christian community.

　▶ **Sister Stanislaus Kennedy**, and the organisation she founded, helps young people who are out of home here in Ireland.

　▶ **Mother Teresa**, and the religious order she founded, helps the poorest of the poor in India and elsewhere.

　▶ **Brother Roger Schutz**, and the religious order he founded, built an ecumenical community in Taize.

　▶ **Archbishop Desmond Tutu** brings peace and justice to people of all races in South Africa.

　▶ **Christian parents** everywhere love and care for their children on a daily basis.

　▶ **Christian teenagers** follow their parents' good example and regularly support the work of voluntary organisations at home and abroad.

Test Yourself

1. What is the meaning of the term 'vocation'?

_____

2. How do people fulfil their Christian vocation today?

_____

_____

3. What is the meaning of the term 'mission'?

_____

4. How do Christians bear witness to the love of God in the world today?

_____

_____

_____

Exam Questions

---

1. A. a. One parable that Jesus told his followers is: (Tick ✓ the correct box.) ....2009(O)

The Crossing of ❑   The Raising of ❑   The Return on ❑
the Red Sea.   Jairus' Daughter.   the Prodigal Son.

  b. Describe in detail what happened in **one** parable that Jesus told his followers.

  Name of parable: _____

B. a. Outline **two** points that Jesus taught his followers about the Kingdom of God in a parable you have studied.

  Name of parable: _____

  b. Explain **one** reason why Jesus used parables to teach his followers about the Kingdom of God.

---

2. In the parables Jesus tells people what the Kingdom of God is like. ....2005(O)

Outline what is revealed about the Kingdom of God in **one** parable (and **one** miracle) you have studied.

---

3. This drawing is based on the miracle of Jesus raising Lazarus from the dead. ....2006(H)

A. Pick **one** thing from the drawing which shows how people reacted to the miracles of Jesus.

B. Name **one** other miracle that Jesus performed.

C. State **two** characteristics of the Kingdom of God that can be seen in one of Jesus' miracles.

Adapted from Octopus Books Limited

---

4. A. a. Name **one** example of a parable told by Jesus. ....2014(H)

  b. Describe the story Jesus told in the parable that you have named above.

B. a. Outline **one** characteristic of the Kingdom of God that Jesus preached in the parable which you have named in part Aa) above.

  b. Explain **two** reasons why Jesus used parables to teach people about the Kingdom of God.

---

5. Outline **two** characteristics that Jesus preached about the Kingdom of God in his parables. ....2012(H)

NOTE: *This is an essay question.*

---

6. a. 'Turning water into wine' is one example of a miracle that Jesus performed. ....2014(O)
Name **another** example of a miracle that Jesus performed.

  b. Describe what happened in **one** miracle performed by Jesus.

---

7. The "special place of the poor" is a characteristic of the Kingdom of God as preached by Jesus. ....2003(H)

  a. Outline **one** miracle that Jesus performed and explain how it shows this characteristic in action.

  b. Describe **one** example of how this characteristic of the Kingdom of God can be seen in the actions of Christians today.

8. This picture is based on the miracle of Jesus raising Jairus' daughter. ....2011(H)

A. Pick **one** thing from this picture which suggests that it is based on the miracle of Jesus raising Jairus' daughter.

B. Give **another** example of a miracle that Jesus performed.

C. State **two** reasons why Jesus performed miracles.

www.qwickstep.com

9. A. a. 'Feeding the Five Thousand' is one example of a meal that Jesus shared with others. ....2012(O)
Name **another** example of table-fellowship from the life of Jesus.

b. Outline what happened in the example of table-fellowship from the life of Jesus that you have named in part a) above.

B. a. Describe what Jesus taught his disciples about the Kingdom of God in a meal that he shared with others.

b. Outline **another** example of how Jesus' words or actions taught people about the Kingdom of God.

10. Tick ✓ **one** of the following characteristics of the Kingdom of God and explain ....2004(H)
how it can be seen in an example of table-fellowship from the life of Jesus:

Special place of the poor ❏   Love of neighbour ❏   Treatment of sinners and outcasts ❏

11. This drawing is based on Jesus calling his disciples. ....2010(O)

A. Pick **one** thing from the drawing which suggests that it is based on Jesus calling his disciples.

B. The name of the sea where Jesus called his first disciples was (Tick ✓ the correct box.)
The Dead Sea ❏   The Mediterranean Sea ❏   The Sea of Galilee ❏

C. State **one** thing Jesus asked his disciples to do.

www.ebibleteacher.com

12. This picture is based on Jesus teaching his disciples. ....2008(H)

a. Pick **one** thing from this picture which shows that the teaching of Jesus was important to his disciples.

b. Name **one** of the first disciples of Jesus.

c. State **two** things that Jesus taught his disciples about the Kingdom of God.

www.hithcc.org

13. A These headlines might have appeared in Palestine at the time of Jesus. ....2007(O)

a. Tick ✓ **one** of the following headlines and name **one** event from the life of Jesus which it could describe.

Jesus welcomes sinners	Jesus treats women as equals	Jesus says the poor are blessed	Love your enemies says Jesus
The Galilee Gazette	*The Bethlehem Bulletin*	*The Nazareth News*	*The Jerusalem Journal*
❏	❏	❏	❏

b. Describe what happened in the event from the life of Jesus which you have named.

B. Explain why people were surprised by what Jesus said about the Kingdom of God.

Conflict with Authority

KEY CONCEPT

Conflict with Authority: a clash or struggle with people in power.

Conflict with Authority

◆ Jesus' teaching and miracles attracted a large following in Galilee and other parts of Palestine. His teaching about love and forgiveness was different from that of other Jewish rabbis. Yet Jesus' message brought him into conflict with people of power and authority in the Jewish religion such as:

▶ The Pharisees - Jewish laymen, experts on the Law of God in the local synagogues.

▶ The Sadducees - Jewish priests in the Temple in Jerusalem and members of the Sanhedrin.

Jesus was accused of...

◆ **Mixing with Social Outcasts**
because he was friendly with sinners, non-Jews and others who were regarded as unclean and unsuitable for Jewish society. People such as:

● Tax collectors.   ● Romans
● Samaritans   ● People with leprosy

Read:

Jesus and Levi the tax collector. (Luke 5:27-32)
Jesus and the Samaritan woman. (John 4:1-30)
Jesus heals a Roman officer's servant. (Matt 8:5-13)
Jesus heals people with leprosy. (Luke 17:11-19)

▶ They said: Jesus was unfit to be a rabbi because he mixed with social outcasts.

▶ Jesus said: his mission was to show that the love of God is for all people, everyone has a place in the Kingdom of God.

◆ **Breaking Jewish Laws**
because he healed people on the Sabbath, a day when all physical work was forbidden.

Read: *Jesus heals a man with a paralysed hand.* (Luke 6:6-11)

▶ They said: they knew the law and Jesus had broken it.

▶ Jesus said: he had the right to interpret the law and to help people, even on the Sabbath.

◆ **Blasphemy** (serious disrespect to God)
because he claimed to have power to forgive sins.

Read: *Jesus heals a paralysed man.* (Luke 5:17-26)

▶ They said: only God can forgive sins.

▶ Jesus said: his power to heal and forgive sins came directly from God.

◆ **Receiving his power from the Devil**
because he was able to expel evil spirits.

Read:

Jesus and a man with an Evil Spirit. (Mark 1:21-28)
Jesus heals a boy with an Evil Spirit. (Mark 9:14-29)
Jesus and Beelzebul. (Mark 3:20-30)

▶ They said: his power to work miracles came from the Devil.

▶ Jesus said: his power to work miracles came directly from God.

Jesus in the Temple (Mark 11:15-19)

◆ Jesus and his disciples went to the Temple in Jerusalem for the festival of Passover. Jesus was annoyed at the way the Temple priests allowed traders and money changers to operate in the Court of Gentiles.

◆ The Sadducees became angry when Jesus publicly defied them and chased the traders and moneychangers out of the Temple.

◆ The Pharisees and Sadducees agreed that Jesus could not be allowed to teach or challenge their authority any longer. He had to be stopped.

Test Yourself

1. Who were the religious authorities in Palestine at the time of Jesus?

_____

_____

_____

_____

_____

2. List the main accusations against Jesus and his teaching.

_____

_____

_____

_____

_____

_____

_____

_____

3. How did Jesus' words or actions in the Temple bring him into conflict with the Jewish authorities?

_____

_____

_____

_____

_____

_____

_____

The Last Supper

KEY CONCEPTS

Passover: a Jewish festival to celebrate the Exodus.

Eucharist: a Christian service of thanksgiving. In the Catholic Church the Eucharist is a sacrament.

Memorial: something done to honour and remember someone or something.

Sacrifice: something of value (one's life, for example) offered to God for the sake of others.

Passover

◆ The Last Supper is the name of the meal Jesus hosted and shared with his disciples on the eve of Passover.

◆ Passover is a Jewish festival to celebrate the Exodus. At the time of Jesus this annual event attracted thousands of pilgrims to the Temple in Jerusalem.

◆ The Passover meal is a high point of the Passover festival. It helps Jews remember and re-live what happened at the very first Passover. (Exod 12:21-28)

Jewish families in Egypt sacrificed a lamb to God and sprinkled its blood on the doorpost of their homes so the Angel of Death would pass over and they would be saved.

◆ At the annual Passover meal since that event:
  ▶ Prayers of thanks are offered to God.
  ▶ Roast lamb and bitter herbs are eaten.
  ▶ A cup of wine is blessed and given to everyone to drink.
  ▶ Unleavened bread is blessed, broken and shared among everyone.

Eucharist

◆ Eucharist is a Christian service of thanksgiving. Jesus' Passover meal with his disciples became the first Eucharist.

◆ While they were together, Jesus took the bread, said a prayer of thanks to God and gave it to his disciples saying, "This is my body".

◆ Then Jesus took a cup of wine, said a prayer of thanks to God and gave it to his disciples saying, "This is my blood". "Do this in memory of me".

The Last Supper.

◆ Jesus gave the bread and wine of Passover a new meaning when he connected it with his own suffering and death.

◆ Jesus asked his disciples to continue the table-fellowship of the Last Supper. The Christian Eucharist today is based on the words and actions of Jesus at the Last Supper.

NOTE: the precise meaning of the Eucharist varies in the different Christian Churches.

Memorial

◆ The Jewish Passover meal and the Christian Eucharist are both memorial occasions to honour and remember an important person or event.

◆ Jesus asked his followers to remember him by sharing a special meal together.

◆ The Eucharist is a meal that helps Christians to remember and make present Jesus' sacrificial death and his resurrection.

Sacrifice

◆ Jesus tried to tell his disciples that his death would be no ordinary death. His death would be a sacrifice offered to God for the sake of others. Jesus would be the new Passover lamb.

◆ Jesus' death would set everyone free to live in the Kingdom of God.

◆ The disciples were confused. They only fully understood the meaning of Jesus' words and actions after the resurrection.

Test Yourself

1. What do Jews remember and celebrate at Passover?

_____

_____

_____

_____

2. At the Last Supper what new meaning did Jesus give to the bread and wine of Passover?

_____

_____

_____

_____

3. In what way is the Last Supper:
   a. a memorial?

_____

_____

_____

_____

   b. a sacrifice?

_____

_____

_____

_____

Arrest and Trial of Jesus

KEY CONCEPT

Conflict with Authority: a clash or struggle with people in power.

Conflict with authority

◆ After the Last Supper, Jesus went with his disciples to the Garden of Gethsemane. He knew his words and actions as a travelling teacher had brought him into conflict with authority.

◆ While Jesus prayed, Judas arrived with the Temple guards and Jewish authorities. The disciples tried to defend Jesus but they later fled, all except Peter who followed at a distance.

◆ Jesus was arrested and led away to face trial. It was going to be an unfair trial as the Pharisees and Sadducees had already decided to get rid of Jesus because:

▶ He had publicly challenged their authority.

▶ His claim to be the Messiah might cause a revolt against the Romans.

Pilate washes his hands of Jesus and sentences him to death.

The Religious Trial	*The Political Trial*
◆ Jesus was brought to the house of the High Priest. It was late at night.	◆ Jesus was taken to the governor's palace the next morning.
◆ Jesus was questioned by Caiaphas, the High Priest and leader of the Sanhedrin. Caiaphas wanted to find out how serious a threat Jesus actually was.	◆ Jesus was questioned by Pilate the Roman Governor of Palestine. Pilate tried to find out if Jesus was a political troublemaker.
◆ Jesus was asked if he was the Messiah. He said he was, adding that he had a special relationship with God.	◆ Jesus was asked if he was King of the Jews. He replied that he was a king but his kingdom was not of this world.
◆ The Sanhedrin were furious and found Jesus guilty of blasphemy (a religious offence against God).	◆ Pilate thought Jesus was innocent, but under pressure from the Sanhedrin agreed that he was breaking Roman law by claiming to be a king. Pilate found Jesus guilty of treason (a political offence against the Roman Empire).
◆ Jesus had broken Jewish law, so it was decided he must be put to death. However the Sanhedrin did not have the power to execute him.	◆ Jesus had broken Roman law and so Pontius Pilate sentenced him to death.

Test Yourself

1. Place the correct response in each column.

Jesus on trial	The Religious Trial	The Political Trial
a. Where did Jesus' trial take place?		
b. Who questioned Jesus?		
c. What was Jesus asked?		
d. How did Jesus respond?		
e. Of what crime was Jesus accused?		
f. What rule of law was Jesus alleged to have broken?		

2. Why did the Sanhedrin send Jesus to Pilate after they had sentenced him to death?

_____

_____

_____

_____

3. Explain why Pilate finally agreed to sentence Jesus to death.

_____

_____

_____

_____

_____

4. What impact do you think the arrest and trial of Jesus had on Peter and the disciples?

_____

_____

_____

_____

_____

_____

_____

_____

Death of Jesus

OBJECTIVE:
Re-tell the Gospel account
of Jesus' death
on the cross.

KEY CONCEPTS

Sacrifice: something of value (one's life, for example) offered to God for the sake of others.

Martyrdom: a willingness to suffer and die for one's beliefs or a special cause.

Sacrifice

◆ Crucifixion was a cruel punishment used to deter people from opposing Roman rule. Jesus was led out to be crucified on the day Christians call **Good Friday**.

◆ Jesus had to carry his cross through the streets of Jerusalem. A large crowd followed, weeping and wailing for him. Simon, a man from Cyrene, was forced to help him carry the cross.

◆ At Calvary, the place of execution, soldiers nailed Jesus to the cross. He suffered for almost six hours before he gave up his spirit and died.

◆ Jesus offered his life to God for the sake of others. Christians believe his death was a sacrifice to save people from sin, and so enter the Kingdom of God.

Martyrdom

◆ Jesus' death was a form of martyrdom, as he suffered and died because of his beliefs. Jesus' mission was to teach people about God's love and to show people how to live the way God wants.

◆ According to Jewish law, bodies had to be buried before the Sabbath. The body of Jesus was taken down and hastily laid in a borrowed tomb. The embalming of the body would take place after the Sabbath.

◆ Everything was done quickly, a large stone was rolled in front of the tomb. A guard was placed at the entrance to ensure the tomb was not disturbed. The Sanhedrin did not want Jesus' followers to remove the body.

Test Yourself

1. Describe what happened on the day Jesus died on the cross.

_____

_____

_____

_____

2. Jesus was crucified like a common criminal. What impact do you think this had on Peter and the disciples?

_____

_____

_____

3. Explain how Jesus' death was a form of martyrdom.

_____

_____

The Resurrection

KEY CONCEPTS

Resurrection: the central Christian belief that Jesus rose from the dead three days after he was crucified.

Transformation: a complete change in the appearance and nature of Jesus after the resurrection.

Presence: the fact that Jesus exists and is truly present here and now.

Resurrection

◆ The Resurrection is the fundamental Christian belief that three days after he was crucified, Jesus rose from the dead. The Gospel accounts of the resurrection report that:

▶ On Sunday, when the Jewish Sabbath was over, a group of women arrived at the tomb to finish anointing the body of Jesus. They saw that the large stone sealing the tomb had been rolled back and the tomb was empty.

The empty tomb.

▶ A messenger from God told them "Jesus is not here, he is risen from the dead.".

▶ The women were shocked and rushed to tell the disciples who did not believe them. Peter, one of the disciples, went to see for himself. The tomb was indeed empty and Jesus' burial cloth was lying on the ground.

▶ No-one actually saw Jesus rise from the dead. Yet the New Testament states that more than 500 people in Palestine met and talked to him after the resurrection. (1 Corinthians 15:3-8)

Transformation

◆ The disciples did not immediately recognise Jesus when he appeared to them after the resurrection.

◆ Jesus had changed, there was a transformation in him. His bodily appearance was altered after the resurrection; he was different yet somehow everything about him was still the same.

◆ Jesus' followers found it difficult to explain that Jesus was alive but in a new way.

◆ After the resurrection, Jesus appeared to:
  ▶ Mary Magdalene at the tomb. (John 20:11-18)
  ▶ Disciples on the road to Emmaus. (Luke 24:13-35)
  ▶ Disciples in a house in Jerusalem. (John 20:19-25)
  ▶ Thomas in a house in Jerusalem. (John 20:24-29)
  ▶ Disciples beside Lake Galilee. (John 21:1-14)

Presence

◆ After the resurrection, the risen Jesus appears and is present to the disciples. His presence is experienced by all of them.

◆ Common themes in the Gospel accounts of Jesus' appearances after the resurrection include:

1. The disciples are grieving.

2. Jesus appears unexpectedly.

3. Jesus is transformed. The disciples either:
   ▶ Do not recognise him at first.
   ▶ Are shocked and frightened at seeing him.

4. Jesus comforts them with a greeting.

5. Jesus does something that they recognise.

6. The disciples are overwhelmed with joy and peace because Jesus is with them.

7. Jesus tells them to spread the Good News.

Test Yourself

1. How did the disciples react to the news that Jesus had risen from the dead?

_____

_____

_____

_____

2. In what way was Jesus transformed after the resurrection?

_____

_____

_____

_____

3. What impact did the presence of the risen Jesus have on the disciples?

_____

_____

_____

_____

_____

4. Select one Gospel account of Jesus' appearance to his disciples and answer the questions below.

An Appearance of the Risen Jesus

- Where did Jesus appear to the disciples? _____

- How were the disciples feeling that day? _____

- Did they recognise Jesus straight away? _____

- How did Jesus greet them? _____

_____

- Did Jesus do anything familiar that they recognised? _____

_____

- How did the disciples respond to Jesus? _____

_____

- Did Jesus ask the disciples to do anything? _____

_____

_____

Section B - The Death and Resurrection of Jesus

Exam Questions

1. **A.** Jesus was in conflict with members of each of the following groups. ....2003(O)

Tick ✓ **one** and *explain* why Jesus was in conflict with this group.

Pharisees ☐   Romans ☐   Sadducees ☐

B.

CHIEF PRIESTS CRITICISE JESUS *Capital News*	LEADERS SAY JESUS IS A TROUBLEMAKER *Galilee Times*	ANGRY SCENES AS JESUS OVERTURNS TABLES IN TEMPLE *Jerusalem Herald*

These headlines might have appeared when Jesus came into conflict with people in power.

Imagine you are a journalist covering the events in the life of Jesus. Write a newspaper report describing **one** of the times Jesus was in conflict with people in power.

a. What was the event?   b. What did Jesus say or do?

c. How did the people in power react?   d. Why did they react in this way?

---

2. **A.** Outline the role of the Pharisees in the religious life of people in Palestine at the time of Jesus. ....2004(H)

B. Describe **one** incident from the life of Jesus when he was in conflict with a Pharisee.

C. Imagine you are a Pharisee in this conflict. Outline your reason for opposing Jesus.

---

3. **A.** Describe **one** incident from the life of Jesus that led to his death. ....2007(H)

B. Outline **two** reasons why the incident you have described above led to the death of Jesus.

C. Outline how Jesus' death affected the people who were following him.

---

4. This picture is based on a Gospel account of Jesus celebrating the Last Supper. .... 2007(H), 2014(H)

(Source: www.theliterates.ca)

A. Pick **one** thing from this picture which suggests that it is based on Jesus' celebration of the Last Supper.

B. According to the Gospels which **one** of the following people was present at the Last Supper with Jesus? (Tick ✓ the correct box)

PAUL ☐   PETER ☐   PRISCILLA ☐

C. State **two** reasons why Jesus celebrated the Last Supper.

---

5. **A.** a. The person most associated with the arrest of Jesus in the ....2010(O) Garden of Gethsemane was – (Tick ✓ the correct box)

Barabbas ☐   Herod ☐   Judas ☐

b. Outline **two** ways in which the first disciples were affected by the arrest of Jesus in the Garden of Gethsemane.

B. Imagine you were an eyewitness to the last events of Jesus' life -

Jesus on trial ☐   Jesus on trial ☐   The crucifixion ☐
before the Sanhedrin   before Pilate   and death of Jesus

Tick ✓ **one** of the events listed above and describe what happened in the event you have ticked.

6. A. Give **two** reasons why the Sanhedrin was important in Palestine at the time of Jesus. .... 2008(H), 2013(H)

 B. Outline what happened when Jesus was brought before the Sanhedrin.

---

7. A. a. Below you will find a list of some of the events leading up to the death of Jesus. ....2005(H)

 Number these events in the order in which they occurred.

 Number 1 should be the first event and number 5 should be the last event.

Number	Event
	The Crucifixion
	Jesus is brought to Pontius Pilate
	Jesus is brought before the Sanhedrin
	The Last Supper
	Temple guards arrest Jesus

 b. What was the role of the Sanhedrin in Palestine at the time of Jesus?

 c. What position did Pontius Pilate hold in the political life of Palestine at the time of Jesus?

 B. Imagine you were one of the disciples who witnessed Jesus' death and was present when Jesus appeared after his resurrection.

 a. Describe the impact that the death of Jesus had on your life.

 b. Describe **one** of the appearances of the risen Jesus you witnessed and the effect it had on you.

---

8. a. In the Christian tradition the term 'sacrifice' refers to _____ ....2011(H)

 b. Outline how sacrifice can be seen in **one** event from the life of Jesus.

---

9. This picture is based on a Gospel account of the resurrection of Jesus. ....2012(O)

 A. Pick **one** thing from this picture which suggests that it is based on the resurrection of Jesus.

 B. On which of the following days of the week did the disciples of Jesus first discover his resurrection from the dead? (Tick ✓ the correct box)

 Friday ☐   Saturday ☐   Sunday ☐

 C. State **one** way that the first Christians were affected by the resurrection of Jesus.

www.arabchurch.com

---

10. ....2011(H)

● MEMORIAL   ● MISSION

Examine how the experience of **one** of the above played a part in the development of the first Christian communities.

NOTE: *This is an essay question.*

Pentecost

KEY CONCEPT

Pentecost: the day the apostles received the Holy Spirit and began spreading the message of Jesus.

- In the New Testament, St. Luke wrote two books to enable Christians to have faith in Jesus.
  - **The Gospel of Luke** about the life, death and resurrection of Jesus.
  - **The Acts of the Apostles** about the actions of the apostles and the early Church.
- Jesus appeared to the disciples many times after the resurrection, and continued to teach them about the Kingdom of God.
- Then Jesus appeared to the disciples for the last time before he ascended to heaven.

  He told them:
  - to go out and tell the whole world about his life and his teachings.
  - that he would send the Holy Spirit to help them do this work.

  Jesus then returned to God the Father in Heaven.

Pentecost

- In Jerusalem, fifty days after the resurrection, the Holy Spirit came upon the disciples.
- The experience of Pentecost was hard to put into words, it was like the disciples were on fire with the Spirit of God. It made them brave and strong and eager to continue the work that Jesus had begun.
- On the day of Pentecost the apostles received the Holy Spirit and began spreading the message of Jesus. Peter and the apostles went out in public to announce the Good News that:
  - Jesus had risen from the dead.
  - Jesus was the promised Messiah.
- In Jerusalem a large number of people were baptised and became followers of Jesus.
- Pentecost is the birthday of the Christian Church.

Test Yourself

1. Before he ascended to Heaven:
   a. what new work did Jesus give the disciples to do?

   _____

   b. what promise did Jesus make to the disciples?

   _____

2. What happened to Jesus' disciples on the day of Pentecost?

   _____

   _____

   _____

3. Why is Pentecost important in the life of the Christian Church?

   _____

   _____

   _____

Early Faith Communities

KEY CONCEPT

People of God: Christian communities past and present who believe in God and follow the teaching of Jesus.

◆ After Pentecost the apostles, guided by the Holy Spirit, began their work in the city of Jerusalem. They started:
- teaching the Good News,
- healing illness and disability,
- baptising new believers
- celebrating the Eucharist in people's homes.

People of God

◆ Under the guidance of the apostles, small groups of believers formed themselves into communities. They followed Jesus' teaching about the Kingdom of God and became known as Christians, the new People of God.

Characteristics of the first Christian communities:

Faith: They had faith in Jesus the Messiah, the Son of God.

Worship: On Sunday, the day of resurrection, they met in each others homes and celebrated 'the breaking of bread', the Eucharist, as Jesus had requested.

Way of Life: They shared everything with each other and helped people in need.

◆ The first followers of Jesus may not have realised that they were starting a new community of faith. They were simply a group of Jews who:
▶ Believed Jesus was the Messiah.
▶ Followed Jesus' commandment to love God and love their neighbour.

◆ Over time they began to see that their faith, worship and way of life was different to other Jews. At a certain point they realised they could no longer continue being Jews. They became Christians, followers of Jesus Christ.

Persecution

◆ In Jerusalem, the Sadducees warned the apostles against preaching the message of Jesus in the Temple. The apostles continued their work even though they were threatened and sometimes imprisoned.

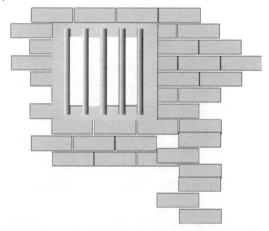

◆ Jesus' followers were soon brought before the Sanhedrin. Stephen, one of their number, was accused of blasphemy and stoned to death. Widespread persecution followed, forcing many Christians out of Jerusalem to other parts of Palestine.

◆ The apostles left Jerusalem too. They began to spread the message of Jesus among new Christian communities that were becoming established throughout Palestine.

◆ The first Christian communities consisted only of Jews. Eventually Gentiles (non-Jews) were welcomed and accepted.

◆ Christians came to realise that Jesus' message of the Kingdom of God was not only for Jews, but for all people, in Palestine and beyond.

Test Yourself

1. The first Christians were known as...

_____

2. Where was the first Christian community established?

_____

_____

_____

3. How did Peter and the apostles serve the Christian community in Jerusalem?

_____

_____

_____

_____

_____

_____

4. What were the characteristics of the early Christian communities?

_____

_____

_____

_____

_____

_____

5. What factors caused the message of Jesus to spread beyond the city of Jerusalem?

_____

_____

_____

_____

_____

_____

_____

St. Paul

KEY CONCEPT

Missionary: one who is sent on a journey to spread the Gospel by preaching, or by example.

Missionary

◆ St. Paul is the most outstanding Christian **missionary** of the early Church. He spread the Christian message beyond Palestine to the rest of the Roman Empire.

◆ **St. Paul** was originally a Jew, a strict Pharisee who persecuted Christians in Jerusalem. He became a follower of Jesus as a result of a religious experience on the road to Damascus.

◆ Paul felt called by God to spend the rest of his life as a Christian missionary.

Guided by the Holy Spirit he began to:

▶ Preach the Good News of Jesus Christ.

▶ Baptise new believers.

▶ Establish new Christian communities throughout the Roman Empire.

◆ Paul set out on three missionary journeys, travelling by land and sea to towns and cities around the Mediterranean. As a Roman citizen who spoke four languages, he could move freely from place to place and be understood wherever he went.

◆ St. Paul brought the Gospel to Gentiles (non-Jews) all over the Roman Empire.

Characteristics of early Christian communities.

◆ Paul taught each new Christian community to:

Faith: have faith in Jesus the Son of God.

Worship: worship on Sunday, meet in each others homes and celebrate the breaking of bread.

Way of Life: follow a way of life which meant sharing everything, and helping people in need.

◆ He wrote letters, or epistles, offering support and advice to each community he established.

◆ St. Paul was arrested and brought to Rome where he was martyred for his faith in 65CE.

Test Yourself

1. What happened on the road to Damascus?

_____

2. What work did Paul do as a Christian missionary?

_____

_____

_____

3. What were the characteristics of the Christian communities established by St. Paul?

_____

_____

_____

_____

_____

Modern Faith Communities

KEY CONCEPTS

People of God: Christian communities, past and present, who believe in God and follow the teaching of Jesus.

People of God

- The Roman Catholic Church is an example of a community of faith. Its members are known as People of God.

- Like the first Christian communities, members of the Catholic Church:
  - Have **faith** in Jesus, the Son of God.
  - On Sunday they **worship** together and celebrate the Eucharist.
  - Lead a caring **way of life** and help people in need.

- A Catholic parish is an example of a modern Christian community. The priest is the leader of this community. Lay people are baptised Christians called to put Jesus' teachings into practice in their daily lives.

- Priests and lay people are modern disciples of Jesus. Both work together to make Jesus' message of the Kingdom of God a reality in the parish.

- Lay people can serve the parish community in various ways. Different roles are available to people according to their gifts and talents, for example:
  - In Parish Liturgies, as a:
    - Minister of the Word.
    - Minister of the Eucharist.
    - Member of the church choir.
    - Sacristan.
  - In Parish Development, as a:
    - Member of the parish council.
    - Member of a team preparing children and families for the sacraments of Baptism, Eucharist and Confirmation.
  - In Voluntary Organisations, as a:
    - Member of the St. Vincent de Paul Society.
    - Fundraiser for Trocaire.
    - Volunteer helping people in need at home and abroad.

Test Yourself

1. Who were the People of God (i) in the early faith communities? _____

   (ii) in modern faith communities. _____

2. What inspires Catholics to serve in their parish community?

   _____

   _____

   _____

3. Compare a parish community today with the first Christian communities founded by the apostles.

   _____

   _____

   _____

   _____

   _____

New Titles for Jesus

KEY CONCEPTS

Son of Man: a title that shows the human nature of Jesus, and the fact that his suffering and death is a sacrifice to benefit all humanity.

Son of God: a title that shows the divine or holy relationship between Jesus and God the Father.

Christ/Messiah: a title meaning "anointed one"; Jesus is a spiritual leader sent by God.

A new understanding of Jesus

◆ In the early years of the Christian Church, the apostles thought a lot about Jesus' true identity.

◆ The apostles needed to understand the connection between God and the risen Jesus so that they could tell others what they believed.

◆ The apostles did not use the term 'God' for Jesus straight away. Instead they used certain words from the Old Testament such as:
- **Son of Man**.
- **Son of God**.
- **Christ/Messiah**

◆ These terms were already familiar to the Jews. So when the apostles applied them to Jesus, their listeners immediately grasped their significance and understood what the disciples were trying to say.

Jesus of Nazareth

Son of Man (Mark 10:32-34)

◆ This is the only title Jesus applied to himself to indicate who he was.

◆ On the way to Jerusalem Jesus took his disciples aside and explained to them what the title Son of Man means:

▶ Jesus is like all humanity, he has feelings and will suffer and die like everybody else.

▶ Jesus is different in that he is sent by God to establish the Kingdom of God on Earth. His suffering and death is a sacrifice that will benefit everyone.

Son of God (Mark 15:33-39)

◆ A title the early Christians used for Jesus but only after the resurrection.

◆ In ancient times an extremely good or holy person was referred to as 'a son of God'.

◆ This term takes on an additional meaning when applied to Jesus. He is not simply the best or the holiest person who ever lived. Jesus' life and work shows that he has a unique and very close relationship with God.

◆ Jesus is not just <u>**a**</u> son of God, he is <u>**the**</u> Son of God.

Christ/Messiah (Mark 8:27-30)

- This title came into proper use after the resurrection, although the disciples attempted to use it for Jesus before that.

- Both words, Christ/Messiah, mean the 'anointed one', that is someone chosen by God to carry out a special task.

- All Jewish kings including King David were anointed at the beginning of their reign. The Jews expected the promised Messiah to be another great king who would bring peace and liberty to Jews in Palestine.

- However Jesus' idea of the 'anointed one' was different from that of the disciples and other Jews at the time.

  For Jesus, the Messiah is not a political leader but a spiritual one who must suffer, die and rise again. His kingdom is a spiritual kingdom in people's hearts, not a political kingdom in a particular place.

- After the resurrection the disciples finally understood and believed. Jesus Christ the Messiah was specially chosen to do God's work not just in Palestine but among all people everywhere.

Test Yourself

1. Why did the apostles promote the use of certain titles for Jesus?

   _____

   _____

   _____

   _____

2. When Jesus refers to himself as Son of Man, in what way is he the same as all human beings, and in what way is he different?

   _____

   _____

   _____

   _____

3. What did the apostles mean when they referred to Jesus as the Son of God?

   _____

   _____

   _____

   _____

4. How is Jesus' understanding of the Messiah different to the Jewish expectation of the Messiah?

   _____

   _____

   _____

   _____

   _____

Exam Questions

1. Below you will find a list of events that occurred after the death of Jesus. ....2012(H)

Number **each** event in the order in which it occurred.

Number 1 should be the first event and number 3 should be the last event.

Number: *Events that occurred after the death of Jesus:*

_____ ● Jesus appears to his disciples.

_____ ● Jesus ascends into heaven.

_____ ● Jesus is buried.

2. a. JESUS' ASCENSION ☐ PENTECOST☐ ....2013(H)

Tick ✓ **one** of the above and describe what happened in the event.

b. Outline how the first Christians were affected by the event that you have ticked above.

3.

masbury.files.wordpress.com

This picture is based on the first Christians' ....2009(O) experience of Pentecost.

A. Pick **one** thing from this picture which shows that it is based on the first Christians' experience of Pentecost.

B. The first Christians experienced Pentecost after the death of Jesus. (Tick ✓ the correct box)

True ☐ False ☐

C. State **one** effect the experience of Pentecost had on the first Christians.

4. A. Examine the way in which the Jewish religion was structured in Palestine ....2010(H) at the time of Jesus.

B. a. Describe **two** difficulties the first Christians faced after the death of Jesus.

b. Outline **one** way in which the first Christians dealt with the difficulties they faced after the death of Jesus.

5. Describe **one** way in which Jesus' teaching about the Kingdom of God ....2005(H) influenced the way of life in the first Christian communities.

6. A. Name the founder/ earliest followers of the religion of Christianity. ....2003(H)

B. Describe **one** important event that inspired the earliest followers of this religion.

C. Briefly explain how the event described above can be seen as inspiration for the followers of this faith today.

7. ● Son of God   ● Son of Man   ....2006(H)

Outline what **one** of the above titles shows about the early Christians' understanding of Jesus.

---

8. ● MESSIAH   ● NEW CREATION   ....2010(H)

Examine **one** of the above titles for Jesus referring to the following points:

i. The meaning of the title for the Jewish people at the time of Jesus.

ii. The new understanding of Jesus seen in the use of the title by the first Christians.

NOTE: *This is an essay question.*

---

9. "One of them was Andrew, Simon Peter's brother. ....2003(H)
At once he found his brother Simon and told him,
'We have found the Messiah.' (This word means 'Christ'.)
Then he took Simon to Jesus."
(John 1:40-42 *Good News Bible*)

a. Describe **another** incident from the Gospels when people used the title "Messiah" for Jesus.

b. Explain how the use of this title influenced the faith and practice of the early Christian community.

---

10. Imagine you have to give a talk on the way the Early Christians used the ....2013(H)
following titles for Jesus:

● NEW CREATION   ● SON OF MAN

Outline the points that you would make in your talk on the meaning of **one** title and
explain how the use of this title shows the Early Christians' new understanding of Jesus.

NOTE: *This is an essay question.*

Section C - Foundations of Religion: Judaism

The *Syllabus Aims* in this section are:

◆ To explore in detail a major world religion.

◆ To examine the impact of this religion on it's followers today, and on other individuals and communities.

Key Concepts in Judaism *(Section C)* *Page*

Judaism - the Context

KEY CONCEPTS

Location: the part of the world where the religion of Judaism began.

Cultural context: the whole way of life of people living in the place where Judaism began.

Location

◆ Judaism is a major world religion with over eighteen million members in the world today. Jews believe in one God, Yahweh, whom they call 'Lord'. The religion of Judaism was founded by Abraham about 4,000 years ago.

◆ Canaan was the location, or the place, where the religion of Judaism began. Canaan was located in the **Fertile Crescent**, an arc (or crescent) of good land that stretched from Egypt all the way to the city of Ur in Mesopotamia.

◆ Ur and Babylon were important city states in Mesopotamia. At the time of Abraham:

  ▶ The Babylonian Empire ruled one part of the Fertile Crescent, including the city of Ur.
  ▶ The Egyptian Empire ruled the other part, including the land of Canaan.

Cultural Context

◆ The cultural context is the way of life of the people living in the Fertile Crescent at the time of Abraham. Different groups of people travelled through this vast region, some were merchants and travellers, others were nomads.

◆ Nomads were large family groups who migrated from place to place in search of pasture for their animals. They were self-sufficient and traded their surplus in the markets along the way.

◆ Abraham, a founder of Judaism, became a nomad in later life. He set out from the city of Ur in Mesopotamia and travelled to the land of Canaan, a distance of over 1000 miles (1600km).

◆ Ur was an advanced city in Abraham's time and had active trading links with other cities. Most people were polytheists and worshipped different gods. The temple in Ur was an important centre of moon worship in Mesopotamia.

  People visited Ur from far and wide
  ▶ to trade in the city.
  ▶ to worship in the temple.

The journey of Abraham

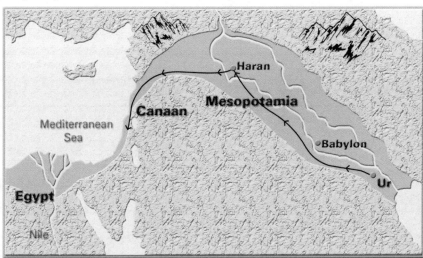

Test Yourself

1. Where did the religion of Judaism begin?

_____

_____

_____

2. What was the Fertile Crescent in ancient times?

_____

_____

3. How did the nomadic people of the Fertile Crescent live in the time of Abraham?

_____

_____

_____

_____

_____

_____

_____

4. What was the religious belief and practice of people in the Fertile Crescent at the time of Abraham?

_____

_____

_____

_____

5. Outline the importance of the city of Ur in ancient times as:
   a. a trading centre.

_____

_____

_____

_____

   b. a religious centre.

_____

_____

_____

_____

Exam Questions

---

1. a. Tick ✓ **one** of the following world religions you have studied: .... 2004(H)

☐ Buddhism   ☐ Hinduism   ☐ Islam   ☐ Judaism

Tick ✓ **one** country on the map below where the world religion you have chosen began.

b. Briefly describe **one** thing about the way people lived in the country you have chosen at the time this world religion began.

---

2.   Buddhism ☐   Hinduism ☐   Islam ☐   Judaism ☐   .... 2009(H)

Tick ✓ **one** of the major world religions above that you have studied.

a. Name **one** part of the world associated with the founding story of the major world religion you have ticked above. Hinduism

b. Describe the way people lived in the part of the world you have named above at the time the world religion began.

---

3. A. Tick ✓ **one** of the following world religions that you have studied: .... 2010(O)

BUDDHISM ☐   HINDUISM ☐   ISLAM ☐   JUDAISM ☐

B. a. Name *either* **one** person *or* **one** group associated with the founding story of the world religion you have ticked above.

   b. Outline how *either* **one** person *or* **one** group played an important part in the founding of the world religion you have ticked above.

Abraham

KEY CONCEPTS

Founder: the person who established a religion.

Vision: a vivid dream or mental image of something important.

Founder

◆ **Abraham**, a founder of the religion of Judaism, lived about 4000 years ago in the city of Ur in Mesopotamia.

◆ Abraham worshipped the gods of nature like everyone else, but then began to wonder about the need for so many gods. Around this time his family left Ur and travelled to Haran.

Vision

◆ In Haran, Abraham had a vision, a dream of something important. God spoke to him saying "Leave your country, your people, and your father's house and go to the land I will show you." (Genesis 12:1)

◆ Abraham showed great faith and set off across the Fertile Crescent with his wife, his nephew, and all their goods and animals. They travelled south and eventually settled in the land of **Canaan**, which became known as the Promised Land.

◆ In Canaan Abraham had a second vision. He believed God made a **covenant** (a sacred agreement) with him. God asked Abraham to believe in and worship the one all-powerful God.

◆ If Abraham did as God told him, God promised him:
  ▸ many descendants.
  ▸ the land of Canaan.

The Covenant was the beginning of a special relationship between God and the Jewish people.

◆ Following another vision, God blessed Abraham and his wife Sarah and in their old age the couple had a son named Isaac. When the child was eight days old he was circumcised.

Ever since, male circumcision is a sign that Araham's descendants have a special relationship with God.

Test Yourself

1. Why did Abraham make the long journey to the land of Canaan?

_____

_____

2. What was the covenant God made with Abraham and his descendants?

_____

_____

3. How would you describe Abraham and his relationship with God?

_____

_____

_____

Moses

OBJECTIVE:
Identify key moments in
the life of Moses,
a founder of Judaism.

> **KEY CONCEPTS**
>
> **Founder**: the person who established a religion.
>
> **Vision**: a vivid dream or mental image of something important.

Founder

◆ **Moses** is a founder of the religion of Judaism.

◆ Abraham's descendants migrated from Canaan and were forced into slavery in Egypt. Moses, a descendant of Abraham, was adopted, raised and educated as an Egyptian prince.

Vision

◆ When Moses stopped to pray in the desert he saw a bush go on fire. Then he had a vision, a dream of something important. God spoke to him.

"I am sending you to the King of Egypt so that you can lead my people out of his country." (Exodus 3:10)

◆ Moses eventually went to the Pharoah and demanded that God's people be set free. The Pharaoh refused, but was forced to change his mind when a number of plagues and disasters occured in the land.

The Passover

◆ The Jews followed Moses' instructions and sprinkled the blood of lambs on their doorposts. The Angel of Death passed over their houses and they were spared from disaster.

◆ The Jews gave thanks and had a Passover celebration. They ate a special meal of roast lamb, bitter herbs and bread made without yeast.

The Exodus

◆ Moses then led God's people through the Red Sea where the Pharaoh's army could not follow. The Jew's escaped, they were free at last. This is the Exodus, the great event of Jewish history.

The Ten Commandments

◆ When they reached Mount Sinai, Moses went up the mountain alone to pray. There he had another vision. God renewed the covenant with Moses and the Jewish people.

◆ God gave Moses the Laws and the Ten Commandments. (The Ten Sayings.)

◆ The Ten Commandments gave details of how God wanted the Jewish people to live. They must:

  ▶ Believe in one powerful God.

  ▶ Create a good and just society.

Test Yourself

1. What occurred at the first Passover in Egypt?

_____

_____

_____

2. Explain the meaning of the Exodus.

_____

_____

_____

3. Why are the Ten Commandments so important in the religion of Judaism?

_____

_____

Sacred Text

OBJECTIVE:
Name the primary source of information about Judaism.
Trace the development of its sacred texts from the oral tradition to the written word.

KEY CONCEPTS

Sacred text: the book of holy or sacred writings of a community of faith.

Oral Tradition: stories and religious teaching that a people pass on by word of mouth.

Evidence: information about a religious tradition collected from different sources.

Revelation: the way in which God chooses to make himself known to human beings.

Inspiration: the way in which a person is guided by God to pass on a sacred message.

Sacred Text

- The Tenakh is the sacred text of Judaism. It is a collection of thirty nine books and is the primary source of information about Judaism.

- The **Tenakh** is a document of faith. It tells the story of how Judaism began and the beliefs and practices that are important in Judaism.

- The Tenakh has three parts:
  1. The Torah.
  2. The Prophets.
  3. The Writings.

- The **Torah** is the holiest and most important part of the Tenakh.
  The five books of the Torah contain:
  ▸ Jewish teaching on Creation.
  ▸ The story of Abraham and Moses.
  ▸ The Law and the Ten Commandments.

- Most of the Torah is in Hebrew and is handwritten on scrolls for use in the synagogue.

- The **Talmud** is a sacred text, based on the Torah. It was written by rabbis who were experts on the Torah.

- The Talmud explains how the laws in the Torah can be applied to all aspects of people's daily life.

Oral Tradition

- The history of the Jewish people began with Abraham, then Moses, and later the Prophets.

- The detail of their story was carefully remembered and passed on from generation to generation by word of mouth.

- The oral tradition or oral stage of Jewish scripture lasted for many centuries.

- The history of God's intervention in the life of the Jewish people was eventually written down. Many authors undertook the task; it developed slowly over 1,000 years.

Evidence

- The evidence or information about Judaism was collected from different sources. Eventually the work of the different scriptural authors was gathered together in one volume.

- God inspired scribes (Jewish writers) to select and edit the sacred writings.

- In 90CE the seal of approval was given to 39 books, the result was the Tenakh, or the Hebrew Bible as it exists today.

- In 500CE the Talmud was written, up to then the rabbi's teaching on the Torah had been passed on orally, by word of mouth.

Revelation

◆ **Revelation** is the way in which God chose to make himself known to human beings. God made himself known first to Abraham, and then to Moses. God revealed himself more fully to Moses than to anyone else.

◆ God revealed his holy name - Yahweh. God revealed that he is good, fair and just.

◆ God gave the Torah to Moses on Mount Sinai. Most Jews believe the words in the Torah are the actual words of God himself. The Torah is therefore treated with great respect by Jewish people.

Inspiration

◆ Jews believe that all other parts of the Tenakh, the Prophets and Writings, were inspired by God.

◆ **Inspiration** is the way in which a person is guided by God to pass on a sacred message. The human authors of the remaining parts of the Tenakh were guided by God to pass on a sacred message to the Jewish people.

◆ God worked through these human authors.

◆ The writers used their own words and style of writing to say what God wanted them to say.

Test Yourself

1. Name the sacred text of Judaism?

_____

2. What is the connection between the Torah and the Talmud?

_____

_____

_____

3. Why do Jews regard the Torah as the most sacred part of the Tenakh?

_____

_____

_____

4. Outline the development of the Jewish sacred text from the oral tradition to written word.

_____

_____

_____

_____

5. How was the will of God revealed to the Jewish people?

_____

_____

_____

_____

1. a. Pick **one** of the following world religions that you have studied: .... 2003(H)

 ◆ BUDDHISM ◆ HINDUISM ◆ ISLAM ◆ JUDAISM

 Name the world religion: _____

 Name the founder/earliest followers of the world religion: _____

 b. Describe **one** important event that inspired the founder/earliest followers of this world religion.

 c. Briefly explain how the event described above can be seen as inspiration for the followers of this faith today.

---

2. Tick ✓ **one** of the following world religions you have studied: .... 2006(O)

 ❑ Buddhism ❑ Hinduism ❑ Islam ❑ Judaism

 a. Describe how religious belief had an effect on the life of an important person in the story of the world religion you have ticked above.

---

3. Tick ✓ **one** of the following world religions that you have studied: .... 2014(O)

 BUDDHISM ❑ HINDUISM ❑ ISLAM ❑ JUDAISM ❑

 a. Name the founder/earliest followers of the world religion that you have ticked above.

 b. Describe an example of how trust in God/gods/the divine was shown by the founder/earliest followers of the world religion that you have ticked above.

---

4. a. ❑ Buddhism ❑ Hinduism ❑ Islam ❑ Judaism .... 2007(H)

 Tick ✓ one of the world religions above that you have studied:

 (i) Name **one** key person / group of people associated with the founding story of the world religion you have ticked above.

 (ii) Explain why the person / group of people you have named is important in the founding story of the world religion you have ticked above.

 b. Outline **one** way in which the story of the earliest followers influences members today in the world religion you have ticked.

 c. Explain how the world religion you have ticked above is linked to another major world religion.

---

5. Tick ✓ **one** of the following world religions that you have studied: .... 2009(O)

 BUDDHISM ❑ HINDUISM ❑ ISLAM ❑ JUDAISM ❑

 a. Name **one** sacred text that is associated with the world religion you have ticked above.

 b. Explain **two** reasons why a sacred text is important for members of a world religion.

---

6. Tick ✓ **one** of the following world religions that you have studied: .... 2013(O)

 BUDDHISM ❑ HINDUISM ❑ ISLAM ❑ JUDAISM ❑

 a. Name **one** sacred text that is most associated with the world religion which you have ticked above.

 b. Outline **two** reasons why the sacred text that you have named above is valued by the members of the world religion that you have ticked above.

7. a. Below you will find a list of the stages involved in the development of a sacred text. ....2013(O)

Number each stage in the order in which it occurred.

Number 1 should be the first stage and number 3 should be the last stage.

Number	Stages in the Development of a Sacred Text
	An account of the founding story was written down.
	Events took place associated with the founding story.
	Information about the founding story was passed on by word of mouth.

b. Outline what was involved in **one** of the stages in the development of the sacred text that you have named in question *6a* above.

---

8. **A.** Tick ✓ **one** of the following world religions that you have studied: ....2006(O)

   ❏ Buddhism   ❏ Hinduism   ❏ Islam   ❏ Judaism

   a. Name a text that is sacred for members of the world religion you have ticked above.

   b. Give **one** reason why this text is sacred for members of the world religion ticked above.

B. Sacred texts have been passed on by word of mouth and by written word.

   Describe what happened in the development of the sacred text you have named above at either the word of mouth stage *or* the written word stage.

---

9. Tick ✓ **one** of the following major world religions that you have studied: ....2012(H)

   BUDDHISM ❏   HINDUISM ❏   ISLAM ❏   JUDAISM ❏

   a. Name **one** sacred text that is most associated with the world religion that you have ticked above.

   b. Outline what was involved in **two** stages in the development of the sacred text that you have named above.

---

10. **A.** a. In religious traditions the term 'revelation' involves God/the divine ....2012(O)
   communicating with people.
   (Tick ✓ the correct box)   True ❏   False ❏

   b. Tick ✓ **one** of the following world religions that you have studied:

   BUDDHISM ❏   HINDUISM ❏   ISLAM ❏   JUDAISM ❏

   Describe **one** example of revelation from the story of the world religion that you have ticked above.

B. a. Read the list of religious names and the list of world religions given below.

   Match **one** religious name to the world religion with which it is most associated.

Religious Names	World Religions		Religious Name	World Religion
Allah	Buddhism	Answer:		
Yahweh/YHWH	Hinduism			
Enlightened One	Islam			
Brahman	Judaism			

11. a. In religious traditions the term 'revelation' means _____   ....2009(O)

b. Describe **one** example of revelation from the story of the founder/earliest followers of the world religion you have studied.

---

12. a.   ◆ BUDDHISM   ◆ HINDUISM   ◆ ISLAM   ◆ JUDAISM   ....2014(H)

Name a sacred text that is associated with **one** of the above world religions.
Explain **two** reasons why it can be described as a document of faith.

SACRED TEXT: _____   WORLD RELIGION: _____

b. Describe what happened from the oral to the written stages in the development of the sacred text that you have named above.

---

13.   ◆ BUDDHISM   ◆ HINDUISM   ◆ ISLAM   ◆ JUDAISM   ....2009(H)

Discuss the importance of a sacred text in **one** of the above major world religions that you have studied.

NOTE: *This is an essay question.*

Belief and Practice

KEY CONCEPTS

Creed/ethic: the summary of a religion's deeply held beliefs and moral principles.

Practice: customs and rituals that show a person's religious faith.

Creed/ ethic

◆ A **creed** is a summary of a religion's deeply held beliefs. The Shema is a Jewish prayer and the nearest thing to a creed in the religion of Judaism. It is a summary of Jewish belief about God.

"Hear O Israel, the Lord is our God, the Lord alone. You shall love the Lord your God with all your heart and with all your soul and with all your might." (Deut 6:4-5)

Main Jewish beliefs

◆ Jews believe:
  ▶ In **one God**, Yahweh, who is good and all powerful, the creator of the world.
  ▶ That they are God's **chosen people**.
  ▶ God made a **covenant** with Abraham and Moses, and they must be faithful to it.
  ▶ God gave Moses the **Torah** containing the Ten Commandments to help Jewish people live good and holy lives.

Practice

◆ **Practice** is the set of customs and rituals that show a person's religious faith. Jews put their religious beliefs into practice through:
  ▶ Daily rituals such as:
    - Saying the Shema morning and evening.
    - Wearing tefillin (containing the Shema) at prayer times.
    - Touching the mezuzah (containing the Shema) on the doorframe of their homes.
  ▶ Weekly rituals such as:
    - The celebration of the Sabbath.
  ▶ Annual rituals such as:
    - The celebration of religious feasts and festivals.
  ▶ Life changing rituals such as:
    - The circumcision of a baby boy after birth.
    - Bar mitzvah and bat mitzvah.
    - Wedding ceremonies.
    - Death and mourning.

Test Yourself

1. What is the Shema?

   _____

2. What are the central beliefs of Judaism?

   _____

   _____

   _____

3. How do Jews put their religious beliefs into practice?

   _____

   _____

   _____

   _____

Prayer

OBJECTIVE:
Outline the importance
of prayer
in the religion of Judaism.

> **KEY CONCEPT**
>
> **Prayer**: the act of communicating with God.

Prayer

- **Prayer** is how Jewish people communicate with God.

- Abraham and Moses, the founders of Judaism, communicated with God through prayer.

- All male Jews over thirteen years of age are expected to pray three times a day, morning, afternoon and evening.

Ways to Pray

- ▶ **Personal prayer**: when Jews pray by themselves at home during the week.

- ▶ **Communal prayer**: when Jews pray with others as a community. Two examples are:
  - going to the synagogue to pray on the morning of the Sabbath.
  - praying together as a family at home on the Sabbath and during religious festivals.

Different types of Prayer

- The Psalms are the great prayers of Judaism. The Book of Psalms contains different types of prayers; for example there are:

  - ▶ Prayers of **Praise and Thanksgiving** thanking God for some good thing that happened.

  - ▶ Prayers of **Petition** asking God for help with something special.

  - ▶ Prayers of **Penitence** expressing sorrow for some wrongdoing and asking God for forgiveness.

- The Shema (Deut. 6:4-9) is the most important Jewish prayer. The Siddur is the Jewish prayer book. It has the main 'set' prayers which are said every day and on the Sabbath.

- Jewish men dress for prayer in the synagogue. A kippah is put on the head, a tallit around the shoulders and a tefillin tied to the forehead and left arm.

Test Yourself

1. When do Jewish people pray?

   _____

   _____

2. How do Jewish people pray?

   _____

   _____

   _____

   _____

3. Identify different types of prayer in the Jewish tradition.

   _____

   _____

   _____

   _____

The Sabbath

KEY CONCEPT

Ritual: an occasion when people use symbolic objects, words and actions to express what is deeply important to them.

◆ The Jewish Sabbath, or 'Shabbat' in Hebrew, begins at sunset on Friday and ends at sunset on Saturday. It is sacred time marked by religious rituals in the home and in the synagogue.

Ritual

◆ A ritual is an occasion when people use symbolic objects, words and actions to express what is deeply important to them. Certain things are always said and done on the Jewish Sabbath.

Preparing for the Sabbath

◆ On Friday afternoon, all work is finished and a meal is prepared. The table is set with special care. It is covered with a white tablecloth, two candlesticks, a wine glass, a dish of salt and two loaves of plaited bread called challah.

Welcoming the Sabbath

◆ At sunset the mother performs a short ritual. She lights the two candles and says a special prayer to welcome the Sabbath.

The Kiddush

◆ The Sabbath meal begins with the Kiddush. The father says a blessing over the glass of wine, sprinkles salt on the bread, breaks it and gives a piece to everyone to eat.

The Sabbath Meal

◆ The family enjoy the Sabbath meal of kosher food prepared according to Jewish rules about diet and hygiene. The meal always ends with a prayer of thanksgiving.

The Sabbath Day

◆ On Saturday morning Jewish families attend a service in the synagogue. The Sabbath is different to all other days; it is a holy day and a day of rest.

The Havdalah

◆ The Sabbath ends at sunset on Saturday. It is marked by a short ritual carried out in the home. The father says a blessing, lights a special plaited candle and passes around a box of sweet smelling spices.

Test Yourself

1. What is the Jewish holy day of the week? When does it begin and end?

_____

_____

2. Describe a ritual performed by a Jewish mother or father in the home during Shabbat.

_____

_____

_____

_____

3. How might celebrating the Sabbath strengthen family ties in the Jewish community?

_____

_____

Place of Worship

KEY CONCEPTS

Worship: the way people of faith praise and honour God in prayer and at religious services.

Place of worship: a building or place where people go to pray and worship God or gods.

Ritual: an occasion when people use symbolic objects, words and actions to express what is deeply important to them.

Worship

◆ **Worship** is the way people of faith praise and honour God in prayer and at religious services. Jews praise and honour God when they pray at home and attend services in the synagogue.

◆ Men and women cover their heads in the synagogue; it is a way of showing respect for God. Men usually wear ceremonial clothes such as a Kippah (a prayer cap), a Tallit (a prayer shawl) and a Tefillin (small leather boxes containing a tiny scroll).

◆ For Jews, worship in the synagogue is mainly prayers and readings from scripture.

Place of Worship

◆ A synagogue is a **place of worship**, it is where Jews go to pray and worship God. A Jewish symbol such as the Magen David, or Star of David, usually decorates the front of the building.

◆ A synagogue is a plain rectangular building, one wall of which faces the holy city of Jerusalem. There are no pictures or statues inside a synagogue; Jewish law forbids the use of images that depict God.

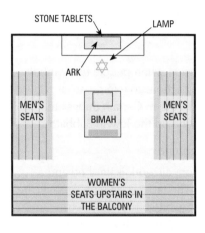

Diagram of a synagogue interior.

The Synagogue

◆ A synagogue has the following features.

The Ark:	A special cabinet where the scrolls of the Torah are kept. A curtain is draped in front of it. The Ark is the focal point of the synagogue.
Scrolls of the Torah:	The books of Moses handwritten on scrolls. Each scroll is covered in a mantle and kept in the Ark.
Everlasting Light:	A lamp that burns day and night in front of the Ark. It is a symbol of God's everlasting presence in the world.
Stone Tablets:	The Ten Commandments in Hebrew on stone tablets above the Ark.
Bimah:	A raised platform in the centre of the synagogue with a reading desk for the scrolls of the Torah.
Seating:	Men sit downstairs, women sit upstairs in a balcony, everyone faces the Ark.

Ritual

◆ A ritual is an occasion when people use symbolic objects, words and actions to express what is deeply important to them. **The Sabbath service** in the synagogue helps Jews express what is deeply important to them.

◆ The service is in Hebrew and lasts about an hour. The **rabbi** leads the prayers, reads the Torah and preaches a sermon. He is assisted by a cantor who leads the singing.

◆ The most important part of the Sabbath service is when the Sefer Torah (the handwritten copy of the Torah) is taken from the Ark and read to the people.

◆ The curtain in front of the Ark is drawn aside and everyone stands to show respect for the Law of God in the Torah.

◆ The scroll is carried in procession around the synagogue and up the steps of the bimah.

◆ Everyone sits and listens respectfully as the rabbi reads the Torah aloud. The Torah is the Word of God for Jewish people.

◆ When the reading and the sermon are over, the scroll is carried back to the Ark. The service ends with a blessing.

Test Yourself

1. Name the main features in a Jewish place of worship.

_____

_____

_____

_____

2. What is the role of the rabbi at the Sabbath service in the synagogue?

_____

_____

_____

_____

3. Describe the central ritual at the Sabbath service in the synagogue. What is its significance?

_____

_____

_____

_____

_____

_____

_____

Pilgrimage

KEY CONCEPTS

Pilgrimage: a journey made by a pilgrim to a shrine or a sacred place.

Ritual: an occasion when people use symbolic objects, words and actions to express what is deeply important to them.

Pilgrimage

◆ **Pilgrimage** is a journey made by a pilgrim to a sacred place. People go on a pilgrimage to pray and get closer to God.

◆ The **Western Wall** in Jerusalem is the holiest site in the religion of Judaism. Jews go there to pray, although pilgrimage is not compulsory in Judaism.

◆ The Ark of the Covenant was originally kept in the Temple in Jerusalem.

◆ After the Temple was destroyed in 70CE it was never rebuilt again. The Western Wall is all that remains.

◆ Prayer is the main form of worship at this sacred place.
  ▸ Private prayer - facing the wall.
  ▸ Public prayer - in which pilgrims attend services and bar mitzvahs near the wall.

Ritual.

◆ A **ritual** is an occasion when people use symbolic objects, words and actions to express what is deeply important to them. A pilgrimage is a ritual occasion for people of faith. Jewish pilgrims who go to the Western Wall in Jerusalem:
  ▸ Wash their hands before going to pray as a sign of their purity of heart.
  ▸ Cover their heads as a sign of respect.
  ▸ Face the wall to pray.
  ▸ Pray using a prayer book.

As pilgrims offer their prayer to God they can:
  ▸ Stand near the wall.
  ▸ Place their hand or forehead on the wall.
  ▸ Push tiny slips of paper containing prayers between the cracks in the wall.

◆ Tourists may visit the Western Wall too but they must stand further back and not disturb the pilgrims who go there to pray.

Test Yourself

1. Why do Jews go on pilgrimage to Jerusalem?

_____

_____

_____

2. What symbolic actions do Jewish pilgrims perform when they worship at the Western Wall?

_____

_____

_____

3. What do you think is the main difference between the experience of a pilgrim and a tourist at the Western Wall?

_____

_____

_____

Religious Festivals

KEY CONCEPTS

Calendar/sacred time: days and weeks set aside every year for a religious purpose.

Festivals: sacred time marked by fasting or celebration to remind people of key events and beliefs in their faith.

Symbol: something visible that represents something else that is invisible.

Calendar/Sacred Time

◆ **Sacred time** is the days and weeks set aside every year for a religious purpose. Jews set aside sacred time each year to remember and celebrate important events in their religion.

◆ Judaism follows a lunar calendar, which means the dates of Jewish festivals vary from year to year.

◆ Some festivals are more important than others, for example Yom Kippur is the holiest day of the Jewish year. Pesach (or Passover) is a major festival; it is celebrated by Jews in every part of the world.

Time	Festival	To celebrate
Autumn	● **Rosh Hashanah**	The Jewish New Year. A ram's horn is blown to call people to return to God.
	● **Yom Kippur**	The holiest day of the year, a day of prayer and fasting for the forgiveness of sin.
Winter	● **Hanukkah**	The time the Jews had a successful protest against foreign rulers in Palestine in 165 BCE. The Jews took back the Temple and rededicated it to the one true God.
Spring	● **Pesach (Passover)**	The time of the Exodus when Moses led the Jews to freedom from slavery in Egypt.
Summer	● **Shavuot**	The time God gave Moses the Torah (the Law and the Ten Commandments) on Mount Sinai.

Festivals/Symbol

◆ **Festivals** are sacred time marked by fasting or celebration that remind Jews of the key events and important beliefs in their faith.

◆ The festivals help Jews to focus on their faith. It is a time to think and pray and be united with Jews everywhere past and present.

◆ Rosh Hashanah and Yom Kippur are two festivals celebrated in autumn.

Rosh Hashanah

◆ Rosh Hashanah is:
  ▶ The first day of the Jewish New Year.
  ▶ A day for remembering and giving thanks to God for the creation of the world.

◆ At the synagogue service on New Year's morning, the shofar (a ram's horn) is blown loudly. It reminds people to return to God and live better lives.

◆ A reading from scripture tells how Abraham was willing to sacrifice his son Isaac, such was the depth of Abraham's obedience to God.

◆ During the following ten days Jewish people must put right whatever they have done wrong.

Yom Kippur

- Yom Kippur is:
  - ▶ The holiest day in the Jewish Year.
  - ▶ A day of prayer and fasting for the forgiveness of sin.

- A **symbol** is something visible that represents such things as thoughts, feelings or beliefs that are invisible and difficult to put into words. Jews fast for the full day on **Yom Kippur**. Fasting is a symbol. It represents their feelings of sorrow for any wrong they have done and their desire for forgiveness.

- On Yom Kippur many Jews spend much of the day praying in the synagogue. Everything in the synagogue is covered in white. The colour white symbolises God's willingness to forgive their sins.

- A reading from scripture tells how the High Priest entered the Holy of Holies in the Temple once a year, to offer sacrifice to God to make amends for the sins of the Jewish community.

- At the end of the synagogue service the shofar is blown for the last time. It is a reminder to be faithful to God and do good in the year ahead.

Test Yourself

1. Name two important festivals in the Jewish calendar: _____

   _____

2. Select either Rosh Hashanah or Yom Kippur and state:

   a. When it occurs: _____

   _____

   b. What event is remembered at this sacred time: _____

   _____

   _____

   c. What Jews do during this festival: _____

   _____

   _____

   d. Why this festival is important for Jewish people: _____

   _____

   _____

3. **a.** What symbolic words and actions are used at the festival of Rosh Hashanah **or** Yom Kippur?

   _____

   _____

   b. Explain the meaning of each symbol identified.

   _____

   _____

   _____

Pesach - Passover

> ## KEY CONCEPTS
>
> **Festival**: sacred time marked by fasting or celebration to remind people of key events and beliefs in their faith.
>
> **Rite**: the pattern of words and actions used in a religious ceremony.
>
> **Symbol**: something visible that represents something else that is invisible.
>
> **Ritual**: an occasion when people use symbolic objects, words and actions to express what is deeply important to them.

Festival

- **Pesach (Passover)** is an important week-long festival that takes place in spring. It is sacred time when Jews remember the Exodus and give thanks to God for their escape from slavery in Egypt. The festival of Pesach celebrates their freedom.

- The Seder, or Passover meal, is the high point of the festival. The Seder is a special meal combined with a religious service. It takes place in the family home on the eve of Pesach.

- The Seder table is set with traditional food and drink.

Rite

- A **rite** is the pattern of words and actions used in a religious ceremony. The Seder meal in every Jewish household always follows the same order of events. This order, or rite, is written in a book called the Haggadah.

- The father of the family begins the service. He lights two candles, fills glasses of wine for everyone and says a blessing.

- The youngest child asks "Why is this night different from all other nights?". The father responds by telling the story of the Exodus, and explaining the meaning of the symbols on the Seder plate.

Symbol

- A **symbol** is something visible that stands for, or represents, something that is invisible. Each item of food on the Seder plate is a symbol. It stands for, or represents, something in the Exodus event.

The Seder Plate

Lamb bone	A symbol of the Passover lamb that was killed so that its blood could be sprinkled on the doorposts of Jewish houses.
Horseradish	A bitter root vegetable - a reminder of the years of bitter slavery in Egypt.
Haroset	A mix of apples, nuts, honey and spices that stands for the mud bricks used to make the pharaoh's buildings in Egypt.
Green herbs	Parsley or lettuce to remind everyone that Pesach is a Spring festival.
Egg	A symbol of new life in a new land.

- Other important items on the table are:
  - **Matzot** (unleavened bread) a reminder of the flat bread eaten on the first Passover night.
  - **Salt Water** a reminder of the tears shed when the Jews were slaves in Egypt.
  - **Wine** a reminder of the promise God made to Moses.

Ritual

◆ A **ritual** is an occasion when people use symbolic objects, words and actions to express what is deeply important to them. The Seder meal at the festival of Pesach is a ritual.

◆ At the Seder meal, readings from scripture are accompanied by certain symbolic actions that help Jews express what is deeply important to them.

▶ Wine is sipped.
  It tastes of the freedom promised by God.

▶ Parsley is dipped in salt water.
  It tastes of sorrow that people still suffer from slavery and oppression.

▶ Matzot is broken and shared out.
  It symbolises the unleavened bread prepared in the rush for freedom.

▶ Bitter herbs are dipped in the haroset.
  It tastes of the bitter misery of working as slaves in Egypt.

▶ A drop of wine is spilt from the wine glasses.
  It shows sadness for all those who still suffer in the world today.

The Seder plate.

◆ Jews gather together at the annual Seder meal to celebrate their freedom and to think of those who still lack freedom in the world today.

◆ The service ends with a blessing.

Test Yourself

1. What do Jews celebrate at the festival of Pesach?

_____

_____

_____

2. What book contains the rite outlining the way the Seder is to be conducted?

_____

3. Explain the meaning of the symbolic food on the Seder plate.

_____

_____

_____

_____

_____

_____

4. How does the ritual of the Seder meal communicate the experience of the Exodus?

_____

_____

_____

_____

_____

Rites of Passage

KEY CONCEPTS

Ritual: an occasion when people use symbolic objects, words and actions to express what is deeply important to them.

Ceremony: the solemn or formal actions performed on a ritual occasion.

Rite: the pattern of words and actions used in a religious ceremony.

◆ A rite of passage is the name given to an occasion that marks the passing from one stage of life to another. Religions mark important moments in life such as:
  ▶ Birth. ▶ Maturity of faith. ▶ Marriage. ▶ Death.

Ritual

◆ A **ritual** is an occasion when people use symbolic objects, words and actions to express what is deeply important to them. In Judaism birth, maturity of faith, marriage and death are ritual occasions. Symbolic actions are used to express Jewish beliefs about God's presence in people's lives at such times.

Ceremony/ Rite

◆ **Bar Mitzvah** is a rite of passage. At a special **ceremony** in the synagogue, a thirteen year old boy becomes 'Bar Mitzvah' and is considered mature enough to:
  ▶ Take responsibility for his own faith and obey the Law of God like other Jewish men.

  ▶ Read the Torah at religious services in the synagogue.

◆ A special **rite**, or pattern of words and actions, is used at a bar mitzvah ceremony.
  ▶ The rabbi welcomes the boy and his family to the synagogue service.
  ▶ The boy wears a kippah (prayer cap), tallit (prayer shawl), tefillin (box strapped to the arm and forehead) and holds a siddur (prayer book) - all symbols of his new role as an adult Jew.
  ▶ He is called forward to read a passage in Hebrew from the Torah.
  ▶ The rabbi reminds him of his duty to keep the Law of God like all Jewish men, and publically announces that the young man is now a 'Son of the Law'.
  ▶ The boy receives a blessing from his father who says a prayer on his behalf. All the family have a festive meal and a celebration after the ceremony.

◆ **Bat Mitzvah** is a short ceremony for twelve year old girls who become 'Daughters of the Law'.

Test Yourself

1. What ceremony marks a young Jewish boy's entry into adulthood?

_____

2. Outline the rite of a bar mitzvah ceremony.

_____

_____

_____

_____

3. Why is a bar mitzvah ceremony so important in the Jewish community?

_____

_____

Exam Questions

1. "Every religion has ideas about God, the world and humanity - ideas that ....2005(H)
shape the beliefs and rituals of that religion."

   A. State a key belief about God from **one** of the following religions.

       ■ Buddhism   ■ Hinduism   ■ Islam   ■ Judaism

   B. Describe how their belief about God influences the way of life of followers of this world religion today.

   C. Outline how the life of an important person in the story of this world religion was influenced by his/her beliefs about God.

2. Tick ✓ **one** of the following world religions that you have studied: ....2010(H)

   BUDDHISM ☐   HINDUISM ☐   ISLAM ☐   JUDAISM ☐

   a. Describe **one** example of the teaching of the founder / earliest followers of the world religion you have ticked above.

   b. Outline how the teaching of the founder / earliest followers influences the way members live today, in the world religion you have ticked above.

3. a. Name a type of prayer associated with one of the following world religions: ....2004(H)

       ■ Buddhism   ■ Hinduism   ■ Islam   ■ Judaism

   b. Give **one** example of the type of prayer named above and explain how it illustrates that type of prayer.

   c. Explain how the type of prayer named above illustrates **one** belief of the world religion you have chosen above.

4. A. a. World religions have special times of the day and / or days of the week set aside for prayer. ....2006(O)

       Tick ✓ **one** of the world religions below and describe one of the special times set aside for daily or weekly prayer in that religion.

       Buddhism ☐   Hinduism ☐   Islam ☐   Judaism ☐

       b. Give **two** reasons why daily or weekly prayer is important for members of a world religion.

   B. Explain the meaning of *either* a sign or symbol which members of a world religion use in daily or weekly prayer.

5. Tick ✓ **one** of the following world religions that you have studied: .... 2006(H), 2012(H)

   BUDDHISM ☐   HINDUISM ☐   ISLAM ☐   JUDAISM ☐

   a. Describe **one** example of how a sacred text is used in worship by the members of the world religion that you have ticked above.

   b. Outline **two** ways in which a sacred text could influence the way of life of members in the world religion that you have ticked above.

6. Tick ✓ **one** world religion you have studied from those listed below and name the ....2006(H) place of worship where members of this world religion regularly gather for prayer.

      Buddhism ❑   Hinduism ❑   Islam ❑   Judaism ❑

    a. Name of place of worship.

    b. Describe the place of worship you have named above.

    c. Explain how the place of worship you have described above can help people to pray.

7. Tick ✓ **one** of the following major world religions that you have studied: ....2011(H), 2014(H)

      Buddhism ❑   Hinduism ❑   Islam ❑   Judaism ❑

    a. Name **one** place of pilgrimage that is most associated with the world religion which you have ticked above.

    b. Explain **two** reasons why the members of the world religion that you have ticked go on pilgrimage to the place which you have named in part a. above.

8. This is a photograph of people taking part in a religious pilgrimage. ....2009(O)

Ruqaiyyah Waris Maqsood 1993

    A. Pick **one** thing from this photograph which shows that these people are taking part in a pilgrimage.

    B. Buddhism ❑   Hinduism ❑   Islam ❑   Judaism ❑

    Tick ✓ **one** of the above world religions and name a place of pilgrimage associated with it.

    C. State **one** reason why members of a world religion would take part in a pilgrimage.

9. Imagine you are bringing a group of young people on a tour to a place of pilgrimage for ....2003(H) members of a major world religion. Pick **one** of the following world religions you have studied:

      ■ Buddhism   ■ Hinduism   ■ Islam   ■ Judaism

Name a world religion.

    A. Name **one** place of pilgrimage connected with your chosen world religion.

    B. Describe **two** rites or rituals that people could participate in or observe at this place of pilgrimage.

    C. Compare **one** aspect of the belief or practice of members of this world religion with that of Christians.

10. Tick ✓ **one** of the following world religions that you have studied: ....2011(O)

      BUDDHISM ❑   HINDUISM ❑   ISLAM ❑   JUDAISM ❑

    a. Name **one** time of year that has religious importance for members of the world religion that you have ticked above.

    b. Explain **two** reasons why the time of year named above has importance for members of the world religion that you have ticked above.

11.   ◆ BUDDHISM ◆ HINDUISM ◆ ISLAM ◆ JUDAISM ....2014(H)

Imagine you are preparing a presentation about a religious festival that is associated with one of the above world religions. Outline the points you would make in your presentation about the religious festival in answer to **each** of the following questions:

    i. What happens during the celebration of the religious festival?

    ii. Why do members of the world religion celebrate the religious festival today?

    NOTE: *This is an essay question.*

12. a. Read the list of religious festivals and the list of world religions given below. ....2014(O)

Match **one** religious festival to the world religion with which it is most associated.

Religious Festivals	World Religions
Diwali	Buddhism
Eid ul Adha	Hinduism
Hanukkah	Islam
Wesak/Vesak	Judaism

Answer:

Religious Festival	World Religion

b. ◆ BUDDHISM   ◆ HINDUISM   ◆ ISLAM   ◆ JUDAISM

Explain **two** reasons why a festival has religious importance for the members of **one** of the world religions listed above.

RELIGIOUS FESTIVAL: _____

---

13. This is a photograph of a young person taking part in a Sacred Thread ceremony. ....2006(O)

www.swaminarayan.org

A. Pick **one** thing from the photograph which shows that this ceremony is celebrating religious faith.

B. Name **one** other ceremony which celebrates a stage in the growth of religious faith.

C. Taking part in a religious ceremony is one way of expressing religious faith. Name **one** other way of expressing religious faith.

---

14. Tick ✓ **one** of the following world religions that you have studied. ....2008(H)

Buddhism ☐   Hinduism ☐   Islam ☐   Judaism ☐

People of faith gather to mark key moments in life such as birth, death etc.

a. Name **one** religious ceremony that marks an important moment in the life of a believer in the world religion you have ticked above.

b. Outline what happens during the religious ceremony you have named above.

---

15. Tick ✓ **one** of the following major world religions you have studied: ....2009(O)

Buddhism ☐   Hinduism ☐   Islam ☐   Judaism ☐

a. Name **one** religious object that is associated with the world religion ticked above.

b. Explain **two** reasons why the religious object you have named in part a) is important for members of the world religion you have ticked above.

---

16.   ◆ BUDDHISM   ◆ HINDUISM   ◆ ISLAM   ◆ JUDAISM ....2010(H)

Imagine that you have been asked to write an article about the religious practice of members in **one** of the above major world religions. Outline the points that you would make in your article referring to the religious practice of early followers and members today.

NOTE: *This is an essay question.*

Development of Judaism

KEY CONCEPTS

Development: the way a community of faith grows and progresses over time.

Commitment: a decision to devote time and energy to the practice of one's religion.

Development and Commitment

◆ Judaism began almost 4,000 years ago. For the first 2,000 years the development of Judaism took place through the energy and commitment of certain people who had great faith in God.

◆ At the beginning there was a **covenant** - a sacred agreement - between God and Abraham.

God promised to look after Abraham and his descendants forever.

Abraham promised that his people would worship and obey God forever.

◆ Ancient Judaism is the story of how the Jewish people lived up to their part of the covenant down through the ages.

1. Abraham

1850 BCE   **Abraham** came to believe that there was only one all-powerful God. Abraham put his trust in God and set off on a journey of faith to the land of Canaan, where God made a covenant with him.

Abraham was told, "I will be your God…You will be my people". God promised Abraham many descendants and the land of Canaan to belong to them forever.

Abraham is the first patriarch, or founding father, of God's chosen people.

2. Moses

As a result of a famine, Abraham's descendants migrated to Egypt but were then forced into slavery.

1250 BCE   **Moses** led the Jews to freedom in an event called the Exodus. He led them out Egypt back toward the Promised Land. At Mount Sinai, God renewed the covenant with Moses and gave him the Law which includes the Ten Commandments. The Jews now had a clear set of rules for worship and behaviour. This was the beginning of Judaism as an organised religion.

3. Joshua

1200 BCE   When Moses died, **Joshua** became leader. He led the Chosen People back into the Promised Land. It was nearly 200 years before the Jews finally took control of Canaan.

4. David

1000 BCE   God chose **David** to be King of Israel. He was anointed, and became Israel's greatest king. He made Jerusalem his capital city. David was faithful to the covenant, and brought the Ark of the Covenant – a casket containing the stone tablets of the Ten Commandments – to Jerusalem.

His son **Soloman** built a magnificent Temple to honour God. The Ark of the Covenant was placed in the 'Holy of Holies'. The Temple became the most important centre of worship for the Jewish people.

5. The Prophets

860 BCE   After Solomon died, Jewish leaders in different parts of the country began fighting among themselves. Two prophets, **Jeremiah and Ezekiel**, called on the Jewish leaders to keep the covenant and turn back to God but they refused to listen.

The country was invaded. The city of Jerusalem was destroyed. The Temple was looted and burned to the ground. The people were taken away as prisoners to Babylon.

6. The Exile

586 BCE   The Jews were forced to work like slaves in **Babylon**. They had disobeyed God's law. They believed the exile from their homeland was their punishment.

The Jews tried to keep their faith alive. They no longer had the Temple but they started to meet in small groups on the Sabbath. They began to pray together and to study the Torah. This was the beginning of the synagogue in Jewish life.

7. Return from Exile

539 BCE The Jews returned to their homeland after fifty years in exile. They rebuilt the Temple and the city of Jerusalem. **Ezra**, and other religious leaders called rabbis, encouraged the Jews to go and worship in the Temple and in the synagogues.

8. Foreign Rulers

Over the next 400 years the Jewish homeland was invaded by one powerful nation after another, first the Persians, then the Greeks and finally the Romans. The Jews had no power in their own land. The most important thing to them now was their religion. They went to worship in the Temple and the synagogue as often as they could.

In **70 CE** a group of Jews called Zealots led a revolt against the Romans. The **Romans** responded with force, destroying the city of Jerusalem and pulling down the Temple - only the western wall was left standing.

9. The Messiah

Throughout the years of foreign rule in Palestine the Jews needed their own leader. Their prophets said that one day a Messiah would come to lead them to freedom. The Jews believed the coming of the Messiah would bring peace to their homeland and to the whole world.

10. Diaspora

After the uprising against the Romans in 70 CE, many Jews were killed. The rest were driven from their homeland and were scattered around the lands bordering the Mediterranean Sea.

Jewish people living outside the Holy Land became known as the Diaspora. Down the centuries, their **rabbis** had a key role in encouraging them to practice their religion in their homes and in the synagogues.

Test Yourself

1. Who were the most important figures in the early development of Judaism? Explain.

_____

_____

_____

_____

2. Judaism Timeline.
   Identify key periods in Jewish history on the diagram below

| 2000 | 1850 | 1250 | 1200 | 1000 | 860 | 586 | 539 | 333 | 63 | 70 | 1948 | 2000 |

NOTE:
❖ BCE = Before common era. CE = Common era.
❖ No one knows the <u>exact</u> dates when some of these events took place.

0

BCE   CE

3. What was the role of the prophets?

_____

4. How did Jews show their commitment to the faith during and after the Exile?

_____

_____

_____

Judaism Worldwide

KEY CONCEPTS

Expansion: the way a religion spreads out into new territories.

Commitment: a decision to devote time and energy to the practice of one's religion.

Persecution: making people suffer because of their race or religion.

Expansion

◆ Jews do not try to convert people to their religion. A person becomes a Jew by being born into the faith.

◆ The expansion of Judaism, i.e. the way it spread into new territories, began following the destruction of the Temple in 70 CE.

◆ The diaspora (Jews forced out of the Holy Land) formed new communities around the Mediterranean and across the Roman Empire. Judaism gradually spread across Europe in the centuries that followed.

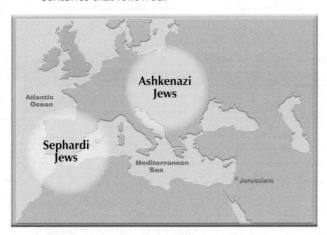

◆ Some Jews moved to Spain, Portugal, and North Africa. The descendants of those early Jewish settlers are called Sephardi Jews.

◆ Other Jews moved to countries in central and eastern Europe. The descendants of these European Jews are called Ashkenazi Jews.

◆ In the 15th century Sephardic Jews were expelled from Spain and Portugal. They went to different countries, some arrived in Ireland and settled on the south coast, in the towns of Limerick, Cork and Waterford.

Commitment and Persecution

◆ Jews throughout Europe paid a high price for their commitment to their faith.

◆ Persecution is about making people suffer because of their race or religion. Down the centuries Jews have endured anti-semitism and suffered persecution because of their beliefs.

◆ In the 18th and 19th century there was a major increase in **anti-semitism** (hatred of Jews) in Eastern Europe. Large numbers of Ashkenazi Jews fled to Western Europe and the United States to escape persecution.

◆ Some Jewish families arrived in Ireland and settled in Dublin and Belfast, where they set up synagogues, shops, and small businesses.

◆ Today about 2,000 Jews live in the Republic and Northern Ireland. There is a total of six synagogues serving the Irish Jewish community: four in Dublin, one in Cork, and one in Belfast.

◆ The worst persecution of the Jews took place in the 1930's and 1940's under Hitler and the Nazis. During World War II, thousands of Jews died every day in death camps across Europe.

◆ Jews refer to the suffering and death in the concentration camps as the 'Shoah' or **'Holocaust'**. Six million Jews died in the Holocaust, over 1.5 million were children.

Israel

◆ After World War II, many Jewish refugees went to Palestine. The United Nations returned it to the Jews as their homeland in 1948. The new country is called Israel.

◆ There are 18 million Jews worldwide, one quarter of that number live in Israel. The majority of Jews outside Israel live in the USA.

Test Yourself

1. Did the expansion of Judaism in Europe take place quickly or slowly over the centuries? Explain your answer.

_____

_____

_____

_____

2. What is anti-semitism? How did it affect Jews in Europe in the 15th, 18th and 19th centuries?

_____

_____

_____

_____

_____

_____

3. What form of persecution was visited on the Jewish population of Europe in the 20st century?

_____

_____

_____

_____

4. What is the distribution of the Jewish population in the world today?

_____

_____

_____

_____

Branches of Judaism

> **KEY CONCEPTS**
>
> **Schism**: a division or split within a community of faith.

Schism

◆ A **schism** is a division or split within a community of faith. Judaism was united for thousands of years from the time of Abraham and Moses. Then, during the period of the Enlightenment in the 18th century CE, the world changed rapidly. This had an effect on the development of Judaism. A certain division or schism occured.

◆ Some Jews thought their religion should reform and adapt to a changing world. The majority thought change was unnecessary as the old traditional ways were best.

◆ These two outlooks underpin the two branches of Judaism that exist today:

▶ Orthodox Judaism (Traditional Judaism).

▶ Non-Orthodox Judaism (Reform and Liberal Judaism).

◆ **Orthodox Jews**, the largest group, strictly follow the Torah and the Jewish tradition in all its aspects.

For example, in synagogue services:

▶ Prayers are entirely in Hebrew.

▶ The rabbi is male.

▶ Men and women sit separately.

◆ **Non-Orthodox Jews**, the smaller group, follow the Torah and Jewish tradition less strictly than Orthodox Jews.

For example, in synagogue services:

▶ Prayers may be said in the local language.

▶ The rabbi may be male or female.

▶ Men and women sit together.

Test Yourself

1. Name the two main branches of Judaism.

_____

_____

2. When did this divisions occur in Judaism?

_____

_____

_____

3. What are the main differences between the two branches of Judaism?

_____

_____

_____

_____

_____

Exam Questions

---

1. a. In a religious tradition the term 'expansion' refers to _____ .... 2011(O)

   b. Outline what happened during a time of expansion in **one** of the following world religions:

       ◆ BUDDHISM ◆ HINDUISM ◆ ISLAM ◆ JUDAISM

---

2. ■ Buddhism ■ Hinduism ■ Islam ■ Judaism .... 2010(H)

   a. Each world religion has gone through a time of growth after it first began.

   Name *either* **one** person *or* **one** group who played an important part in the growth of a major world religion listed above.

   b. Outline the way in which *either* a person *or* a group played an important part in the growth of a major world religion listed above.

---

3. ■ Buddhism ■ Hinduism ■ Islam ■ Judaism .... 2006(H)

Briefly describe a time of growth and development in **one** of the above world religions.

---

4. A. In the history of every world religion there are important moments. .... 2004(O)

   Tick ✓ **one** of the following words which describes such a moment:

   Expansion ❏   Schism ❏

   Explain how the word you have ticked describes an important moment in the story of **one** of the following world religions:

      ■ Buddhism ■ Hinduism ■ Islam ■ Judaism

  B. a. Sometimes people suffer persecution because of their religious commitment.
     Describe **one** example of persecution in the story of **one** of the following world religions:

     ■ Buddhism ■ Hinduism ■ Islam ■ Judaism

    b. Outline **one** effect this persecution could have on a follower of your chosen world religion.

---

5.   ◆ BUDDHISM ◆ HINDUISM ◆ ISLAM ◆ JUDAISM   .... 2013(H)

Describe what happened during a time of persecution in **one** the world religions listed above and outline how it affected the members of the world religion.

NOTE: *This is an essay question.*

---

6.   ■ Buddhism ■ Hinduism ■ Islam ■ Judaism .... 2008(H)

In the history of world religions there are key moments that shape their development.

Profile the way in which **one** of the above world religions has been shaped by experiencing a time of *either* persecution *or* expansion.

NOTE: *This is an essay question.*

The Jewish Community

OBJECTIVES:
Describe a key leadership role in the Jewish community.

Outline the benefit of interfaith dialogue and the links between Judaism and Christianity.

KEY CONCEPTS

Community structure: the way a community of faith is organised.

Leadership: the task of a leader in guiding a community of faith.

Education: the way the faith is passed on within a community of faith.

Dialogue: open and honest discussion between the major world religions.

Community Structure

◆ **Community structure** is the way a community of faith is organised. The Jewish community has its own network of roles and relationships.

◆ There are no priests and there is no single overall leader in Judaism.
- The rabbi.   - The cantor.   - The scribe.
- The mohel.   - The shochet.

all make an important contribution to the religious life of Jewish people.

◆ A clear structure holds the community together, enabling it to run efficiently.

Leadership

◆ **Leadership** is the task of a leader in guiding a community of faith.

◆ Each country has a Chief Rabbi who is the senior leader of the Jewish community in that country.

◆ Each synagogue employs its own rabbi. He is a layman with a deep knowledge of the Torah and the Talmud, and a firm commitment to the Jewish way of life.

◆ **The rabbi** has a key role in the Jewish community:
  ▶ Leading the prayers in the synagogue on Shabbat.
  ▶ Teaching the Law and helping people to apply it to their daily lives.
  ▶ Conducting weddings and funerals, and preparing young people for their bar mitzvah (boys) and bat mitzvah (girls).
  ▶ Visiting the sick.
  ▶ Advising Gentiles (non-Jews) about Jewish affairs.

Education

◆ **Education** is the way the faith is passed on within a community of faith. Jewish children's religious education begins at an early age, mainly in the home, because the home is the centre of Jewish religious life.

◆ Children also attend classes in the synagogue in preparation for their bar mitzvah. The rabbi teaches them to read and speak Hebrew, and to learn the beliefs and practices of Judaism.

Dialogue

◆ **Dialogue** is open and honest discussion between the major world religions. Many believe it is important that people of different religions have discussions about their religious beliefs and practices.

◆ In 1942, the **Council of Christians and Jews** was formed to promote good relations between Christian and Jewish communities. There are now over 50 branches in cities throughout Britain and Ireland.

◆ Interfaith dialogue between Christians and Jews:
  ▶ Encourages respect and understanding.
  ▶ Reduces prejudice and intolerance.

◆ The two faith communities can learn about each others traditions;
  ▶ they can recognise the similarities.
  ▶ they can be candid about the differences.

Christianity and Judaism

◆ Some similarities and differences between Christians and Jews. They:

Share a belief in:

▶ One God.

▶ Life after death.

▶ God's final Judgement.

▶ The Ten Commandments.

Have different beliefs about:

▶ The nature of God.

▶ The expectation of a Messiah.

▶ The person of Jesus Christ.

▶ The status of the Bible and the Tenakh.

Test Yourself

1. How does the role of the rabbi benefit the Jewish community?

_____

_____

_____

_____

_____

_____

_____

2. What religious education do Jewish children receive either at home or in the synagogue?

_____

_____

_____

_____

3. What are the advantages of inter-faith dialogue between Christians and Jews?

_____

_____

_____

_____

_____

_____

Jewish Identity

> **KEY CONCEPTS**
>
> **Follower/ discipleship**: persons called to follow the teaching and way of life of a religious leader.
>
> **Tradition**: the wisdom and teaching of a community of faith handed down from generation to generation.

Follower/Discipleship

◆ Judaism is a monotheistic religion. Down the ages Jews have learned to remain faithful to the covenant that God made first with Abraham and later with Moses.

◆ To be a Jew is to:
  ▶ Belong to the religion of Judaism.
  ▶ Believe in one all-powerful God.
  ▶ Follow a way of life based on the Torah, the Law of God.

◆ There are over 18 million Jews in the world today, mainly in the United States, Russia, France and Britain.

Tradition

◆ Tradition is the wisdom and teaching of a community of faith handed down from generation to generation. The wisdom and teaching of Judaism is contained in the Tenakh and the Talmud.

◆ Down the centuries, Jewish rabbis studied the sacred texts and passed on their knowledge and understanding to the Jewish people, guiding them in the right way to live.

◆ Identity is the set of distinct characteristics by which a person or group is recognised. Jewish identity is about the many beliefs and customs unique to Jews and the religion of Judaism.

The symbol of Judaism highlights the reign of David, King of Israel.

Jewish Identity

Founders:	Abraham is a patriarch or founding father of Judaism.
Followers:	Orthodox and non-Orthodox Jews follow the teaching that Moses received from God on Mount Sinai.
Beliefs:	Jews are monotheistic. They believe in and worship one all-powerful God. God's special relationship with the chosen people was sealed by the covenant made with Moses on Mount Sinai.
Sacred Text:	The Tenakh, especially the books of the Torah written in Hebrew. The Talmud, is a collection of discussions on the Torah.
Holy Day:	Shabbat, the Jewish holy day of the week, begins at sunset on Friday and ends at sunset on Saturday.
Place of worship:	The synagogue where the scrolls of the Torah are kept in the Ark and read at the Bimah. The family home however is a more important place of Jewish prayer and worship.
Prayer:	Jews pray three times a day. The Siddur is a Jewish prayer book. The Shema is a Jewish prayer and a ststement of Jewish belief. Jewish men may wear a Kippah, Tallit and Tefillin at prayer.
Pilgrimage:	The Western Wall in Jerusalem is sacred and a place of pilgrimage for Jews.
Festivals:	Jews celebrate many major and minor festivals throughout the year. Pesach (Passover) is a major festival, the Seder meal its high point. At Yom Kippur victims of the Holocaust are remembered.
Leadership:	The rabbi is the leader of the local Jewish community.
Lifestyle:	Jews obey moral laws such as the Ten Sayings (Ten Commandments) and follow ritual laws such as eating only kosher food.
Rites of Passage:	Ceremonies mark important moments in life such as birth, marriage and death. Bar-mitzvah marks entry into adult faith.
Symbol:	The Magen David, often called the Star of David, is a symbol of Judaism.

Test Yourself

1. Who is the founder and who are the followers of Judaism?

_____

2. Who were the guardians of the Jewish traditions down through the centuries?

_____

_____

3. Explain the meaning of the following features characteristic of Jewish identity.

- ARK _____
- RABBI _____

- BAR-MITZVAH _____
- SEDER _____

- BIMAH _____
- SHABBAT _____

- COVENANT _____
- SHEMA _____

- CHOSEN PEOPLE _____
- SIDDUR _____

- HEBREW _____
- SYNAGOGUE _____

- HOLOCAUST _____
- TALLIT _____

- JEWS _____
- TALMUD _____

- KOSHER FOOD _____
- TEFILLIN _____

- MAGEN DAVID _____
- TENAKH _____

- MONOTHEISM _____
- TEN COMMANDMENTS _____

- ORTHODOX JEWS _____
- TORAH _____

- PATRIARCH _____
- WESTERN WALL _____

- PESACH _____
- YOM KIPPUR _____

Exam Questions (HIGHER LEVEL)

1. Tick ✓ **one** of the following major world religions that you have studied: .... 2005(H), 2011(H)

BUDDHISM ☐   HINDUISM ☐   ISLAM ☐   JUDAISM ☐

   a. Name a title that is given to a religious leader in the world religion that you have ticked above.

   b. Describe **two** examples of the work of a leader in the world religion that you have ticked above.

2. a. Read the list of religious titles and the list of world religions given below. .... 2003(H), 2009(H)
   One religious title has been matched to the world religion with which it is most associated
   as an example for you. Make **one** other match.

Religious Titles	World Religions
Brahmin	Buddhism
Rabbi	Christianity
Imam	Hinduism
Monk	Islam
Priest	Judaism

Example

Priest	Christianity

Answer

   b.   ● Buddhism   ● Hinduism   ● Islam   ● Judaism
   Outline the way in which the community is structured in **one** of the major world religions listed above.

3. A. a. Read the list of religious symbols and the list of world religions given below. ....2013(H)
   Match **one** symbol to the world religion with which it is most associated.

Religious Symbols	World Religions
The Star of David	Buddhism
The Eight-Spoked Wheel	Hinduism
Om/Aum	Islam
Crescent Moon	Judaism

Answer:

Religious Symbol	World Religion

   b. Tick ✓ **one** of the following major world religions that you have studied:

   BUDDHISM ☐   HINDUISM ☐   ISLAM ☐   JUDAISM ☐   _____
   (Religious Symbol)

   Outline how a religious symbol is associated with the world religion that you have ticked above.

   c. Describe what happened in **one** example of a time when great commitment to faith was shown
   by the members of the world religion that you have ticked in *part A.b.* above.

B. Explain how a connection exists between **two** of the following world religions:
   ◆ Buddhism   ◆ Christianity   ◆ Hinduism   ◆ Islam   ◆ Judaism

4. A tradition can be described as a long established belief or custom. ....2004(H)
   Describe **one** tradition that is popular in one of the following world religions that you have studied.
   Explain its origins and its significance for followers today.

   ■ Buddhism   ■ Hinduism   ■ Islam   ■ Judaism

   NOTE: *This is an essay question.*

Section C - Foundations of Religion: Islam

The *Syllabus Aims* in this section are:

◆ To explore in detail a major world religion.

◆ To examine the impact of this religion on it's followers today, and on other individuals and communities.

Key Concepts in Islam *(Section C)*   *Page*

Islam - the Context

KEY CONCEPTS

Location: the part of the world where the religion of Islam began.

Cultural context: the whole way of life of people living in the place where Islam began.

Location

◆ Islam is a major world religion with over 1 billion members in the world today. Muslims believe in one God, Allah. The religion of Islam was founded by the prophet Muhammad about 1,500 years ago.

◆ **Arabia** in the Middle East is the location, or the place where the religion of Islam began. Arabia is a vast desert land that juts out into the sea between North Africa and Western Asia.

◆ Mecca and Medina, two cities in Arabia, are central to the story of the beginnings of Islam.

The location of Arabia.

Cultural Context

◆ The cultural context is the way of life of the people living in Arabia at the time Islam began. The Arabs were a nomadic desert people who wandered from place to place in search of water and fresh pasture for their animals.

◆ Some Arabs settled in Mecca, a city that grew up around an oasis on the west coast of Arabia. Mecca was an important trading centre on the path of several trade routes going north to the Mediterranean.

◆ Mecca was also an important religious centre and a place of pilgrimage for the nomadic tribes of the Arabian peninsula.

◆ The Arabs were polytheists. They worshipped carved images of their gods at the Ka'ba, a shrine in the centre of Mecca. The tribal people of the desert kept their religious belief and way of life until the arrival of the prophet Muhammad in the 6th century CE.

Test Yourself

1. Where did the religion of Islam begin? _____

2. How did the Arabs live long ago? _____

   _____

   _____

3. Explain the importance of Mecca in ancient times as:

   a. a trading centre. _____

   _____

   b. a religious centre. _____

   _____

   _____

1. a. Tick ✓ **one** of the following world religions you have studied: ....2004(H)

☐ Buddhism   ☐ Hinduism   ☐ Islam   ☐ Judaism

Tick ✓ **one** country on the map below where the world religion you have chosen began.

b. Briefly describe **one** thing about the way people lived in the country you have chosen at the time this world religion began.

2.   Buddhism ☐   Hinduism ☐   Islam ☐   Judaism ☐   ....2009(H)

Tick ✓ **one** of the major world religions above that you have studied.

a. Name **one** part of the world associated with the founding story of the major world religion you have ticked above.

b. Describe the way people lived in the part of the world you have named above at the time the world religion began.

3. A. Tick ✓ **one** of the following world religions that you have studied: ....2010(O)

BUDDHISM ☐   HINDUISM ☐   ISLAM ☐   JUDAISM ☐

B. a. Name *either* **one** person *or* **one** group associated with the founding story of the world religion you have ticked above.

b. Outline how *either* **one** person *or* **one** group played an important part in the founding of the world religion you have ticked above.

Prophet Muhammad

> ### KEY CONCEPTS
>
> **Founder**: the person who established a religion.
>
> **Vision**: a vivid dream or mental image of something important.
>
> **Prophet**: a person chosen by God to give people an important message.

Founder

◆ **Muhammad** is the founder of the religion of Islam. He was born in Mecca, in what is now Saudi Arabia, around 570CE. Muhammad married a wealthy widow, Khadijah, and had six children. He became a successful businessman leading camel caravans across the trade routes of Arabia.

◆ Muhammad was a good man and became troubled by the corruption and violence in Mecca. He went off regularly by himself to the hills outside the city in order to think and to pray.

Vision

◆ One night while praying and fasting in a cave on **Mount Hira**, Muhammad had a vision of something important. He believed the angel Gabriel appeared to him telling him there was one God, Allah, and Muhammad was chosen to be God's messenger.

◆ The experience was unsettling, but later his wife assured him that God had indeed called him to be his prophet. Muhammad continued to receive messages from God throughout his life.

Prophet

◆ Muhammad became a prophet, a person chosen to give people a message from God. He began to preach in the city of **Mecca**, urging people to live good lives and to worship the one God, Allah, not the idols in the Ka'ba.

◆ The Prophet's message was not well received among the business community in Mecca. He was threatened and eventually forced to flee to Medina, 400 km away across the desert. The journey from Mecca to Medina is called the Hijra, and marks the beginning of the religion of Islam.

◆ Under his leadership, the first Muslim community was born in Medina. They began to follow the **Five Pillars**, the moral code of Islam. Some years later Muhammad returned to Mecca with a large army. He met little resistance and took over the city.

◆ Muhammad removed all the idols from the Ka'ba, declaring that it was now a shrine to the one God, Allah. The people converted to Islam and Mecca became the holy city of Islam.

◆ The Prophet died in the year 632CE aged 62 years.

Test Yourself

1. Who is the founder of Islam? _____

2. What extraordinary event occured on Mount Hira?

   _____

   _____

   _____

3. What was the Prophet's message to the people of Mecca?

   _____

   _____

   _____

Sacred Text

OBJECTIVES:

Name the primary source of information about Islam.

Trace the development of its sacred text from the oral tradition to the written word.

KEY CONCEPTS

Sacred text: the book of holy or sacred writings of a community of faith.

Revelation: the way in which God chooses to make himself known to human beings.

Oral Tradition: stories and religious teaching that a people pass on by word of mouth.

Evidence: information about a religious tradition collected from different sources.

Inspiration: the way in which a person is guided by God to pass on a sacred message.

Sacred Text

◆ The Qur'an is the sacred text of Islam. It is the primary source of information about the beliefs and practices of Islam. The Hadith is another sacred text.

◆ **The Qur'an** is a document of faith. Muslims believe the Qur'an is the word of Allah, revealed to Muhammad by the Angel Gabriel.

◆ The Qur'an is written in Arabic and is divided into 114 chapters or suras.

◆ The **Hadith** is a collection of sayings and teachings from the life of Muhammad.

◆ In Islam, there is a clear distinction between:
  ▶ The Qur'an – the direct word of Allah.
  ▶ The Hadith – the teaching of Muhammad.

Revelation

◆ **Revelation** is the way in which God chooses to make himself known to human beings.

Muslims believe that the will of God was revealed to Muhammad through the Angel Gabriel. This revelation began on the night Muhammad had a vision in the cave on Mount Hira. The angel's message was that there is one God, Allah, and Muhammad is his prophet.

◆ Further messages were revealed to the Prophet and were later written down, word for word, in the Qur'an.

◆ Muslims believe the words in the Qur'an are the exact words of God. The Qur'an is therefore treated with great respect by all Muslims.

Oral Tradition

◆ The oral tradition, or oral stage of the Qur'an, lasted for a number of years. The message the Prophet received from the Angel Gabriel was initially passed on by word of mouth.

◆ Not being able to read or write, Muhammad learned the angel's words by heart. He repeated them to his wife and followers; they too learned the angel's message word for word.

◆ Scribes wrote part of the Prophet's message down before his death.

Evidence

◆ **Evidence** is information about a religious tradition collected from different sources. After Muhammad died, all the revelations from oral and written sources were gathered together and written down in one volume.

◆ The Qur'an was written:
  ▸ To ensure the word of Allah was recorded correctly.
  ▸ To preserve the message of Allah for future generations.

Inspiration

◆ **Inspiration** is the way in which a person is guided by God to pass on a sacred message.

Muslims believe Muhammad received sacred messages from God through the angel Gabriel. Muhammad received inspiration or guidance from God to pass on these sacred messages to his followers, who in turn carefully wrote it all down in the Qur'an.

◆ This meant many more people learned about Allah and what Allah wanted them to do.

Test Yourself

1. What is the sacred text of Islam?

_____

2. Outline the development of the Qur'an from the oral tradition to the written word.

_____
_____
_____
_____
_____
_____
_____

3. How was the will of God revealed to Muhammad?

_____
_____
_____
_____

4. What did God inspire Muhammad to do with the sacred messages he received?

_____
_____
_____
_____
_____
_____

1. a. Pick **one** of the following world religions that you have studied: .... 2003(H)

♦ BUDDHISM   ♦ HINDUISM   ♦ ISLAM   ♦ JUDAISM

Name the world religion: _____

Name the founder/earliest followers of the world religion: _____

b. Describe **one** important event that inspired the founder/earliest followers of this world religion.

c. Briefly explain how the event described above can be seen as inspiration for the followers of this faith today.

---

2. Tick ✓ **one** of the following world religions you have studied: .... 2006(O)

❑ Buddhism   ❑ Hinduism   ❑ Islam   ❑ Judaism

a. Describe how religious belief had an effect on the life of an important person in the story of the world religion you have ticked above.

---

3. Tick ✓ **one** of the following world religions that you have studied: .... 2014(O)

BUDDHISM ❑   HINDUISM ❑   ISLAM ❑   JUDAISM ❑

a. Name the founder/earliest followers of the world religion that you have ticked above.

b. Describe an example of how trust in God/gods/the divine was shown by the founder/earliest followers of the world religion that you have ticked above.

---

4. a. ❑ Buddhism   ❑ Hinduism   ❑ Islam   ❑ Judaism   .... 2007(H)

Tick ✓ one of the world religions above that you have studied:

(i) Name **one** key person / group of people associated with the founding story of the world religion you have ticked above.

(ii) Explain why the person / group of people you have named is important in the founding story of the world religion you have ticked above.

b. Outline **one** way in which the story of the earliest followers influences members today in the world religion you have ticked.

c. Explain how the world religion you have ticked above is linked to another major world religion.

---

5. Tick ✓ **one** of the following world religions that you have studied: .... 2009(O)

BUDDHISM ❑   HINDUISM ❑   ISLAM ❑   JUDAISM ❑

a. Name **one** sacred text that is associated with the world religion you have ticked above.

b. Explain **two** reasons why a sacred text is important for members of a world religion.

---

6. Tick ✓ **one** of the following world religions that you have studied: .... 2013(O)

BUDDHISM ❑   HINDUISM ❑   ISLAM ❑   JUDAISM ❑

a. Name **one** sacred text that is most associated with the world religion which you have ticked above.

b. Outline **two** reasons why the sacred text that you have named above is valued by the members of the world religion that you have ticked above.

7. a. Below you will find a list of the stages involved in the development of a sacred text. ....2013(O)

Number each stage in the order in which it occurred.

Number 1 should be the first stage and number 3 should be the last stage.

Number	Stages in the Development of a Sacred Text
	An account of the founding story was written down.
	Events took place associated with the founding story.
	Information about the founding story was passed on by word of mouth.

b. Outline what was involved in **one** of the stages in the development of the sacred text that you have named in question *6a* above.

---

8. **A.** Tick ✓ **one** of the following world religions that you have studied: ....2006(O)

❏ Buddhism   ❏ Hinduism   ❏ Islam   ❏ Judaism

a. Name a text that is sacred for members of the world religion you have ticked above.

b. Give **one** reason why this text is sacred for members of the world religion ticked above.

B. Sacred texts have been passed on by word of mouth and by written word.

Describe what happened in the development of the sacred text you have named above at either the word of mouth stage *or* the written word stage.

---

9. Tick ✓ **one** of the following major world religions that you have studied: ....2012(H)

BUDDHISM ❏   HINDUISM ❏   ISLAM ❏   JUDAISM ❏

a. Name **one** sacred text that is most associated with the world religion that you have ticked above.

b. Outline what was involved in **two** stages in the development of the sacred text that you have named above.

---

10. **A.** a. In religious traditions the term 'revelation' involves God/the divine ....2012(O)
communicating with people.
(Tick ✓ the correct box)   True ❏   False ❏

b. Tick ✓ **one** of the following world religions that you have studied:

BUDDHISM ❏   HINDUISM ❏   ISLAM ❏   JUDAISM ❏

Describe **one** example of revelation from the story of the world religion that you have ticked above.

B. Read the list of religious names and the list of world religions given below.

Match **one** religious name to the world religion with which it is most associated.

Religious Names	World Religions		Religious Name	World Religion
Allah	Buddhism	Answer:		
Yahweh/YHWH	Hinduism			
Enlightened One	Islam			
Brahman	Judaism			

11. a. In religious traditions the term 'revelation' means _____ ....2009(O)

    b. Describe **one** example of revelation from the story of the founder/earliest followers of the world religion you have studied.

---

12. a.   ◆ BUDDHISM   ◆ HINDUISM   ◆ ISLAM   ◆ JUDAISM   ....2014(H)

    Name a sacred text that is associated with **one** of the above world religions.
    Explain **two** reasons why it can be described as a document of faith.

    SACRED TEXT: _____ WORLD RELIGION: _____

    b. Describe what happened from the oral to the written stages in the development of the sacred text that you have named above.

---

13.   ◆ BUDDHISM   ◆ HINDUISM   ◆ ISLAM   ◆ JUDAISM   ....2009(H)

    Discuss the importance of a sacred text in **one** of the above major world religions that you have studied.

    NOTE: *This is an essay question.*

Belief and Practice

OBJECTIVE:
Identify the main beliefs
of Islam
and how these beliefs
are put into practice.

> **KEY CONCEPTS**
>
> **Creed/Ethic**: the summary of a religion's deeply held beliefs and moral principles.
>
> **Practice**: customs and rituals that show a person's religious faith.

Creed

◆ A **creed** is a summary of a religion's deeply held beliefs. The Muslim creed contains six main beliefs, or articles of faith.

Main Muslim beliefs

◆ The six articles of Muslim faith are:

1. Belief in Allah.
2. Belief in Angels.
3. Belief in a Sacred Text.
4. Belief in Prophets.
5. Belief in a Day of Judgement
6. Belief in Pre-destination.

Practice

◆ **Practice** is the set of customs and rituals that show a person's religious faith. Muslims put their religious beliefs into practice when they carry out certain duties known as 'The Five Pillars'.

The Five Pillars of Islam

1. Belief (Shahadah)
   "There is no god but Allah and Muhammad is the prophet of Allah."
   Say this creed as often as possible.

2. Prayer (Salat)
   Pray five times a day.
   On Friday, pray in the mosque.

3. Charity (Zakat)
   Give 2.5% of all savings every year to help those in need.

4. Fasting (Sawm)
   Fast from sunrise to sunset during the holy month of Ramadan.

5. Pilgrimage (Hajj)
   Go on pilgrimage to the holy city of Mecca at least once in a lifetime.

Test Yourself

1. What are the articles of faith in the Muslim creed?

   _____

2. Name the Five Pillars of Islam.

   _____

   _____

   _____

3. Explain how the Muslim creed can be seen in the Muslim way of life.

   _____

   _____

   _____

   _____

   _____

   _____

Prayer

OBJECTIVE:
Outline the importance
of prayer
in the religion of Islam.

> **KEY CONCEPT**
>
> **Prayer**: the act of communicating with God.

Prayer

◆ Muslims communicate with God through **prayer**. Prayer is the second pillar of Islam. The Qur'an states that Muslims must pray five times a day.

◆ **Salat** is a formal prayer. It has a set pattern of words and actions. It can be performed alone or with others, in the home or at the mosque.

◆ Salat is a ritual. Muslims must:
   ▶ Remove shoes.
   ▶ Perform wudu (ritual cleansing).
   ▶ Stand on a prayer mat.
   ▶ Face Mecca.
   ▶ Say the prayers and perform the movements of the rak'ah (stand, bow, kneel, touch the ground with the forehead).

◆ All prayers are from the Qur'an and are said in Arabic.

Ways to Pray

◆ **Personal prayer** - when Muslims pray alone during the week.

◆ **Communal prayer** - when Muslims pray together as part of a community in the mosque on Friday at mid-day prayer. Salat is the ritual prayer performed by the Muslim community in the mosque.

Different types of Prayer

◆ Du'ah are informal personal prayers with no set pattern of words or actions. A person can say them anywhere, anytime, facing any direction, using their own words. Personal prayers may be:
   ▶ Prayers of **praise and thanksgiving** to Allah for some good thing that happened.
   ▶ Prayers of **petition** asking Allah to help with something special.
   ▶ Prayers of **penitence** that express sorrow and regret for some wrongdoing.

◆ Du'ah ends with the person drawing their hands across their face to show that they have received Allah's blessing.

Test Yourself

1. When do Muslims pray?

_____

_____

2. How do Muslims pray?

_____

_____

_____

_____

_____

Place of Worship

KEY CONCEPTS

Place of worship: a building or place where people go to pray and worship God or gods.

Worship: the way people of faith praise and honour God in prayer and at religious services.

Place of Worship

- A mosque is a place of worship; it is where Muslims go to pray and worship Allah. A star and crescent moon, the symbol of Islam, can be seen on top of the mosque.

The Mosque

- Mosques may have a **minaret** from where Muslims are called to prayer five times a day.

- At the mosque, everyone removes their footwear and covers their head as a sign of respect. In the **wudu** area there is running water for ritual cleansing.

- Inside the mosque the **mihrab** is an arch built into one wall; it shows the direction of Mecca. Muslims must pray facing the Ka'ba in Mecca.

- The **minbar** is a pulpit from where a sermon is preached at Friday prayer. A bookstand near the minbar contains a copy of the **Qur'an**, the sacred text of Islam.

- The mosque has no furniture; the floor is usually covered with a carpet. The walls are decorated with verses from the Qur'an (pictures and statues are not allowed).

Worship

- Friday is the holy day of the week for Muslims. The main form of worship in Islam is **Friday mid-day prayer** in the mosque.

- The **imam** is the leader of the mosque. He leads the prayers to honour Allah.
  - At the mihrab, the imam faces Mecca to lead the prayers.
  - Worshippers stand in long straight rows. Everyone follows the imam chanting the creed in Arabic, and performing the prayerful ritual, the rak'ah.
  - At the minbar the imam gives a sermon based on the Qur'an.

- Muslims have a deep respect for the prophet Muhammad but do not worship him, Muslims worship Allah.

Test Yourself

1. Describe a Muslim place of worship.

_____

_____

_____

_____

2. Outline the main features of Friday worship in the mosque.

_____

_____

_____

_____

Pilgrimage

KEY CONCEPTS

Pilgrimage: a journey made by a pilgrim to a shrine or a sacred place.

Ritual: an occasion when people use symbolic objects, words and actions to express what is deeply important to them.

Pilgrimage

◆ A pilgrimage is a journey made by a pilgrim to a sacred place. People go on pilgrimage to pray and get closer to God. Hajj, the pilgrimage to Mecca, is the fifth pillar of Islam.

◆ Muslims are expected to go to **Mecca**, the most sacred place in Islam, at least once in their lifetime.

◆ Mecca is where the prophet Muhammad lived and began to teach about the one God, Allah.

Ritual

◆ A ritual is an occasion when people use symbolic objects, words and actions to express what is deeply important to them. During the Hajj pilgrims perform symbolic actions that express important Muslim beliefs.

◆ In Mecca, pilgrims ritually wash themselves and put on long **white robes** to show that everyone is equal before Allah.

◆ In the courtyard of the Great Mosque, pilgrims walk around the **Ka'ba** seven times.

◆ Pilgrims hurry seven times between the two small **hills of Safa and Marwa** in memory of Abraham's wife's frantic search for water in the desert.

◆ Pilgrims then go to the **Plain of Arafat**, outside Mecca, and stand for a full day listening to sermons and praying to Allah to forgive their sins. This is where Muhammad preached his last sermon.

◆ At the three **pillars in Mina** pilgrims throw stones to show that, like Abraham, they too reject evil and wish to follow Allah.

◆ **Eid-ul-Adha**, the festival of sacrifice, marks the end of the pilgrimage. Sheep are sacrificed in memory of the one that God asked Abraham to sacrifice in place of his son.

◆ When Muslims return home from Mecca, they can give themselves the title 'Hajj' (man) or 'Hajjah' (woman).

Test Yourself

1. Name a Muslim place of pilgrimage. _____

2. What symbolic actions do Muslims perform during the Hajj at:

   ● Mecca? - _____

   ● The Ka'ba? - _____

   ● Safa and Marwa? - _____

   ● Arafat? - _____

   ● Mina? - _____

3. Give two reasons why Muslims go on pilgrimage.

   _____

   _____

   _____

Religious Festivals

KEY CONCEPTS

Calendar/sacred time: days and weeks set aside every year for a religious purpose.

Festivals: sacred time marked by fasting or celebration to remind people of key events and beliefs in their faith.

Calendar/Sacred Time

◆ **Sacred time** is days and weeks set aside every year for a religious purpose. In Islam, sacred time is set aside each year to remind Muslims of what is important in their religion.

◆ Islam follows a lunar calendar which means the dates of Muslim festivals and holy days vary from year to year.

Ramadan

◆ The holiest month is Ramadan. Muslims fast from sunrise to sunset each day during Ramadan. Fasting is one of the Pillars of Islam.

◆ During Ramadan, Muslims spend extra time:
  ▶ at prayer.
  ▶ attending the mosque.
  ▶ reading the Qur'an.
  ▶ giving money to charity (Zakat).

Dhu-al- Hijjah

◆ The other important month is Dhu-Al-Hijjah. This is when the Hajj, the pilgrimage to Mecca, takes place.

◆ The pilgrimage to Mecca is one of the Pillars of Islam. The pilgrimage begins and ends at the Ka'ba, a shrine believed to have been built by Abraham and his son.

Festivals

◆ **Festivals** are sacred time marked by fasting or celebration to remind Muslims of the key events and important beliefs in their faith.

◆ Two Muslim festivals celebrated each year are:
  ▶ Eid-ul-Fitr   - at the end of Ramadan.
  ▶ Eid-ul-Adha - at the end of Hajj, the pilgrimage to Mecca.

◆ These festivals are a time to think and pray and be united with Muslims everywhere.

Eid-ul-Fitr

◆ Eid-ul-Fitr takes place at the end of the holy month of Ramadan.

◆ It is a festival to thank Allah for a successful fast.

◆ Muslims attend the mosque for prayers and give an amount of money to charity.

◆ After prayers, Muslim families gather together to celebrate and share a special meal. Over the following three days, friends and relatives visit each other, exchanging cards and gifts.

Eid-ul-Adha

◆ Eid-ul-Adha takes place at the end of Hajj, the Muslim pilgrimage to Mecca.

◆ It is a festival recalling Abraham's willingness to sacrifice his son to Allah.

◆ Muslims not in Mecca attend their mosque for special prayers, and listen to a sermon recalling the story of Abraham.

◆ After prayers families gather together to share a special meal. Over the following three days friends and relatives visit each other exchanging cards and gifts.

Test Yourself

1. In Islam what happens during the month of:

   a. Ramadan?

   _____

   _____

   _____

   _____

   b. Dhu-al-Hijjah?

   _____

   _____

   _____

   _____

2. Name the two main festivals on the Muslim calendar.

   _____

   _____

3. Choose one festival in Islam.

   a. Name the festival. _____

   b. When does it occur? _____

   c. What religious event is remembered at this sacred time?

   _____

   _____

   _____

   d. How do Muslims celebrate this festival?

   _____

   _____

   _____

   _____

   _____

   _____

Rites of Passage

KEY CONCEPTS

Ritual: an occasion when people use symbolic objects, words and actions to express what is deeply important to them.

Ceremony: the solemn or formal actions performed on a ritual occasion.

Ritual

◆ A rite of passage is the name given to a ritual occasion that marks the passing from one stage of life to another. Religions mark important moments in life such as:

▶ Birth.

▶ Marriage.

▶ Death.

◆ A ritual is an occasion when people use symbolic objects, words and actions to express what is deeply important to them. In Islam birth, marriage and death are ritual occasions.

Ceremony

◆ The **Aqiqah** is a rite of passage. It is a ritual occasion following the birth of a baby, and is a great family event.

◆ Muslims believe a child is a gift from Allah. When a baby is born, the father whispers words from the Qur'an into the child's ear:

"I witness there is no god but Allah and that Muhammad is the messenger of Allah."

◆ When the baby is seven days old the Aqiqah, a naming ceremony, takes place.

▶ The baby's hair is cut. A donation is given to charity; this act brings Allah's blessing upon the child.

▶ The baby is given a name.

▶ An animal is sacrificed in thanksgiving to Allah for the child.

▶ Male children are circumcised as a sign that they belong to the community of Muslims who submit to the will of Allah.

Test Yourself

1. What important moments in the lives of Muslims are marked with religious rituals?

   _____

2. What occurs at the Aqiqah naming ceremony?

   _____

   _____

   _____

3. How are Muslim beliefs evident in the Aqiqah ceremony?

   _____

   _____

   _____

   _____

   _____

Section C - Islam: Rites of Passage and Other Rituals

Exam Questions

1. "Every religion has ideas about God, the world and humanity - ideas that .... 2005(H) shape the beliefs and rituals of that religion."

   A. State a key belief about God from **one** of the following religions.

      ■ Buddhism   ■ Hinduism   ■ Islam   ■ Judaism

   B. Describe how their belief about God influences the way of life of followers of this world religion today.

   C. Outline how the life of an important person in the story of this world religion was influenced by his/her beliefs about God.

---

2. Tick ✓ **one** of the following world religions that you have studied: .... 2010(H)

   BUDDHISM ☐   HINDUISM ☐   ISLAM ☐   JUDAISM ☐

   a. Describe **one** example of the teaching of the founder / earliest followers of the world religion you have ticked above.

   b. Outline how the teaching of the founder / earliest followers influences the way members live today, in the world religion you have ticked above.

---

3. **a.** Name a type of prayer associated with one of the following world religions: .... 2004(H)

      ■ Buddhism   ■ Hinduism   ■ Islam   ■ Judaism

   b. Give **one** example of the type of prayer named above and explain how it illustrates that type of prayer.

   c. Explain how the type of prayer named above illustrates **one** belief of the world religion you have chosen above.

---

4. **A. a.** World religions have special times of the day and / or days of the week set aside for prayer. .... 2006(O)

      Tick ✓ **one** of the world religions below and describe one of the special times set aside for daily or weekly prayer in that religion.

      Buddhism ☐   Hinduism ☐   Islam ☐   Judaism ☐

      b. Give **two** reasons why daily or weekly prayer is important for members of a world religion.

   B. Explain the meaning of *either* a sign or symbol which members of a world religion use in daily or weekly prayer.

---

5. Tick ✓ **one** of the following world religions that you have studied: .... 2006(H), 2012(H)

   BUDDHISM ☐   HINDUISM ☐   ISLAM ☐   JUDAISM ☐

   a. Describe **one** example of how a sacred text is used in worship by the members of the world religion that you have ticked above.

   b. Outline **two** ways in which a sacred text could influence the way of life of members in the world religion that you have ticked above.

6. Tick ✓ **one** world religion you have studied from those listed below and name the ....2006(H) place of worship where members of this world religion regularly gather for prayer.

Buddhism ☐   Hinduism ☐   Islam ☐   Judaism ☐

a. Name of place of worship.

b. Describe the place of worship you have named above.

c. Explain how the place of worship you have described above can help people to pray.

---

7. Tick ✓ **one** of the following major world religions that you have studied: .... 2011(H), 2014(H)

Buddhism ☐   Hinduism ☐   Islam ☐   Judaism ☐

a. Name **one** place of pilgrimage that is most associated with the world religion which you have ticked above.

b. Explain **two** reasons why the members of the world religion that you have ticked go on pilgrimage to the place which you have named in part a. above.

---

8. This is a photograph of people taking part in a religious pilgrimage. ....2009(O)

Ruqaiyyah Waris Maqsood 1993

A. Pick **one** thing from this photograph which shows that these people are taking part in a pilgrimage.

B. Buddhism ☐   Hinduism ☐   Islam ☐   Judaism ☐

Tick ✓ **one** of the above world religions and name a place of pilgrimage associated with it.

C. State **one** reason why members of a world religion would take part in a pilgrimage.

---

9. Imagine you are bringing a group of young people on a tour to a place of pilgrimage for ....2003(H) members of a major world religion. Pick **one** of the following world religions you have studied:

■ Buddhism   ■ Hinduism   ■ Islam   ■ Judaism

Name a world religion.

A. Name **one** place of pilgrimage connected with your chosen world religion.

B. Describe **two** rites or rituals that people could participate in or observe at this place of pilgrimage.

C. Compare **one** aspect of the belief or practice of members of this world religion with that of Christians.

---

10. Tick ✓ **one** of the following world religions that you have studied: ....2011(O)

BUDDHISM ☐   HINDUISM ☐   ISLAM ☐   JUDAISM ☐

a. Name **one** time of year that has religious importance for members of the world religion that you have ticked above.

b. Explain **two** reasons why the time of year named above has importance for members of the world religion that you have ticked above.

---

11.   ◆ BUDDHISM   ◆ HINDUISM   ◆ ISLAM   ◆ JUDAISM ....2014(H)

Imagine you are preparing a presentation about a religious festival that is associated with one of the above world religions. Outline the points you would make in your presentation about the religious festival in answer to **each** of the following questions:

i.   What happens during the celebration of the religious festival?

ii. Why do members of the world religion celebrate the religious festival today?

NOTE: *This is an essay question.*

12. a. Read the list of religious festivals and the list of world religions given below. ....2014(O)

Match **one** religious festival to the world religion with which it is most associated.

Religious Festivals	World Religions
Diwali	Buddhism
Eid ul Adha	Hinduism
Hanukkah	Islam
Wesak/Vesak	Judaism

Answer:

Religious Festival	World Religion

b. ◆ BUDDHISM ◆ HINDUISM ◆ ISLAM ◆ JUDAISM

Explain **two** reasons why a festival has religious importance for the members of **one** of the world religions listed above.

RELIGIOUS FESTIVAL: _____

---

13. This is a photograph of a young person taking part in a Sacred Thread ceremony. ....2006(O)

www.swaminarayan.org

A. Pick **one** thing from the photograph which shows that this ceremony is celebrating religious faith.

B. Name **one** other ceremony which celebrates a stage in the growth of religious faith.

C. Taking part in a religious ceremony is one way of expressing religious faith. Name **one** other way of expressing religious faith.

---

14. Tick ✓ one of the following world religions that you have studied. ....2008(H)

Buddhism ☐ Hinduism ☐ Islam ☐ Judaism ☐

People of faith gather to mark key moments in life such as birth, death etc.

a. Name **one** religious ceremony that marks an important moment in the life of a believer in the world religion you have ticked above.

b. Outline what happens during the religious ceremony you have named above.

---

15. Tick ✓ one of the following major world religions you have studied: ....2009(O)

Buddhism ☐ Hinduism ☐ Islam ☐ Judaism ☐

a. Name **one** religious object that is associated with the world religion ticked above.

b. Explain **two** reasons why the religious object you have named in part a) is important for members of the world religion you have ticked above.

---

16. ◆ BUDDHISM ◆ HINDUISM ◆ ISLAM ◆ JUDAISM ....2010(H)

Imagine that you have been asked to write an article about the religious practice of members in **one** of the above major world religions. Outline the points that you would make in your article referring to the religious practice of early followers and members today.

NOTE: *This is an essay question.*

Islam Worldwide

> **KEY CONCEPTS**
>
> **Development**: the way a community of faith grows and progresses over time.
>
> **Commitment**: a decision to devote time and energy to the practice of one's religion.
>
> **Expansion**: the way a religion spreads out into new territories.

Development

◆ **Development** is the way a community of faith grows and progresses over time. The development of Islam took place rapidly during the lifetime of the prophet Muhammad.

Key moments in the beginning of Islam

▸ Muhammad is born in 570CE in the city of Mecca in Arabia.

▸ Muhammad and Khadijah get married.

▸ The Angel Gabriel appears to Muhammad in a vision in a cave on Mount Hira. Muhammad began to preach in Mecca about the one God, Allah.

▸ The Hijra: Muhammad and his followers are forced to flee from Mecca to Medina.

▸ Muhammad returns to Mecca and establishes the Ka'ba as a place of worship to Allah.

▸ The prophet Muhammad dies in 632CE after returning from a pilgrimage to Mecca.

▸ After his death the messages the prophet received from Allah through the Angel Gabriel are written down in the Qur'an.

Commitment

◆ The history of Islam is the story of how Muslims have been faithful to the Qur'an down through the centuries.

◆ Muslims show their **commitment** to the Qur'an, and the religion of Islam, in the way they devote time and energy to carrying out duties known as the **Five Pillars**:

1. Belief. 2. Prayer. 3. Charity. 4. Fasting. 5. Pilgrimage.

The Five Pillars are the foundation of the Muslim way of life.

Expansion

◆ The **expansion** or spread of Islam began early on. By the time of Muhammad's death, most of Arabia was converted to Islam.

◆ One hundred years after Muhammad's death, Islam had spread beyond Arabia into northern Africa, India, and across the Mediterranean Sea into Spain and Portugal.

◆ In the Middle Ages, Islam spread to Palestine.

◆ In the fifteenth century, the great Christian centre of Constantinople was conquered by Muslim forces and was re-named Istanbul.

◆ By the seventeenth century, the power and wealth of three Islamic Empires in the Middle East was at its height.

◆ Islam was not just spread by wars and fighting. Muslim traders brought the message of Islam to countries in the East where it won many converts.

◆ Today there are over one billion followers of Islam. The majority live in the Middle East and in North and West Africa.

◆ Over two million Muslims live in Britain and over fifty thousand Muslims live in Ireland.

GLOBAL DISTRIBUTION OF ISLAM TODAY

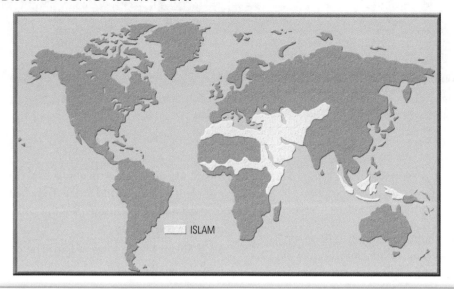

ISLAM

Test Yourself

1. Who is the most important figure in the early development of Islam, and why?

_____

_____

_____

_____

_____

_____

2. How far had Islam spread in the first hundred years after the Prophet's death?

_____

_____

_____

3. How did Muslims show their commitment to the faith down through the ages?

_____

_____

_____

_____

4. What is the distribution of the Muslim community of faith in the world today?

_____

_____

_____

_____

Division in Islam

KEY CONCEPT

Schism: a division or split within a community of faith.

Schism

◆ A division, or schism, occurred in the religion of Islam fifty years after the death of the prophet Muhammad.

◆ The Prophet died without appointing a successor. A disagreement arose about leadership, about who should succeed Muhammad as leader of the Muslim community.

◆ There was a bitter dispute between:
  ▶ Muhammad's immediate family who became known as Shi'ah Muslims, and
  ▶ Muhammad's tribe who became known as Sunni Muslims.

◆ Shi'ah and Sunni formed separate groups; these divisions still exist today.

◆ **Shi'ah Muslims** make up about 10% of the Muslim population of the world today. They believe that God gave Ali, their first leader, the ability to interpret the Qur'an.

Most Shi'ah Muslims live in Iran, The Lebanon, Afghanistan and India.

◆ **Sunni Muslims** make up about 90% of Muslims in the world today. They regard themselves as orthodox, or true followers of Muhammad and his teaching. They believe Muhammad was the 'Final Seal of the Prophets' and no one after him received special knowledge from God.

Sunni Muslims are the most powerful group in Islam.

◆ Sunni and Shi'ah have been in conflict with each other down the centuries. There is disagreement about the Qur'an, and especially over control of the sacred shrine, the Ka'ba, in Mecca.

Test Yourself

1. Name the two main groups within Islam. Which one is in:

   a. the majority? _____

   b. the minority? _____

2. What issue caused the division in Islam in the beginning?

   _____

   _____

   _____

   _____

3. What do Sunni and Shi'ah Muslims believe about who has authority to interpret the Qur'an?

   _____

   _____

   _____

Exam Questions

1. a. In a religious tradition the term 'expansion' refers to _____ ....2011(O)

   b. Outline what happened during a time of expansion in **one** of the following world religions:

   ◆ BUDDHISM ◆ HINDUISM ◆ ISLAM ◆ JUDAISM

---

2. ■ Buddhism   ■ Hinduism   ■ Islam   ■ Judaism ....2010(H)

   a. Each world religion has gone through a time of growth after it first began.

   Name *either* **one** person *or* **one** group who played an important part in the growth of a major world religion listed above.

   b. Outline the way in which *either* a person *or* a group played an important part in the growth of a major world religion listed above.

---

3. ■ Buddhism   ■ Hinduism   ■ Islam   ■ Judaism ....2006(H)

   Briefly describe a time of growth and development in **one** of the above world religions.

---

4. **A.** In the history of every world religion there are important moments. ....2004(O)
   Tick ✓ **one** of the following words which describes such a moment:

   Expansion ☐   Schism ☐

   Explain how the word you have ticked describes an important moment in the story of **one** of the following world religions:

   ■ Buddhism   ■ Hinduism   ■ Islam   ■ Judaism

   B. a. Sometimes people suffer persecution because of their religious commitment.
   Describe **one** example of persecution in the story of **one** of the following world religions:

   ■ Buddhism   ■ Hinduism   ■ Islam   ■ Judaism

   b. Outline **one** effect this persecution could have on a follower of your chosen world religion.

---

5. ◆ BUDDHISM   ◆ HINDUISM   ◆ ISLAM   ◆ JUDAISM ....2013(H)

   Describe what happened during a time of persecution in **one** the world religions listed above and outline how it affected the members of the world religion.

   NOTE: *This is an essay question.*

---

6. ■ Buddhism   ■ Hinduism   ■ Islam   ■ Judaism ....2008(H)

   In the history of world religions there are key moments that shape their development.

   Profile the way in which **one** of the above world religions has been shaped by experiencing a time of *either* persecution *or* expansion.

   NOTE: *This is an essay question.*

The Muslim Community

OBJECTIVE:
Describe a key leadership role in the Muslim community.

Outline the benefit of inter-faith dialogue and the links between Islam and Christianity.

KEY CONCEPTS

Community structure: the way a community of faith is organised.

Leadership: the task of a leader in guiding a community of faith.

Education: the way the faith is passed on within a communty of faith.

Dialogue: open and honest discussion between the major world religions.

Community Structure

◆ **Community structure** is the way a community of faith is organised. The Muslim community has its own network of roles and relationships.

◆ There are no priests and there is no single overall leader in Islam.

◆ The role of imam is a key role in the Muslim community. The imam makes an important contribution to the religious life of Muslims.

Leadership

◆ **Leadership** is the task of a leader in guiding a community of faith. The imam is the religious leader in the mosque. Each community elects its own imam. He is a well-respected layman with a good knowledge of the Qur'an and a deep commitment to the Muslim way of life.

◆ The **imam** has a key leadership role in the Muslim community:

  ▶ Leading the prayers and giving the sermon at Friday mid-day prayer in the mosque.

  ▶ Teaching the Qur'an.

  ▶ Assisting at marriages and funerals.

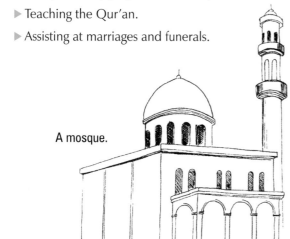

A mosque.

Education

◆ **Education** is the way the faith is passed on within a community of faith. Muslim children's religious education starts at an early age. They attend the mosque for special classes after school and at the weekend.

◆ In the mosque Muslim children learn Arabic in order to read the Qur'an, and study the beliefs and practices of Islam.

Dialogue

◆ **Dialogue** is open and honest discussion between the major world religions. Many believe it is important that people of different religions have open and honest discussions about religious belief and practice.

◆ In Ireland the **Three Faiths Forum** has established links between the three monotheistic religions: Judaism, Christianity and Islam. Members, for example, participate in inter-faith services to mark special occasions.

◆ Interfaith dialogue between Christians, Jews and Muslims:

  ▶ encourages respect and understanding.

  ▶ reduces prejudice and intolerance.

◆ The different faith communities can learn about each other's traditions:

  ▶ they can recognise the similarities.

  ▶ they can be candid about the the differences.

Christianity and Islam

◆ Some similarities and differences between Christians and Muslims. They:

Share a belief in:
- ▶ one God.
- ▶ life after death.
- ▶ God's final Judgement.
- ▶ prayer, fasting and charity.

Have different beliefs about:
- ▶ the nature of God.
- ▶ the person of Jesus Christ.
- ▶ the role of the Prophet Muhammad.
- ▶ the status of the Bible and the Qur'an.

Test Yourself

1. How does the role of the imam benefit the Muslim community?

_____

_____

_____

_____

_____

_____

2. What religious education do Muslim children receive in the mosque?

_____

_____

_____

3. How important is inter-faith dialogue between Christians and Muslims?

_____

_____

_____

_____

_____

_____

_____

Muslim Identity

KEY CONCEPTS

Follower/ discipleship: persons called to follow the teaching and way of life of a religious leader.

Tradition: the wisdom and teaching of a community of faith handed down from generation to generation.

Follower/Discipleship

◆ Islam is a monotheistic religion. The prophet Muhammad taught his followers to believe in one God, Allah.

◆ A Muslim belongs to the religion of Islam, and follows a way of life based on the Qur'an and the teaching of the Prophet Muhammad.

◆ There are over 1 billion Muslims in the world today, mainly in the Middle East, North Africa and parts of Asia.

◆ About fifty thousand followers of Islam live in Ireland. The first mosque opened in Dublin in 1975. As the Muslim community grew, other mosques were established in Cork, Galway, Limerick and Belfast. The Islamic Cultural Centre in Dublin caters for the religious, educational and social needs of the Muslim community.

Tradition

◆ Tradition is the wisdom and teaching of a community of faith handed down from generation to generation. The wisdom and teaching of Islam is contained in the Qur'an, and the Hadith, another sacred text.

◆ Down the centuries, Muslim **imams** studied the sacred texts and passed on their knowledge and understanding to the Muslim people, guiding them in the right way to live.

◆ Identity is the distinct characteristics by which a person or group is recognised. Muslim identity is about the many beliefs and customs unique to Muslims and the religion of Islam.

The symbol of Islam highlights the Five Pillars and the lunar calendar of the Islamic year.

Muslim Identity

Founder:	The most important teacher in the religion of Islam is the prophet Muhammad.
Followers:	Sunni and Shi'ah Muslims follow the teaching of the Qur'an and the prophet Muhammad.
Beliefs:	Muslims are monotheistic. They believe in and worship one God, Allah. The main beliefs are the Articles of Faith and The Five Pillars.
Sacred Text:	The Qur'an is the sacred text of Islam. For Muslims, it is the word of Allah.
Holy Day:	Friday is the holy day of the week. All Muslim men are expected to attend the mosque on Friday for mid-day prayer.
Place of worship:	The mosque is the Muslim place of worship. It features: a wudu area for washing; a mihrab facing Mecca; a minbar for preaching sermons.
Prayer:	Muslims pray five times a day, performing rak'ah, a ritual prayer.
Pilgrimage:	The Ka'ba in the city of Mecca is the holiest site and place of pilgrimage in Islam.
Festivals:	Eid-ul-Fitr takes place at the end of Ramadan. Eid-ul-Adha celebrates the end of Hajj, the Muslim pilgrimage to Mecca.
Leadership:	There is no single overall leader in Islam. The imam is the religious leader in the mosque.
Lifestyle:	Muslims strictly follow the Five Pillars, and eat only halal or lawful food. Men and women do not mix socially and women follow a strict dress code.
Rites of Passage:	Ceremonies mark important times in a person's life e.g. the aqiqah naming ceremony at birth.
Symbol:	The star and crescent moon is the symbol of Islam.

Test Yourself

1. Who is the founder and who are the followers of Islam?

   _____

   _____

2. Who were the guardians of the Muslim tradition down through the centuries?

   _____

   _____

   _____

3. Explain the meaning of the following features characteristic of Muslim identity.

   ● ALLAH _____   ● MIHRAB _____

   _____   _____

   ● AQIQAH _____   ● MOSQUE _____

   _____   _____

   ● EID-UL-ADHA _____   ● MONOTHEISM _____

   _____   _____

   ● EID-UL-FITR _____   ● MUSLIMS _____

   _____   _____

   ● FIVE PILLARS _____   ● PROPHET _____

   _____   _____

   ● HAJJ _____   ● QUR'AN _____

   _____   _____

   ● HALAL _____   ● RAK'AH _____

   _____   _____

   ● HIJRA _____   ● RAMADAN _____

   _____   _____

   ● IMAM _____   ● SHI'AH _____

   _____   _____

   ● KA'BA _____   ● STAR AND CRESCENT MOON _____

   _____   _____

   ● MECCA _____   ● SUNNI _____

   _____   _____

   ● MINBAR _____   ● WUDU _____

   _____   _____

Exam Questions (HIGHER LEVEL)

1. Tick ✓ **one** of the following major world religions that you have studied: .... **2005(H), 2011(H)**

BUDDHISM ☐   HINDUISM ☐   ISLAM ☐   JUDAISM ☐

   a. Name a title that is given to a religious leader in the world religion that you have ticked above.

   b. Describe **two** examples of the work of a leader in the world religion that you have ticked above.

2. a. Read the list of religious titles and the list of world religions given below. .... **2003(H), 2009(H)**
One religious title has been matched to the world religion with which it is most associated
as an example for you. Make **one** other match.

Religious Titles	World Religions
Brahmin	Buddhism
Rabbi	Christianity
Imam	Hinduism
Monk	Islam
Priest	Judaism

Example	Priest	Christianity

Answer		

   b.   ● Buddhism   ● Hinduism   ● Islam   ● Judaism
Outline the way in which the community is structured in **one** of the major world religions listed above.

3. A. a. Read the list of religious symbols and the list of world religions given below. ....**2013(H)**
Match **one** symbol to the world religion with which it is most associated.

Religious Symbols	World Religions
The Star of David	Buddhism
The Eight-Spoked Wheel	Hinduism
Om/Aum	Islam
Crescent Moon	Judaism

Answer:	Religious Symbol	World Religion

   b. Tick ✓ **one** of the following major world religions that you have studied:

BUDDHISM ☐   HINDUISM ☐   ISLAM ☐   JUDAISM ☐   _____

                                                      (Religious Symbol)
Outline how a religious symbol is associated with the world religion that you have ticked above.

   c. Describe what happened in **one** example of a time when great commitment to faith was shown
by the members of the world religion that you have ticked in *part A.b.* above.

  B. Explain how a connection exists between **two** of the following world religions:
    ◆ Buddhism   ◆ Christianity   ◆ Hinduism   ◆ Islam   ◆ Judaism

4. A tradition can be described as a long established belief or custom. ....**2004(H)**
Describe **one** tradition that is popular in one of the following world religions that you have studied.
Explain its origins and its significance for followers today.

   ■ Buddhism   ■ Hinduism   ■ Islam   ■ Judaism

NOTE: *This is an essay question.*

Section D - The Question of Faith

The *Syllabus Aims* in this section are:

◆ To explore the situation of faith today

◆ To identify the beginning of faith in the asking of questions and the search for meaning

◆ To recognise expressions of human questioning in modern culture.

◆ To identify the characteristics of religious faith.

◆ To examine challenges to religious faith today.

◆ To offer opportunities for the exploration of, and reflection on, personal faith positions.

Key Concepts in the Question of Faith *(Section D)*   *Page*

Religion Today

KEY CONCEPTS

Religious belief: a set of ideas about God, or gods, that people accept as true.

Religious practice: the things people do to express their religious belief.

Religious Belief

◆ **Religious belief** is the set of ideas people have about God or gods that they accept as true. The central beliefs in Christianity, for example, are summarised in a special prayer called 'The Apostle's Creed'. These beliefs include:

▶ Belief in God the Father, Son and Holy Spirit.

▶ Belief in life after death.

▶ Belief in a final Judgement that involves heaven and hell.

◆ Social surveys routinely investigate levels of religious belief in Ireland and in other countries.

◆ Two 'European Values Surveys' found a consistently high level of religious belief among Roman Catholics in Ireland over the period 1981-1999.

Religious Belief in **Ireland**

1981	95% believe in God.
1999	96% believe in God.

Religious Practice

◆ **Religious practice** consists of the things people do to express their religious belief. When people have deep religious beliefs they do things to show or express those beliefs.

Christians, for example, express their religious beliefs through:

▶ Praying.

▶ Participating in weekly religious services.

▶ Celebrating annual religious festivals.

▶ Going on pilgrimages.

▶ Obeying a code of behaviour.

◆ Social surveys investigate the levels of these religious practices in Ireland and elsewhere.

◆ Two 'European Values Surveys' found a decline in religious practice in Ireland over the period 1981-1999.

Religious Practice in **Ireland**

1981	87% go to Mass once a week.
1999	65% go to Mass once a week.

◆ The surveys show that in Ireland:

▶ Religious practice has changed.

▶ Church attendance had dropped by almost a quarter.

But:

▶ Religious belief has not changed.

▶ Belief in God has remained at a consistently high level over the same period.

◆ Religious belief remains strong in Ireland but this is not reflected in equally high levels of church attendance.

◆ Although it is a fact that religious practice is falling in Ireland, at 65% it is still one of the highest rates of religious practice in the world.

Religious Belief and Practice in Ireland

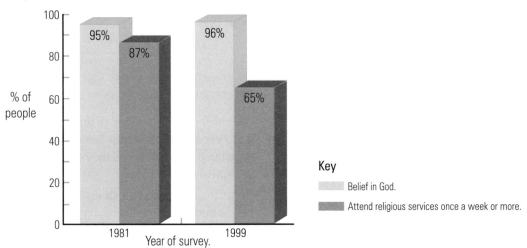

Key

Belief in God.

Attend religious services once a week or more.

Test Yourself

1. Give examples of religious belief and religious practice in the Christian tradition.

_____

_____

_____

_____

_____

_____

_____

2. In the European Values Survey:

   a. What proportion of Irish people believe in God? _____

   b. Has belief in God changed over the twenty year period? _____

   c. What proportion of Irish Catholics attend Mass? _____

   d. Has Mass attendance gone up or down over the twenty year period? _____

3. What are the implications of this change in religious practice for Catholics in Ireland and elsewhere?

   _____

   _____

   _____

   _____

   _____

Religion in a Changing World

KEY CONCEPT

Religious practice: the things people do to express their religious belief.

Religious Practice

◆ **Religious practice**, or the way people express their religious belief, has changed in Ireland over the last century.

◆ In the past, Irish Catholics expressed their faith by regularly attending Mass and the sacraments, and participating in such devotional practices as:

- ▶ The Rosary.
- ▶ The Angelus.
- ▶ Stations of the Cross.
- ▶ Benediction.
- ▶ The Station.
- ▶ The Parish Mission.

◆ Factors that caused a change in Mass attendance and devotional practice include:

- ▶ The influence of **migration**. People moved from the countryside to towns and cities in search of work. This led to a decline in religious practice in rural areas.
- ▶ The influence of the **media**. Film and television presented images, values and behaviour that were different from people's religious values and way of life.

▶ The influence of **materialism**. With economic prosperity people work longer hours and may not have the time, energy or inclination to practice their faith.

◆ **The Second Vatican Council** was a meeting of 2,600 bishops in Rome from 1962-1965. It has had an enormous influence on the religious practice of Roman Catholics in the last fifty years.

◆ The Pope and the bishops worked together to find new ways of bringing the teaching of Jesus closer to people in the modern age.

◆ Many important changes were made, covering all aspects of life in the Catholic Church. These included, for example, a greater role for **lay people** e.g. in the celebration of the Mass as Ministers of the Word, Ministers of the Eucharist, and in liturgy preparation groups. Lay people also took on a greater role in the parish as members of the Parish Council.

◆ Today there are less people attending Mass than in the past. However there are more lay people actively involved in church life than ever before.

Test Yourself

1. What was the pattern of religious practice in Ireland in the past?

_____

_____

_____

2. What effect did Vatican II have on the role of lay people in the Church?

_____

_____

_____

3. Was Ireland a more religious country in the past than it is now?

_____

_____

_____

Religion and Young People

KEY CONCEPTS

Religious belief: a set of ideas about God, or gods, that people accept as true.

Religious practice: the things people do to express their religious belief.

Religious Belief, Religious Practice

◆ Major influences on the religious belief and practice of adolescents include:
  ▶ Family: parents, grandparents, siblings.
  ▶ Peers: friends and acquaintances.
  ▶ Education: school, teachers.
  ▶ Religion: religious leaders, experience of worship.
  ▶ Media: television, magazines, internet.

◆ According to social research, the greatest influence on the religious belief and practice of young people is:
  a) The family.   b) The peer group.

◆ Research carried out in the UK and Australia shows that **parents** have the strongest influence on the religious belief and practice of young people.

◆ Research carried out in Ireland found that young people's outlook on religion was usually shared by their **peers**.

Parents

◆ The values of parents are a critical factor in young people's attitude to religion. Children pick up whether or not religion is valued in the home.

◆ Parents may encourage or discourage religious belief and practice. The example of parents has more of an influence on the religiousness of their teenage sons and daughters than any other factor.

Peers

◆ How friends and classmates view religion, and whether or not they practice it, has implications for the young person's attitude to religion.

◆ The effect of the peer group is strong in adolescence and can lead to peers sharing a similar outlook on religious belief and practice.

Test Yourself

1. What are the two primary influences on the religious belief and practice of adolescents?

_____

_____

2. How do parents influence the religious outlook of their sons and daughters?

_____

_____

_____

3. How do friends influence the religious outlook of one another?

_____

_____

_____

Exam Questions

1. *"When I was young everyone I knew believed in God and* ....2005(H)
churches all over Ireland were crowded every Sunday…" - Pat, born 1940.

   a. Is there a difference between religious practice in Ireland today and religious practice when Pat was young?
(Tick ✓ **one** box)   Yes ❑   No ❑

   b. Explain why you think there is / is not a difference in religious practice in Ireland today.

   c. Apart from going to church, outline **one** other way in which young people today express religious belief.

   d. The findings of surveys show that many young people today believe in God.
Give **two** reasons why many young people today believe in God.

2. a. Outline **two** ways in which religious practice has changed in Ireland .... 2008(H), 2014(O)
in the last one hundred years.

   b. Explain **two** reasons why religious practice has changed in Ireland in the last one hundred years.

3. Imagine you have been asked to write an article for a local magazine about ....2014(H)
religious practice in Ireland over the last hundred years. Outline what you
would write in your article making reference to **each** of the following:

   i. Changes in religious practice.   ii. Influences on religious practice.

4. This is a photograph of people practising their religion. ....2007(O)

   A. Pick **one** thing from this photograph which shows that these people are
practising their religion.

   B. State **another** way in which people can practise their religion.

   C. Describe **one** thing that can influence the way in which people practise
their religion.

Flame Tree Publishing

5.   ● Family ● Friends ● Media ● School   .... 2003(O), 2005(H), 2009(H)
Choose **three** of the above and explain how each can influence the religious beliefs of a teenager.

6. a. Tick ✓ **one** of the following world religions that you have studied: ....2010(O)
   BUDDHISM ❑   CHRISTIANITY ❑   HINDUISM ❑   ISLAM ❑   JUDAISM ❑

   Outline **two** religious beliefs associated with the world religion you have ticked above.

   b. FAMILY ❑   MEDIA ❑   (Tick ✓ **one** option and outline how it could influence the religious beliefs of a teenager.)

7.

SERVICE OF LIGHT
SCHOOL HALL
JUNE 1ST
8.30 to 10.30pm

A time for
Singing Hymns
Reading Scripture
and Silence

ALL WELCOME

This is a photograph of a poster for a religious event. ....2013(O)

   A. Pick **one** thing from this poster which suggests that it is inviting
people to a religious event.

   B. State **one** factor that could influence a person's religious practice.

   C. Give **one** reason why religious practice is important for the
members of a community of faith.

*(Source: Adapted from SoftKey Multimedia
& Expert Software INC)*

Questions about Life

OBJECTIVES:
Examine experiences of awe and wonder.
Show that human beings tend to ask questions about the meaning of life.

KEY CONCEPTS

Awe and wonder: feelings inspired by mysterious aspects of life.

Reflection: thinking deeply about some aspect of life.

Question: the act of asking questions e.g. about the meaning of life.

Questioner: the person who asks questions and seeks the truth.

Awe and Wonder

◆ Awe and wonder are feelings inspired by the more mysterious aspects of life. People can experience deep joy and admiration at the mysterious nature of:

▶ the universe

▶ the natural world

▶ other human beings

◆ People of all ages can feel a sense of joy and amazement at:

▶ **The universe.**
The scale of the universe is vast.
Our galaxy the Milky Way, for example, contains over a hundred billion stars. Add to that the millions of other galaxies elsewhere in the universe - it's immense!

▶ **The natural world**.
In the natural world there are large-scale wonders such as:
- the Grand Canyon in the US.
- the Aurora Borealis of the Northern Hemisphere.
And small-scale wonders such as:
- the detail of a spiders web.
- the colours of a sunset.

▶ **Human beings**.
There are also moments when we marvel at the special reality of other human beings such as:
- a new baby.
- a good friend.
- a loving parent or grandparent.
- a person who has achieved some amazing feat.

Reflection

◆ Everyone can recall a moment when they felt awe and wonder that lead them to reflect on the mystery of:

▶ the universe.

▶ the natural world.

▶ human life.

◆ Reflection involves taking time to stop and examine something in our experience, and to think deeply about it.

◆ A personal experience of awe and wonder can lead to personal reflection on the mystery of life. This in turn can prompt questions about the actual meaning of life itself.

Question/Questioner

◆ When we stop to wonder and reflect on the mystery of the universe, the mystery of the natural world, and the mystery of human life, what sort of questions do we ask?

◆ We might ask typical questions such as:

▶ Why is there a universe?

▶ How did the world begin?

▶ Why does anything exist?

▶ What is life for?

▶ Why do people suffer?

▶ What happens when we die?

▶ What do I want to do with my life?

◆ Deep questions such as these help us to explore the mystery of life.

◆ We all have the capacity to question and to seek the truth, and are able to ask fundamental questions about the meaning of life.

Test Yourself

1. What kind of experiences fill you with awe and wonder?
   Select one experience from your own life.

   a. The experience - What is it? Describe it.

   _____

   _____

   _____

   _____

   b. The reflection – write the thoughts that came to you on that occasion.

   _____

   _____

   _____

   _____

   _____

   _____

2. People reflect on life at all stages of their development.
   Give examples of the kind of questions each of the following might ask about life:

   • Small children: _____

   _____

   • Teenagers: _____

   _____

   • Parents: _____

   _____

   • Retired People: _____

   _____

3. When you think deeply about life, what sort of questions do you ask?
   List the questions that **you** ask about the meaning of life.

   _____

   _____

   _____

   _____

   _____

   _____

Search for Meaning

> **KEY CONCEPTS**
>
> **Search**: the deep human need to find meaning in life.
>
> **Meaning**: to find or to have a sense of purpose in life.
>
> **Meaninglessness**: failing to find meaning or purpose in life.
>
> **Humanism**: a belief system that rejects religion and makes sense of life through human reason alone.

Search

◆ **Search** - the deep human need to find meaning in life. Human beings have an in-built need to find meaning in life. We are restless, constantly searching for a purpose in life.

◆ From time to time we stop and think about our lives. We have a need to understand what our life, and life in general, is all about. At such times we might listen to our favourite music, finding inspiration in the words of a song.

◆ When we find ourselves asking deep questions about our existence, we are in fact searching for meaning and purpose in life.

Meaning, Meaninglessness

◆ What gives people a sense of purpose in life? In our society, people find **meaning** and purpose in life by devoting themselves to one or more of the following:
  ▶ their family.
  ▶ their work.
  ▶ their friends.
  ▶ their sport.
  ▶ their music.
  ▶ their leisure activities.
  ▶ their politics.
  ▶ their religion.
  ▶ their social life.
  ▶ their voluntary activities.
  ▶ their educational achievements.

◆ These are the main ways in which people find some meaning in life. However there are people who fail to find meaning or purpose in any human activity. For them everything is meaningless, nothing has any meaning or value at all.

◆ People of faith, who believe in God, find their **religion** gives the most meaning to their lives.
  ▶ For Jews: belief in the Lord God and following the Torah gives meaning to their lives.
  ▶ For Muslims: belief in Allah and the teaching of the Qur'an gives meaning to their lives.
  ▶ For Christians: belief in Jesus and his teaching in the Gospels gives meaning to their lives.

◆ Jews, Muslims and Christians believe their faith gives true meaning and purpose to life.

Humanism

◆ Humanists do not believe in God and do not belong to any community of faith. In **Humanism** religious ideas are rejected in favour of making sense of life through the power of human reason alone.

◆ Humanists believe life here on earth is the only reality. There is no God or gods or any power greater than the human person.

◆ A humanist does not turn to God or religion for answers to life's big questions, reason and human experience alone is sufficient.

Test Yourself

1. **a.** Name a song, a film, a book or a TV programme that has something to say about our search for meaning and purpose in life.

_____

_____

b. What does it identify as the most important thing in life?

_____

_____

_____

2. How might a person's family or their job give a sense of meaning and purpose to their life?

_____

_____

_____

_____

_____

3. Identify at least one source of meaning in your own life. What is it? Why is it important?

_____

_____

_____

_____

_____

_____

4. State one basic difference between a religious and a humanist outlook on life.

_____

_____

_____

_____

Exam Questions

---

1. This is a photograph of a young girl playing with a balloon. ....2003(O)

A. Pick **one** thing from the photograph which suggests that this is an experience of awe and wonder for the girl.

B. Some experiences that might make a person react with awe and wonder are a birth, the beauty of nature, and music. What does the expression "awe and wonder" mean?

C. Experiences of awe and wonder make people ask questions about the meaning of life. Give an example of **one** such question.

Veritas - Adapted

---

2. Some experiences in life can give a person a sense of awe and wonder: .... 2007(H), 2010(H)

The beauty of nature...   *The power of nature...*

The birth of a child...

Outline how an experience in life could make a person wonder and ask questions about the meaning of life.

---

3. This is a photograph of a person taking time for reflection. ....2012(O)

A. Pick **one** thing from this photograph which suggests that this person is involved in reflection.

B. In religious traditions the term 'reflection' refers to ...

C. State **one** reason why having time for reflection is important for the members of a community of faith.

www.gurusoftware.com/images

---

4. Explain **two** reasons why reflection is important for a person ....2010(H)
when searching for the meaning of life.

---

5. *"And will the new young flowers die?* .... 2004(O), 2004(H), 2006(O)
And will the new young people die?
And why?" - Poem from a three year old by Brendan Kennelly.

a. Pick **one** of the above questions and explain how it is typical of a child's search for meaning.

b. Explain how the questions a person may ask in his/her search for meaning could change as he/she develops from childhood into adulthood.

c. People sometimes express questions about the meaning of life in art, music, film and books.
Tick ✓ **one** of the following and explain how people express questions about the meaning of life in this way.

Art ☐   Music ☐   Film ☐   Books ☐

6. People often express their thoughts and feelings about the meaning of life .... 2010(O), 2013(H) in music, art, literature etc.

Describe **one** example of how a question about the meaning of life is expressed today in youth culture – music, art etc.

7. *People sometimes turn to religion as a source of meaning in life.* .... 2005(H), 2013(H)

Describe an example of how the teaching of **one** of the following world religions could help believers find answers in their search for the meaning of life.

● BUDDHISM   ● CHRISTIANITY   ● HINDUISM   ● ISLAM   ● JUDAISM

8. 1. Outline **two** ways in which people search for meaning in life. .... 2008(H), 2010(H)

2. a. What does the term 'reflection' mean?

   b. Explain **two** reasons why reflection can help people in their search for the meaning of life.

3. Outline the way in which religion can help a person in his/her search for the meaning of life.

4. ✦ Family   ✦ Friends   ✦ Work

   Outline the way in which **one** of the above can help a person in his/her search for the meaning of life.

9. a. Briefly explain how religious faith can grow out of the questions that a person asks .... 2006(H) in his/her search for meaning.

b. Describe **two** other factors that can influence personal faith.

c. People today express the search for meaning in many ways.

Give **two** examples of how the search for meaning is expressed in today's world and give a brief account of each example.

10. Which of the following give non-religious answers to questions about the meaning of life? .... 2014(O) (Tick ✓ the correct box)

HUMANISM ☐   MONOTHEISM ☐

11. a. Tick ✓ **one** of the statements below that is most associated with the .... 2013(O) humanist way of looking at life. (Tick ✓ the correct box)

☐ *A relationship with God gives meaning to a person's life.*

☐ *When searching for the meaning of life a person should not turn to religion.*

b. Explain how Humanism is associated with the idea expressed in the statement that you have ticked above.

12. Humanism can be described as a non-religious way of looking at the world. .... 2014(O), 2005(H)

Briefly explain the way Humanism has of looking at the world.

13. Describe **one** way in which Humanism could challenge a person's religious belief. .... 2009(H)

God in Scripture

OBJECTIVE:
Describe various images
of God and their sources
in the Old and New
Testaments.

◆ Images of God from scripture can help people to
form their own image of God. People have always
found it helpful to have an image or a picture of
God in their minds. Christians, for example,
believe that the **Bible** reveals or shows us what
God is like.

Jewish Scripture

◆ In Jewish scripture when people speak of God
they use metaphors. They compare God to what
they already know from their own experience.

◆ In the **Old Testament** familiar images:
   ▶ from nature,
   ▶ from human life,
   help people to know what God is like.

◆ Images of God from nature.
   God is like:
   ◉ An eagle..... that is powerful.
   ◉ The rain ..... that nourishes.
   ◉ A tree......... that shelters.
   ◉ A rock .... that protects.
   ◉ Fire .... that is a guiding light.
   ◉ A bird......... that defends.

◆ Images of God from human life.
   God is like:
   ◉ A king .... who reigns.
   ◉ A judge .... who is fair and just.
   ◉ A mother...... who comforts you.
   ◉ A father........ who created you.
   ◉ A potter........ who moulds you.
   ◉ A shepherd... who guides you.

◆ In Judaism, God is the one all powerful Yahweh
who created the universe and formed a special
relationship with his chosen people, the Jews.

Christian Scripture

◆ Christian scripture teaches that the best image of
God is an actual person, Jesus the Son of God.
Christians believe Jesus came on Earth to show
people who God is.

◆ In the **New Testament**, Jesus showed people what
God is like by:
   ▶ His parables – the things he said.
   ▶ His miracles – the things he did.

◆ The **parables** of Jesus.
   Jesus told parables to help people understand the
   goodness of God. Jesus said God is like:
   ▶ A good shepherd. (Luke 15:4-6)
   ▶ A good housekeeper. (Luke 15:8-10)
   ▶ A generous host. (Luke 14:15-24)
   ▶ A good parent. (Luke 15:11-32)

◆ The **miracles** of Jesus.
   People could see what God is like when Jesus:
   ▶ Healed the sick.
   ▶ Forgave sinners.
   ▶ Was friendly to outcasts.
   ▶ Gave up his life out of love for all.

◆ Jesus wanted his followers to think of God as a
good, loving and caring person. Someone who is
close to them and always looking after them.
A God they can trust.

◆ Two key Christian teachings that are central to Christian faith in God are:

▶ The Incarnation.

▶ The Trinity.

The Incarnation is the Christian belief that in Jesus, God became a human being. It means Jesus is fully God and fully human.

The Trinity is the Christian belief that in the one God there are three distinct and equal persons; the Father, Son and Holy Spirit. So when Christians speak of God they mean *the Father*, *the Son*, and *the Holy Spirit*.

God is...

✧ **The Father** who creates the world.

✧ **The Son** (Jesus) who saves the world.

✧ **The Holy Spirit** who helps people to follow the way of Jesus.

Test Yourself

1. How is God understood in the Old Testament or Jewish scriptures?

_____

_____

_____

_____

_____

_____

2. How is God understood in the New Testament or Christian scriptures?

_____

_____

_____

_____

_____

_____

_____

3. Explain what Christians mean by:

a. the Incarnation. _____

_____

_____

b. the Trinity. _____

_____

_____

Our image of God

OBJECTIVE:
Describe your own image
of God and identify
its source.

KEY CONCEPT

Personal faith: a person's own religious beliefs and response to God.

◆ Everyone has certain ideas of what God is like, although it can sometimes be difficult to find just the right words to say what we mean.

◆ Christians, for example, find it useful to form an **image** or a mental picture of God in their mind. It makes God more real for them.

◆ Our images of God help us to imagine what God is like. But our images cannot describe God completely, as God is a mystery to the human mind.

◆ The **source** of our image of God has to do with where our image of God comes from.

Our idea of God could be based on:

▶ Stories we have heard from scripture.

▶ Pictures we have seen.

▶ Songs and hymns we have listened to.

▶ Our own personal experience of everyday life; its joys and sorrows, hopes and disappointments.

Personal Faith

◆ **Personal faith** is a person's own religious beliefs and response to God. It is our relationship with God arising out of our own personal experience.

a) List some **experiences** that you had in life that give you a hint of what God is like.

_____

_____

_____

_____

b) Pick one **word** that sums up your sense of God from these experiences. _____

c) What picture or **image** of God comes into your mind because of these experiences?

_____

_____

_____

◆ Our words and images can express what God is like, but they will never fully capture who God is.

Test Yourself

1. **a.** What is your image of God? _____

_____

   b. Can you explain why it is a good image of God? _____

_____

_____

2. **a.** What is the main source of your image of God? _____

   b. How did this source shape your image of God? _____

_____

3. How can a person's experience of life affect their faith in God? _____

_____

_____

_____

Stages of Faith

OBJECTIVE:
Differentiate between childhood faith and mature faith.
Outline the development from one stage to the other.

KEY CONCEPTS

Trust: being able to rely on a person with complete confidence.

Faith: a strong inner belief and trust in God.

Stages of faith: the development of a person's relationship with God from childhood faith to mature faith.

Childhood faith: a simple trust in God and an acceptance of one's parents' faith.

Mature faith: a close relationship with God and an active commitment to one's faith.

Trust

◆ **Trust** is being able to rely on a person with complete confidence. People learn about trust early in life. When small children feel loved by their parents it gives them the assurance, as they get older, that they can trust other people and life in general.

Faith

◆ **Faith** is a strong inner belief and trust in **God**. When a person is able to put their trust in God, this is faith. Someone who trusts God believes that:
  ▶ God loves them.
  ▶ God will always be there for them.
  ▶ God will not let them down.
  Having faith in God is about trusting God.

Stages of Faith

◆ People's religious faith can grow and develop throughout their lifetime

◆ Experts who study religious faith tell us that people go through different stages in their relationship with God.
  The **stages of faith** are:
  ▶ Childhood faith - an imitative faith.
  ▶ Adolescent faith - a questioning faith.
  ▶ Mature faith - an active commitment to one's faith.

  Each stage has its own unique characteristics.

Childhood Faith

◆ **Childhood faith** is a simple trust in God and an acceptance of one's parents' faith. Children's **image of God** as a father or grandfather figure is based on their experience of the love of parents and family members.

◆ Through the love of parents and grandparents, children develop a basic trust in the goodness of people and life in general. They learn to trust God in a similar way.

◆ Children accept the religious belief and practices of their parents and imitate what they do without question.

Adolescent Faith

◆ The adolescent's **image of God** is more that of a friend, someone to turn to, talk to, and who can always be relied upon. This image is based on the adolescent experience of friendship and acceptance in the peer group.

◆ Adolescents realise that the world is not always a good place, there is evil and injustice, and bad things do happen to good people. Adolescents begin to question how God can allow this to happen.

◆ Doubts and questions are necessary and important at this stage of faith development as young people try to work out their own position on religious issues.

Mature Faith

- **Mature faith** involves a close relationship with God and an active commitment to one's faith. A person can reach the stage of mature faith any time between the late teens and middle age.

- A person's **image of God** at this stage is that of a loving presence surrounding them and being close to them. This image is based on personal experience of knowing that what matters most in life is love of God, and the love and care of other people.

- People of mature faith, while aware that suffering and injustice exists in the world, are able to trust in the goodness of God.

- People of mature faith have made the decision to give time to God and to live good moral lives caring for others.

Test Yourself

1. How do people learn:

   a. to trust other human beings? _____

   b. to trust God? _____

2. What is religious faith? _____

   _____

   _____

3. Name the different stages of religious faith.

   _____

   _____

   _____

4. How do children learn to have faith in God?

   _____

   _____

5. Why is doubt and questioning in adolescence important in the development of religious faith?

   _____

   _____

   _____

6. Outline the characteristics of mature religious faith.

   _____

   _____

   _____

   _____

   _____

1. A. World religions refer to God by different names. Tick ✓ **one** of the names listed below: ....2005(O)

Allah ☐   Brahman ☐   Jesus ☐   Yahweh / YHWH ☐

With which world religion is the name you have ticked above associated?

B. a. Describe the image of God in a world religion you have studied.

   b. Outline a story from the sacred text of a world religion you have studied in which the image of God described above can be found.

2. a. 'God as Father' is an example of an image of God associated with a major world religion. ....2013(O)
Name **another** image of God that is associated with a major world religion.

   b. Tick ✓ **one** of the following world religions that you have studied:

BUDDHISM ☐   CHRISTIANITY ☐   HINDUISM ☐   ISLAM ☐   JUDAISM

Outline **one** belief about God/gods/the divine that is associated with the world religion which you have ticked above.

3. a. Describe **one** image of God that you have studied. ....2012(H)

   b. Outline how **one** source may have shaped the image of God that you have described above.

4. This is a picture of a child's image of God. ....2010(O)

   A. Pick **one** thing from this picture which suggests that it is based on an image of God.

   B. State **one** thing this image shows about the child's understanding of God.

   C. Give **one** other example of an image of God.

Garrod & Lofhouse Ltd.

5. A. a. Describe **one** image of God that you have studied. .... 2003(H), 2008(O)

   b. Outline **one** way in which a person's image of God can change from childhood to adolescence.

B. Describe **two** ways in which a young person can express his/her religious beliefs.

6. *And God is one God! There is no God but He.* .... 2004(O), 2007(O)

A. Explain how this prayer is an example of monotheism.

B. a. Describe **two** things that are typical of a child's faith.

   b. Describe **one** thing that is typical of mature faith.

7. Explain **one** reason why a person's image of God may change as he/she grows ....2012(H)
from childhood to adulthood.

8. ● ADOLESCENT FAITH   ● MATURE FAITH   ....2010(H)

Outline the main characteristics of each of the above stages of faith development using the following headings:

i. Relationship with God/the Divine.   ii. Main Influences on Faith.

NOTE: *This is an essay question.*

Signs of Religious Faith

OBJECTIVE

Explain how religious faith finds expression in prayer, worship and a certain way of life.

KEY CONCEPTS

Prayer: the way people of faith communicate with God.

Worship: the way people of faith praise and honour God in prayer and at religious services.

◆ If people have a feeling of deep trust or faith in God, they will express that through prayer, worship and the way they live their lives.

◆ It is natural that a person's inner faith in God will find expression in outer ways, such as wanting to:
  ▸ Pray to God.
  ▸ Worship God.
  ▸ Live the way God wants.

These outward behaviours are signs of the person's inner faith.

Prayer

◆ People of faith have a relationship or a friendship with God. **Prayer** is the way people of faith communicate with God.

◆ In order to build a strong relationship with God people need to communicate with God often. This involves spending time talking and listening to God in prayer.

Worship

◆ **Worship** is the way people praise and honour God at religious services, for example in churches, synagogues and mosques. People show their faith when they worship God.

◆ When a person attends a religious service to worship God, it is a sign that their relationship with God really matters to them.

Way of Life

◆ Religious faith is expressed in the way people try to live good lives. For Christians, this means following the teaching of Jesus.

"Love God and love your neighbour as yourself."
(Matthew 22:37-39)

Test Yourself

1. What human behaviours are a sign that a person has faith in God?

_____

_____

_____

_____

_____

2. Why do people of faith pray to, and worship God regularly?

_____

_____

_____

_____

Faithful People

KEY CONCEPTS

Polytheism: the belief in many gods.

Monotheism: the belief in one God.

Polytheism

Hinduism is an example of a polytheistic religion. Hindus believe in many gods. Mahatma Gandhi was a Hindu, a man of deep religious faith.

Mahatma Gandhi (1869 – 1948)

◆ Mahatma Gandhi was a devout Hindu, and a lawyer, who spent his life campaigning for human rights. He lived in India at a time when the country was under British rule and people's rights were undermined.

◆ Gandhi's strong Hindu faith led him to believe that love and truth were important, and that all forms of violence were wrong. He led a peaceful campaign for human rights for many years, often fasting as a form of protest.

◆ Gandhi later gave up his profession as a lawyer and became a Hindu holy man, devoting himself full-time to the cause of human rights.

◆ Gandhi's peaceful protests helped to bring an end to British rule in India in 1947. The following year he was shot dead by an assassin in New Delhi.

Monotheism

Christianity is an example of a monotheistic religion. Christians believe in one God. Martin Luther King was a Christian, a man of deep religious faith.

Martin Luther King (1929 – 1968)

◆ Martin Luther King was a Christian minister and a civil rights leader. He lived in America at a time when there was a lot of prejudice against the black community.

◆ Dr. King said racial prejudice was wrong. He believed everyone was created equal in the eyes of God. As a campaigner for civil rights he travelled throughout the U.S. to lead marches and speak at rallies.

◆ Dr. King wanted change to take place peacefully, not through violence. The Christian way of love and peace was better than hatred and violence he said.

◆ In 1964, the American government eventually granted civil rights to all people of colour in America.

Four years later Dr. Martin Luther Kingt was shot by an assassin in Memphis, Tennessee. He was thirty nine years old.

Test Yourself

1. What is the evidence that religious faith influenced the way of life of either Mahatma Gandhi **or** Martin Luther King?

_____

_____

_____

_____

2. Why do you think Mahatma Gandhi and Martin Luther King are regarded as men of deep religious faith?

_____

_____

_____

Exam Questions

1. a. Read the list of religious practices and the list of world religions given below. ....2005(H), 2012(O)

Match **one** religious practice to the world religion with which it is most associated.

Religious Practices	World Religions
Facing Mecca	Buddhism
Sitting in the Lotus Position	Christianity
Wearing a Tefillin	Hinduism
Making a Sign of the Cross	Islam
Offering Incense	Judaism

	Religious Practice	World Religion
Answer:		

b. Outline **two** reasons why religious practice is important for people of religious faith.

2. Prayer is **one** way in which people express religious faith. .... 2011(O)

Name **another** way in which people express religious faith.

3.

This is a photograph of a group of people praying. .... 2003(O)

A. State **one** thing from the photograph which suggests that these people are expressing their religious faith.

B. Give **one** reason why a person might express his/her faith in this way.

C. Participation is part of worship. State how participation can be seen in this photograph.

Flame Tree Publishing 2002

4. a. Name **one** major world religion that is associated with monotheism. .... 2009(H), 2014(H)

b. Explain **one** reason why monotheism is associated with the major world religion that you have named above.

5. a. Name **one** major world religion that is associated with polytheism today. .... 2011(O)

b. Describe **one** example of how polytheism can be seen in the world religion that you have named above.

6. a. ◆ BUDDHISM ◆ CHRISTIANITY ◆ HINDUISM ◆ ISLAM ◆ JUDAISM .... 2010(H)

Oscar Romero is one example of a person whose faith has inspired others.

Name **another** person, associated with one of the world religions listed above, whose faith has inspired others.

b. Outline how the religious faith of the person you have named above can be seen in an event from his/her life.

7. Discuss how the search for peace has been a driving force in the life of a .... 2006(H) person of faith in a world religion you have studied.

NOTE: *This is an essay question.*

Science and Religion

KEY CONCEPTS

World view: a set of ideas about what the world is like.

Creation: a view on the origin of the world and life on Earth.

Fundamentalism: the view that a sacred text is a factual account to be taken literally.

World View

◆ A world view is a set of ideas about what the world is like. Science and religion have a different outlook and different views on life and the universe.

Science is about examining things that can be seen, weighed and measured.

Religion is about belief in things that cannot be seen but can be experienced.

◆ Science and religion have been regarded as rival forms of knowledge since the time of the Enlightenment in the 17th century.

◆ Up to the Enlightenment people saw the world in religious terms. From the time of the Enlightenment people began to see the world in scientific terms.

◆ The idea that religion and science are opposed took hold when the Catholic Church banned the work of two great scientists whose discoveries affect the way we understand the world.
   ▸ Galileo Galilei in the 17th century
   ▸ Charles Darwin in the 19th century.

Scientific World View

Galileo Galilei (1564 -1642), an Italian astronomer and scientist, studied the planets and the stars. He was able to prove that the Earth orbited the sun.

◆ The Church had always taught what the Bible seemed to say – that the Earth was the centre of the universe. Galileo's new ideas contradicted that view. Galileo was put on trial by Church authorities in Rome and his writings were banned.

◆ Years later the Church apologised and went on to accept his findings, but the damage was done. The idea that there was a conflict between science and religion was established.

Charles Darwin (1809 – 1882), a British scientist, put forward the theory of evolution. It stated that all life, including human life, had evolved over millions of years by a process of natural selection.

◆ This theory challenged the religious view in the Bible that life was created in six days. The Church quickly condemned his writings. In the clash between religion and science, it seemed faith and reason were once again opposed to each other.

Creation

Religious World View

◆ A Christian view on the origin of the world and life on Earth is contained in the Bible, in the story of creation in the **Book of Genesis**.

◆ Genesis is not a scientific account of how the world began. It is a religious account explaining why the world came to be. The world was created out of the goodness and love of God.

◆ The writers of Genesis were not scientists but religious Jews who used poetic language to convey important religious truths such as :
   ▸ God created the world.
   ▸ God's world is created by design.
   ▸ God's world is good.
   ▸ God created human beings, the high point of creation.

◆ Unfortunately, Church leaders at the time of Galileo and Darwin failed to distinguish between religious and scientific truth.

Fundamentalism

◆ **Fundamentalism** is an outlook among some religious groups that their sacred text is a factual account and must be taken literally word for word. Fundamentalists reject scientific discoveries that do not match a literal interpretation of their sacred text.

◆ Christian fundamentalists believe the Genesis account of creation is factual: the world was created in six days; each "day" was a 24 hour period.

◆ Today, new advances in Bible research show that the creation accounts in Genesis are not factual accounts of how the world was made. Genesis is a religious account written to help people to understand <u>why</u> the world was made, not <u>how</u> it was made.

Partnership

◆ Many Church leaders today see little conflict between religion and science. Darwin's theory of evolution explains how life began, the book of Genesis explains why it began.

◆ Religion and Science see the world from different points of view. The two forms of knowledge can work together and need not contradict each other. Both add something valuable to our understanding of the world.

◆ It is possible to study the natural world from a scientific point of view and still believe that creation is a gift from God. For example **Pierre Teilhard de Chardin** (1881-1955), a Catholic priest and a renowned scientist, believed that scientific work enriches a person's religious understanding of God and creation.

Test Yourself

1. What is the origin of the uneasy relationship that exists between science and religion?

_____

_____

_____

2. Explain how Christians understood the Genesis account of creation in the past and the way it is understood today.

_____

_____

_____

_____

_____

3. Are science and religion necessarily opposed to one another? Explain your answer.

_____

_____

_____

_____

_____

World Views

KEY CONCEPTS

Reflection: thinking deeply about certain aspects of life.

World view: a set of ideas about what the world is like.

Experiencing God: being aware of God's mysterious presence.

Atheism: a view that denies the existence of God.

Agnosticism: the view that people cannot know for certain whether or not God exists.

Materialism: the view that only material things are real.

Secularism: the view that organised religion should have no direct influence on society.

Reflection

◆ **Reflection** means taking time to think deeply about certain aspects of life. Some of life's big questions, such as whether or not God exists, requires careful thought and reflection.

World View

◆ A **world view** is a set of ideas about what the world is like. It is a framework people use to organise their thoughts about life. It helps them to tie all their ideas together in order to make sense of it.

Experiencing God

◆ **Experiencing God** is about being aware of God's mysterious presence in a deep and quiet way. The majority of people make sense of the world from a religious viewpoint.

◆ Christians, for example, believe in God. They believe God created the world and continues to guide and sustain it out of love.

◆ A Christian's faith in God enables the person to experience God, to be quietly aware of the mysterious presence of God in their life.

A growing number of people in our society make sense of the world from a non-religious viewpoint.

Atheism

◆ **Atheism** is a view that denies the existence of God. Atheists do not believe that God or gods exist. From an atheist's point of view there is no God. God is not real.

Agnosticism

◆ **Agnosticism** is the view that people cannot know for certain whether or not God exists. There is simply not enough evidence to prove it one way or another. Agnostics claim that no one can say for definite that there is a God or that there is no God.

Materialism

◆ **Materialism** is the view that only material things are real. Something is real if it can be physically seen, touched, weighed, and measured.

◆ Materialists believe that the only real things are material things. Nothing else exists. God does not exist.

◆ Materialism also has another related meaning. A materialistic way of life is about having lots of money, lots of possessions and enjoying oneself as much as possible. Accumulating material things becomes important when it is accepted that only material things matter in life.

Secularism

- **Secularism** is the view that organised religion should have no direct influence on society. Secularists are opposed to the influence of religion in public life. Secularists claim God and religion are simply not relevant anymore.

Challenges to Religious Experience: Materialism

- Materialists claim that the only real things are material things. If something can be examined by the senses then it is real. If it cannot, then it is not real and does not exist.

- But we cannot see, hear or touch our ideas, our beliefs, or our feelings, yet most people would agree that these are a real and a very important part of our lives. Humans therefore are both material and spiritual beings.

- God is different. God is not material; God is totally spiritual. Human beings communicate with God through the spiritual aspect of their own nature.

- Materialism poses a challenge to religion and religious experience. It claims that only material things are real. On that basis, the spiritual nature of human beings is not real. God is not real, and religion doesn't matter.

- The materialist outlook can undermine people's confidence in religious truth as a valid form of human knowledge.

Test Yourself

1. How do you think people of faith experience God in their lives?

_____

_____

_____

2. Explain the meaning of the following non-religious world views.

- Atheism _____

_____

- Agnosticism _____

_____

- Secularism _____

_____

- Materialism _____

_____

3. Belief in God is central to Judaism, Christianity, and Islam. How does materialism pose a challenge to religious faith?

_____

_____

_____

_____

_____

_____

Exam Questions (HIGHER LEVEL)

1. A. Describe in detail a religious world view of creation. ....2003(H)

   B. a. Identify **one** similarity between the scientific and religious views of creation
         and explain how they are similar.

      b. Identify **one** difference between the scientific and religious views of creation
         and explain how they are different.

2. a. ◆ BUDDHISM   ◆ CHRISTIANITY   ◆ HINDUISM   ◆ ISLAM   ◆ JUDAISM   ....2013(H)
      Describe an example of the teaching on the creation of the world that is associated
      with **one** of the world religions listed above.

   b. Compare the teaching on the creation of the world that you have described above
      with that found in **another** major world religion.

3.   Buddhism ❑   Christianity ❑   Hinduism ❑   Islam ❑   Judaism ❑   ....2008(H)

   A. Imagine you are doing a project on the creation of the world. Tick ✓ one of the above world religions and
      outline **two** points it teaches about the creation of the world.

   B. Outline **two** points that science teaches about the creation of the world.

   C. Describe **one** similarity between what a religion says and what science says about the creation of the world.

4. a. Describe **one** example of how religion and science have similar views of creation.   ....2014(H)

   b. Explain **one** reason why there has been tension between the religious and scientific views of creation.

5.   *Science and religion offer two very different accounts of how the world began.*   ....2012(H)

   Discuss the evidence for this statement making reference to both the scientific
   and the religious views of creation.

   NOTE: *This is an essay question.*

6. a. A world view that rules out the possibility of anything spiritual or invisible is: ....2004(H)
      (Tick ✓ the correct box)
      Agnosticism ❑   Materialism ❑   Monotheism ❑   Sectarianism ❑

   b. Explain **one** way in which this view could challenge a person's religious faith.

7. Agnosticism and Humanism can be described as non-religious ways of looking at the world.   ....2005(H)

   Briefly explain the way *either* Agnosticism *or* Humanism has of looking at the world.

8. ● MATERIALISM ● SECULARISM ....2013(H)

Outline what is involved in **one** of the ways of looking at the world listed above and describe an example of how it can be seen in society today.

9. Materialism ☐ Secularism ☐ ....2007(H)

A. Tick ✓ **one** of the above and describe what it means.

B. Explain how the religious faith of a person could be challenged by *either* materialism *or* secularism.

10. a. i. ATHEISM ii. AGNOSTICISM .... 2003(H), 2011(H)

Describe what is meant by **each** of the terms listed above.

b. Explain how the religious belief of a person could be challenged by *either* atheism *or* agnosticism.

11. You are taking part in a school debate about the challenges to .... 2007(H), 2011(H)
religious faith in Ireland today.

Outline what you would say about the way in which **each** of the following could challenge a person's religious faith:

● MATERIALISM ● SECULARISM

NOTE: *This is an essay question.*

Section E - The Celebration of Faith

The *Syllabus Aims* in this section are:

◆ To show how ritual and worship have always been part of the human response to life and to the mystery of God.

◆ To identify how communities of faith express their day-to-day concerns in various forms of ritual.

◆ To explore an experience of worship.

Key Concepts in the Celebration of Faith *(Section E)*   *Page*

Places of Pilgrimage

> **KEY CONCEPTS**
>
> **Sacredness:** a thing or a place that is holy and set apart from ordinary life.
>
> **Places of significance:** places or buildings that have a special meaning for people.
>
> **Actions of significance:** actions that have a special meaning for people.

Sacredness

◆ **Sacredness** is a thing or a place that is holy and set apart from ordinary life. In the Christian tradition, it can be a place associated with:
  ▶ Jesus.
  ▶ The Virgin Mary.
  ▶ The Saints.

This special connection with God makes the place holy and sets it apart.

◆ Christians believe God is present in some mysterious way in a sacred place. God's presence makes it holy. Sacred places are therefore different from all other places.

◆ A **pilgrimage** is a journey made by a pilgrim to a sacred place. A pilgrim is a person who goes on a pilgrimage to pray and to become closer to God.

◆ Reasons why people go on pilgrimage:
  ▶ To strengthen their faith in God.
  ▶ To give thanks to God.
  ▶ To seek God's forgiveness.
  ▶ To ask God for help.

◆ It is customary for Christians to go on pilgrimage but they are not obliged to do so. People who go on pilgrimage hope their journey will bring a change of heart, helping them to become closer to God in their everyday life.

Places of Significance

◆ A place can have **religious significance** for people because it is associated with an important person in a religion. He/she may have been born there, lived there, visited there, or be buried there.

◆ In Christianity, a place becomes a centre of pilgrimage because it is:
  ▶ Associated with the life of **Jesus**, e.g.
    ◉ **The Holy Land** - The country where Jesus lived.
      ◉ **Bethlehem** - The site where Jesus is thought to have been born is located in the Church of the Nativity.
      ◉ **Nazareth** - The site believed to be the home where Jesus grew up is in a church dedicated to the Holy Family.
      ◉ **Jerusalem** - The Via Dolorosa is the route Jesus walked on the way to be crucified.

      The site where Jesus was crucified, was buried and rose from the dead on Easter Sunday is in the Church of the Holy Sepulchre.

  ▶ Associated with a vision or apparition of **The Virgin Mary**, e.g.
    ◉ **Lourdes** - The grotto at Lourdes in France is the site where Saint Bernadette had a series of visions of the Virgin Mary in 1858. Bernadette was told to dig the ground and a spring of water appeared which is believed to have sacred healing powers.
    ◉ **Knock** - The parish church at Knock in Ireland is the site where fifteen men and women saw an apparition of the Virgin Mary on the night of August 21st 1879.

- Associated with the life or death of **a saint**, e.g.

  - **Rome -** Two great figures in the early Church St. Peter (Jesus' First Disciple) and St. Paul (the first great missionary) are both buried in Rome. Pilgrims pray at their tombs.

    Catholic pilgrims go to see the Pope and receive his blessing at a public audience in St. Peter's Square in the Vatican.

  - **Croagh Patrick -** Ireland's patron saint is said to have climbed Croagh Patrick, in Co. Mayo, to pray and fast during Lent 441CE. Pilgrims follow his footsteps on 'Pilgrimage Sunday' at the end of July each year. They kneel and pray where Patrick prayed and attend Mass on top of Croagh Patrick.

  - **Lough Derg -** St. Patrick is believed to have paid frequent visits to an island in Lough Derg in Co. Donegal. He went there to pray and fast before continuing his missionary activities.

Actions of Significance

- When people go on pilgrimage to a sacred place they perform special rituals or actions that have a religious significance.

- Catholic pilgrims at **Lourdes**, for example:
  - Pray and light candles in front of the grotto where Our Lady appeared.
  - Bathe in one of the baths fed by the spring well in front of the grotto.
  - Attend Mass in a church near the grotto.
  - Pray the Stations of the Cross.
  - Join in the candle-lit processions after dark.
  - Fill bottles and flasks with holy water to take home to their relatives and friends.

- Catholic pilgrims on **Lough Derg**, for example:
  - Fast and undertake the pilgrimage in bare feet.
  - Attend the all-night prayer vigil.
  - Pray the Stations of the Cross.
  - Receive the Sacrament of Reconciliation.
  - Attend Mass and receive the sacrament of the Eucharist.
  - Attend Benediction.

- For details of:
  - Places of pilgrimage in **Judaism** see page 108.
  - Places of pilgrimage in **Islam** see page 141.

Test Yourself

1. What do Christians mean when they refer to a place as sacred?

   _____

   _____

2. Why do Christians go on pilgrimage to sacred places?

   _____

   _____

   _____

3. What actions of religious significance are performed at one Christian place of pilgrimage?

   _____

   _____

   _____

   _____

Places of Worship

KEY CONCEPTS

Sacredness: a thing or a place that is holy and set apart from ordinary life.

Actions of significance: actions that have a special meaning for people.

Places of significance: places or buildings that have a special meaning for people.

Sacredness

◆ **Sacredness** refers to a thing or a place that is holy and set apart from ordinary life. A church is a building specifically set aside for the honour of God.

◆ Christians gather together in churches to pray and worship God as a community. For many Christians, their church is a holy and sacred place.

Actions of Significance

◆ People use actions when words cannot fully express what it means to encounter the sacred in a sacred place.

◆ Catholics, for example, believe their place of worship is a sacred place. Catholics perform **special actions** when they enter a church. They:
  ▶ Bless themselves with holy water.
  ▶ Genuflect before the Blessed Sacrament.
  ▶ Kneel in a pew and bow their head.
  ▶ Join their hands together in prayer.

Their actions show that when they are in a Catholic church, Catholics believe they are in the presence of God.

Places of Significance

◆ A **church** is a **place of religious significance** for members of the Christian community.

◆ A church building is designed as a place of worship. The design and layout of churches varies in the different Christian traditions. The focus of a church interior will, in general, be on either:
  ▶ the pulpit, or ▶ the altar.

◆ The **pulpit** is the central feature in Methodist, Presbyterian and Baptist Churches, because the main emphasis in Sunday worship is reading and preaching the Word of God in the Bible.

◆ The **altar** is the focal point of Catholic, Anglican and Orthodox church buildings because the Eucharist is the main form of Sunday worship.

◆ The focal point for the Salvation Army and the Society of Friends (Quakers) in their place of worship is not a pulpit or an altar, but the assembly of people gathered together.

Diagram of a Roman Catholic church interior.

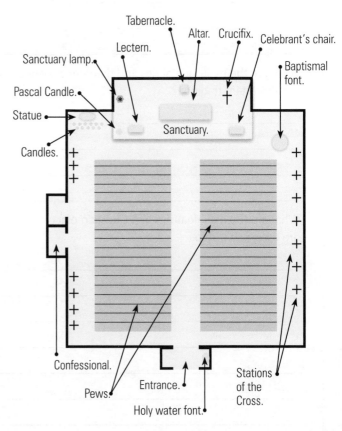

Tabernacle. Altar. Crucifix. Celebrant's chair. Lectern. Sanctuary lamp. Baptismal font. Pascal Candle. Statue. Sanctuary. Candles. Confessional. Entrance. Pews. Holy water font. Stations of the Cross.

Key features in a Catholic church

- **The altar** is where the celebration of the Eucharist takes place. A crucifix is above the altar.
- **The tabernacle** is where the consecrated communion hosts, the Blessed Sacrament, is kept.
- **The sanctuary lamp** is lit to alert people to the presence of Jesus in the Blessed Sacrament.
- **The celebrant's chair** is where the priest sits at Mass.
- **The Lectern** is a stand from where the Bible is read.
- **The baptismal font** is where new members are baptised into the Catholic community of faith.
- **The Pascal candle** is a large candle symbolising that Jesus is the light of the world.
- **The stations of the cross** are fourteen images depicting the events of Good Friday.
- **The statues** are images of Jesus, Mary or the saints.

- **The confessional** is where people receive the sacrament of reconciliation.
- **The pews** are rows of seats where the congregation sit or kneel facing the altar.
- **The stained glass windows** show scenes from the Bible and the lives of the saints.
- **The holy water font** is where people make the sign of the cross as they enter the church.

- Christian traditions which have priests and bishops will have cathedrals. A cathedral is the bishop's church and is the main church in a diocese.

◆ For details of:
  ▶ Places of worship in **Judaism** see page 106.
  ▶ Places of worship in **Islam** see page 140.

Test Yourself

1. What do Roman Catholics do when they enter their place of worship? What meaning do such actions have in the Catholic community?

   _____

   _____

   _____

   _____

2. What are the main similarities and differences between a Catholic church and a church in the Protestant tradition?

   _____

   _____

   _____

   _____

3. What are the main features in a Christian place of worship? Explain how three of these features are used in worship.

   _____

   _____

   _____

   _____

   _____

   _____

   _____

The Liturgical Year

> ### KEY CONCEPT
>
> **Times of significance**: times of the year that have a special meaning for people.
>
> **Actions of significance**: actions that have a special meaning for people.

Times and Actions of Significance

◆ Every religion sets aside special times each year to remember important people and events in the faith. Christianity has a religious calendar that marks special times in the life of Jesus.

◆ Each year the Church remembers and celebrates:
  ▸ The birth of Jesus at Christmas.
  ▸ The death and resurrection of Jesus at Easter.
  ▸ The sending of the Holy Spirit at Pentecost.

◆ The annual cycle of Church seasons is sacred time set aside to honour God.

The Liturgical Year

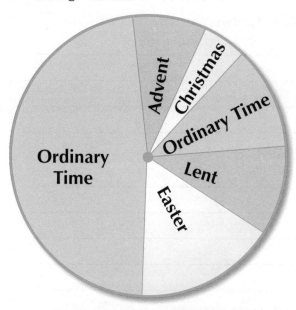

◆ This calendar is used by Roman Catholics and most Anglicans. All Christians observe Christmas and Easter. The Liturgical Year begins on the first Sunday in Advent.

Advent

◆ The season of Advent is the four weeks leading up to Christmas.

◆ Advent is a time when Catholics, for example, prepare to celebrate the birth of Jesus through prayer and attendance at Mass, receiving the sacrament of Reconciliation, and by doing good deeds to help people in need.

Christmas

◆ The Christmas season begins on Christmas day and celebrates the birth of Jesus.

◆ Christmas is the time when Christians focus on an important aspect of their faith - that God became human in Jesus Christ. It is a season of thanksgiving.

◆ Christians attend Mass and religious services, share a special meal and exchange gifts with family and friends.

Ordinary time

◆ The two periods of ordinary time make up most of the liturgical calendar. The Gospel readings at this time focus on the parables and miracles of Jesus.

Lent

◆ The season of Lent lasts forty days (excluding Sundays) and is a time of preparation for Easter. Catholics, for example, make a special effort during Lent to pray, fast and do good deeds to make themselves more aware of the presence of God in their lives.

◆ Ash Wednesday is the first day of Lent. People get ashes on the forehead as a sign that they are sorry for their sins and want to make a fresh start.

Holy Week

◆ In Holy Week, the events leading up to the death and resurrection of Jesus are remembered and celebrated at various ceremonies on:

▶ Holy Thursday. ▶ Good Friday. ▶ Holy Saturday

◆ For details of:
  ▶ Sacred time in **Judaism** see pages 109-112.
  ▶ Sacred time in **Islam** see pages 142-143.

Easter

◆ The season of Easter begins on Easter Sunday and celebrates the resurrection of Jesus Christ.

◆ Easter is the most important season in the liturgical year. Christians believe the resurrection makes it possible for Jesus to be alive and present with his followers today.

◆ The season of Easter lasts for fifty days and ends on the feast of Pentecost, the birthday of the Christian Church.

Test Yourself

1. Identify times of the year that have a special significance for Christians.

_____

_____

_____

_____

2. What do Christians celebrate on: **a.** Christmas Day? **b.** Easter Sunday?

_____

_____

_____

_____

3. What do Christians do to prepare for: **a.** Christmas? **b.** Easter?

_____

_____

_____

_____

4. Why do Christians remember and celebrate significant times in the life of Jesus?

_____

_____

_____

_____

_____

Exam Questions

---

1. This is a photograph of the monastery in Clonmacnoise, Co. Offaly. .... 2005(O)

www.asahi-net.or.jp

    A. State **one** thing from this photograph which shows that Clonmacnoise is a place of religious importance.

    B. Name **one** other place of religious importance.

    C. Give **one** reason why the place you have named above has religious importance for people.

---

2. .... 2010(H)

Lough Derg, Co. Donegal
is a place of religious importance
for members of a community of faith in Ireland.

www.Kandle.ie

a. Name **one** other place in Ireland of importance for members of a community of faith.

b. Explain **two** reasons why the place you have named above has importance for a community of faith.

c. Describe **one** example of the way in which people worship in the place you have named above.

---

3. a. Croagh Patrick is a place of religious importance for a community of faith in Ireland. ....2008(O)
    Name **another** place in Ireland that has religious importance for a community of faith.

    b. Explain **two** reasons why the place you named above has religious importance for a community of faith.

---

4. 1. Explain **two** reasons why Knock is important for members of a community of faith. ....2011(O)

    2. Knock is one place of importance in Ireland for members of a community of faith.
    Name **another** place in Ireland of importance for a community of faith.

    3. RELIGIOUS PILGRIMAGE ☐   RELIGIOUS PRACTICE ☐
    Tick ✓ **one** of the above terms and describe what is involved for members of a community of faith.

    4. a. Outline what is involved in **another** example of either religious pilgrimage or religious practice that is associated with a major world religion that you have studied.

       b. Explain **two** reasons why the religious pilgrimage or religious practice outlined above is important for the members of the major world religion with which it is associated.

5. A. a. Read the list of religious buildings and the list of world religions given below. ....2014(O)

Match **one** religious building to the world religion with which it is most associated.

Religious Buildings	World Religions
Cathedral	Buddhism
Mandir	Christianity
Minaret	Hinduism
Synagogue	Islam
Temple	Judaism

	Religious Building	World Religion
Answer:		

    b. Describe the main features of **one** of the religious buildings listed in *part A.a.* above.

B. a. Outline **one** way that the religious building you have described above could help believers to worship.

    b. Explain **two** reasons why participating in worship is important for the members of a major world religion today.

---

6. Tick ✓ **one** of the following major world religions that you have studied: ....2012(H)

BUDDHISM ☐   CHRISTIANITY ☐   HINDUISM ☐   ISLAM ☐   JUDAISM ☐

  a. Name **one** religious building that has importance for the members of the world religion ticked above.

  b. Describe **two** ways in which the building that you have named above is used by the members of a major world religion.

---

7. Tick ✓ **one** world religion you have studied. ....2006(H)

Buddhism ☐   Christianity ☐   Hinduism ☐   Islam ☐   Judaism ☐

  a. Name the place of worship where members of this world religion regularly gather for prayer.

  b. Describe the place you have named above.

  c. Explain how the place of worship you have described above can help people to pray.

---

8. a. Read the list of religious festivals and the list of world religions given below. ....2012(O)

Match **one** religious festival to the world religion with which it is most associated.

Religious Festivals	World Religions
Diwali	Buddhism
Yom Kippur	Christianity
Eid-ul-Fitr	Hinduism
Wesak Islam	Islam
Easter	Judaism

	Religious Festival	World Religion
Answer:		

  b. Describe **one** example of what is involved in the celebration of a time of year that is regarded as sacred by the members of a world religion.

---

9. a. *Going on pilgrimage is an example of a symbolic action that members of a world religion* ....2014(O)
use to express their faith.

Describe what is involved in **another** symbolic action that the members of a major world religion use to express their faith.

  b. Explain **two** reasons why the members of a major world religion perform symbolic actions to express their faith.

10. A. World religions have special seasons and days of the year which ....2007(O)
are of religious importance for their members.

    a. Name **one** special season *or* day of the year that has importance for members of a world religion you have studied.

    b. Give **one** reason why the time you have named above is important for members of the world religion with which it is associated.

B. a. Name **one** religious ceremony which marks the importance of *either* a special season *or* day of the year in a world religion you have studied.

    b. Outline what happens in the religious ceremony you have named above.

---

11. This is a photograph of a Holy Week procession in Spain. ....2004(H)

The Irish Times

A. State **one** thing from the photograph which suggests that Holy Week is a time of significance.

B. Holy Week is a time of significance for which **one** of the following world religions. (Tick ✓ the correct box)
Buddhism ☐   Christianity ☐   Hinduism ☐   Islam ☐   Judaism ☐

C. Give **two** reasons why Holy Week is a time of significance in the world religion you have ticked above.

Worship

OBJECTIVE:
Identify the elements
of worship at
religious services.

> **KEY CONCEPTS**
>
> Worship: the way people of faith praise and honour God in prayer and at religious services.
>
> Ritual: an occasion when people use symbolic objects, words and actions to express what is deeply important to them.
>
> Participation: being actively involved in an act of worship.

Worship

◆ Worship is the way people of faith praise and honour God in prayer and at religious services. Christians worship God. They set time aside to thank God, for who He is and for what He has done for them.

◆ Christians can worship God privately by themselves, or publicly in the company of others.
  ▶ Examples of private acts of worship:
  - Individual prayer,
  - Meditation,
  - Bible reading.
  ▶ Examples of public acts of worship:
  - The Mass,
  - Holy Communion services,
  - Sacraments,
  - Pilgrimages.

◆ Public or collective acts of worship can be liturgical or non-liturgical.
  ▶ **Liturgical Worship** in Roman Catholic, Anglican and Orthodox Churches is altar centred. The Eucharist is the principal act of worship. There is a set ritual, a book outlines the fixed order of words and actions.
  ▶ **Non-Liturgical Worship** in Methodist, Presbyterian and Baptist Churches is Bible centred. Set rituals are avoided and there is no fixed order of service.

◆ The **elements of a collective act of worship** are:
  ◉ a gathering of a community of faith,
  ◉ in a sacred place,
  ◉ at a sacred time,
  ◉ led by a religious leader,
  ◉ reading from a sacred text,
  ◉ saying prayers,
  ◉ performing sacred rituals,
  ◉ with the participation of the community,

Ritual

◆ A ritual is an occasion when people use symbolic objects, words and actions to express what is deeply important to them. Religious rituals help people of faith express deep beliefs about their relationship with God.

◆ Rituals may involve:
  ▶ Wearing special clothes.
  ▶ Saying special words.
  ▶ Using special actions.

◆ Religious rituals are part of Christian acts of worship at:
  ▶ Mass.
  ▶ Holy Communion Services.
  ▶ Sacraments.
  ▶ Pilgrimages.

◆ Mass in the Catholic Church is an example of an act of worship that involves participation in religious rituals.

A Christian act of worship

The Mass

◆ The Mass (the Sacrament of the Eucharist) is a ritual meal that has its origins in the Last Supper. The words and actions of Jesus are remembered and made present to the Christian community at Mass.

◆ At Mass, **the priest**:

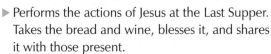

▶ Wears ceremonial clothes.

▶ Reads the Word of God in the Bible.

▶ Repeats the words of Jesus at the Last Supper.

   "This is my body...
   This is my blood...
   Do this in memory of me."

▶ Performs the actions of Jesus at the Last Supper. Takes the bread and wine, blesses it, and shares it with those present.

◆ The sacrament of the Eucharist is the central act of worship in the Roman Catholic Church. The word Eucharist means 'thanksgiving'. Catholics attend Mass to give thanks to God:

▶ For the gift of life.

▶ For what Jesus did in sacrificing his life to save people from sin.

◆ The different parts of the Mass are the:

▶ Introductory Rites.

▶ Liturgy of the Word.

▶ Liturgy of the Eucharist.

▶ Concluding Rites.

Catholics believe:

◆ Jesus is truly present at Mass:

▶ In the gathering of the priest and the people.

▶ In the Word of God in the Bible.

▶ In the bread and wine of the Eucharist.

◆ The bread and wine becomes the body and blood of Jesus Christ at the consecration of the Mass.

◆ Jesus' sacrifice on the cross is made present each time the Eucharist is celebrated.

Participation

◆ **Participation** in worship means being actively involved in sharing an experience of worship with others.

◆ Catholics are encouraged to take a full and active part in the celebration of the Mass.

Lay people participate by taking on the role of:

▶ Minister of the Word.

▶ Minister of the Eucharist.

▶ Altar server.

▶ Choir member.

▶ Participant in processions.

▶ Usher.

▶ Collector.

▶ Flower arranger.

▶ Sacristan.

◆ All lay people in the congregation can actively participate in the Mass by:

▶ Gathering and being present in the right spirit.

▶ Listening actively to the prayers and the readings.

▶ Responding to the blessings, saying the prayers, singing the hymns.

▶ Gesturing - for example thoughtfully performing ritual actions such as blessing oneself, kneeling, standing and giving the sign of peace.

▶ Full participation in the Mass means receiving the Blessed Sacrament in Holy Communion.

◆ For details of:

▶ Worship in **Judaism** see page 106.

▶ Worship in **Islam** see page 140.

Test Yourself

1. Give examples of **a.** private and **b.** public or collective acts of worship in the Christian tradition.

_____

_____

_____

_____

_____

2. What elements of worship can be observed in a Christian church on Sunday?

_____

_____

_____

_____

_____

3. Why do Catholics gather together to worship God at Sunday Mass?

_____

_____

_____

4. Name the different parts of the Mass. Describe one part in detail.

_____

_____

_____

_____

_____

_____

_____

5. How do Christians participate in Sunday worship?

_____

_____

_____

_____

_____

Exam Questions

1. Below are photographs of gestures or positions that people use in prayer. ....2009(O)

www.fotosearch.com

Christine Osborne Pictures

www.img.tebyan.net

Bowing ❏   *Sitting* ❏   *Washing* ❏

Tick ✓ **one** of the above gestures *or* positions and explain the reason why it is used in prayer.

2. A. a. World religions have different places of worship where their members gather .... 2005(O), 2010(O)
for communal prayer. Tick ✓ **one** of the following places of worship and
name the world religion with which it is most associated.

CHURCH ❏   MOSQUE ❏   SHRINE ❏   SYNAGOGUE ❏   TEMPLE ❏

WORLD RELIGION: _____

b. Outline what happens in **one** example of communal prayer for members of the world religion
you have named above.

B. Explain **two** reasons why communal prayer is important for members of a world religion.

3. This is a photograph of people praying. ....2012(H)

www.thecuttingedgenews.com

A. Pick **one** thing from this photograph which suggests that these
people are praying.

B. In religious traditions communal prayer involves _____

C. State **two** reasons why the members of a community of faith
participate in communal prayer.

4. a. In major world religions worship means.... ....2005(H)

b. Briefly outline **one** act of worship you have observed or participated in.

c. Describe **one** religious symbol that is used during an act of worship.

d. Give **three** reasons why people pray during worship.

5.

This is a photograph of a person performing a religious ritual. ....2005(O), 2010(H)

A. Pick **one** thing from this photograph which suggests that this person
is performing a religious ritual.

B. State **two** reasons why people perform religious rituals.

C. Give **one** other example of a religious ritual.

Transedition Limited and Fernleigh Books

6. a. Kneeling is one example of a religious ritual associated with prayer. .... 2008(O), 2013(O)
Name **another** example of a religious ritual associated with prayer.

b. Describe **one** example of a ritual that is involved in communal prayer for the members of a major world religion that you have studied.

7. a. Describe **one** example of a ritual that can be seen in an experience of worship .... 2008(O)
that you have *either* taken part in *or* observed.

b. Explain **two** reasons why people use religious rituals to express their faith.

8. a. ● COMMUNICATING EXPERIENCE ● PARTICIPATION .... 2013(O)
Outline how **one** of the above can be seen in an example of communal prayer in a major world religion.

b. Explain **two** reasons why communal prayer is of benefit to the members of a world religion.

9. A. a. Read the list of religious rituals and the list of world religions given below. .... 2013(H)
Match **one** religious ritual to the world religion with which it is most associated.

Religious Rituals	World Religions		Religious Ritual	World Religion
Blowing a Shofar	Buddhism	*Answer:*		
Giving Dana	Christianity			
Samskaras	Hinduism			
The Sign of the Cross	Islam			
Wudu	Judaism			

b. Tick ✓ **one** of the following major world religions that you have studied:
BUDDHISM ❑   CHRISTIANITY ❑   HINDUISM ❑   ISLAM ❑   JUDAISM ❑

Describe what is involved in a religious ritual that is associated with the world religion that you have ticked above.

B. a. Examine how the religious beliefs of a major world religion are expressed in a religious ritual.

b. Outline **two** ways that the members of a major world religion can benefit from participating in religious rituals.

10. *People have different ways of participating in worship* .... 2008(H)
- gestures, music, readings etc.

Explain how **one** way of participating in worship can help people to communicate with God.

11. ● RITUAL ● PARTICIPATION .... 2012(O)

1. Describe how *either* ritual *or* participation can be seen in a religious ceremony.

2. Describe what happens in a religious ceremony that you have participated in or observed.

3. Explain **one** reason why the members of a community of faith participate in the religious ceremony that you have described in part *2.* above.

12. Profile **two** benefits that communal prayer can have for the members of a community of faith .... 2014(H)

NOTE: *This is an essay question.*

Mystery

KEY CONCEPTS

Reflection: thinking deeply about some aspect of life.

Wonder: a feeling inspired by some mysterious aspect of life.

Encountering mystery: connecting with something mysterious that is beyond human understanding.

Worship as a response to mystery: people responding to mystery by gathering together to perform acts of worship.

Encounter with God: connecting with the mysterious presence of God in acts of worship.

Celebration: a religious ceremony performed in public for a community of faith.

Reflection

◆ **Reflection** involves taking time to think deeply about some aspect of life.

◆ Christians believe in:
 ▶ The invisible presence of God in the world.
 ▶ The Incarnation, the Christian teaching that God became human in Jesus Christ.

◆ For Catholic Christians, this means God's loving presence is everywhere. When people of faith stop to reflect on life, they can see how:
 ▶ God is present among the **people** they meet.
 ▶ God is present in the world of **nature** around them.
 ▶ God is present in a special way in the rituals of the **sacraments** in which they participate.

Wonder

◆ To be filled with wonder is to be filled with awe and amazement at some mysterious aspect of life.

◆ Religion arose out of people's deep sense of wonder at the mystery of the world around them.

◆ From earliest times, people were in awe of:
 ▶ the movement of the sun and the moon.
 ▶ the changing of the seasons.
 ▶ the cycle of birth, life and death.

They struggled to find an explanation for these mysterious events. This is how religion most likely began.

Encountering Mystery

◆ The word 'mystery' refers to something that is beyond human understanding. **Encountering mystery** is to experience something so deep and profound the human mind cannot fully grasp it.

◆ Our **early ancestors** experienced life as deeply mysterious:
 ▶ At first, the ancients believed the sun and the moon had special powers that were able to affect nature and life on earth. They looked at the sun and the moon and regarded them as gods.

◆ The **Jews** came to understand that the power behind the universe is a personal God, not an impersonal force. God revealed himself to be good as well as powerful.

◆ Thousands of years later, **Christians** came to believe that the one God so loved the world that in Jesus, God became human. Jesus lived and died on the Earth and rose again. Christians believe God's caring presence is with each person in the world today.

Worship as a response to Mystery

◆ When people encounter mystery, they respond by gathering together to perform acts of worship.

◆ In Ireland, the Celts (500BCE-500CE) are an example of a people who had a religious response to the mystery of the world around them.

The Celts

Believed in:	◉ The sun and moon as gods.
	◉ An 'otherworld' of invisible gods and goddesses.
Gathered in sacred places:	◉ Woodland groves, hilltops, beside rivers and wells.
Gathered at sacred times.	◉ The winter and summer solstice, the shortest and longest days of the year.
Led by a religious leader:	◉ A druid.
Participated in sacred rituals:	◉ The sun festival, when offerings were made to the gods to celebrate the passage of darkness to light.

Encounter with God

◆ Today people of faith, Christians for example, communicate with the mysterious and invisible presence of God through acts of worship.

Christians

Believe in:	◉ The invisible presence of God.
	◉ That God became human in Jesus Christ.
Gather in sacred places:	◉ Churches and places of pilgrimage.
Gather at sacred times.	◉ On Sunday, the Christian Sabbath, the holy day of the week.
	◉ At Christmas, the Christian festival of thanksgiving, celebrating the birth of Jesus Christ.
	◉ At Easter, the Christian festival celebrating the Pascal Mystery: that Jesus died, rose from the dead and will come again at the end of time.
	◉ At other times in the Liturgical Year.
Led by a religious leader:	◉ A priest or a minister.
Participate in sacred rituals:	◉ In the Sacrament of the Eucharist - a service of thanksgiving.
	◉ In the other sacraments e.g. baptism at birth, anointing of the sick at death.
	◉ On pilgrimage.

Celebration

◆ A celebration is a religious ceremony performed in public for a community of faith. The **Eucharist** is the central act of worship for many in the Christian community of faith.

◆ Participation in worship is the way Christians respond to the mystery of God's presence in their lives.

Test Yourself

1. What mysterious aspects of life filled our early ancestors with awe and wonder?

_____

_____

_____

2. How did people relate to the mystery of life down through the ages?

_____

_____

_____

_____

_____

3. Describe the religious response of the ancient Celts to the mystery of life.

_____

_____

_____

_____

4. How do Christians encounter and respond to the mystery of God today?

_____

_____

_____

_____

_____

_____

5. What might be the outcome when a person of faith stops to reflect on life?

_____

_____

_____

_____

_____

1. This is a photograph of young people holding candles. .... 2004(H)

Alain Pinoges/CIRIC

A. Pick **one** thing from the photograph which suggests that this is an experience of reflection for these young people.

B. What is reflection?

C. Give **two** reasons why it is important for a person to have time for reflection.

2. *In worship people sometimes give expression to their experience of mystery in life.* .... 2009(H)

i. Examine how **one** situation in life could be an experience of mystery for a person.

ii. Describe **one** example of worship and explain how it allows a person to express the experience of mystery in life.

NOTE: *This is an essay question.*

3. A.

Statement Number 1	Statement Number 2	Statement Number 3 ....2003(H)
"Every human person is a mystery, which must be learned slowly, reverently, with care, tenderness and pain, and is never learned completely." - Anon	"I can see nothing plain; all's mystery. Yet sometimes there is a torch inside my head that makes it all clear, but when the light is gone I have but images…" W. B. Yeats	"A mystery is not a wall against which you run your head, but an ocean into which you plunge. A mystery is not a night; it is the sun, so brilliant that we cannot gaze at it…" - E. Joly

a. Which of the above statements best describes encountering mystery in life? Explain your choice.

b. People often look back on life and recognise the experience of mystery at certain times and in certain places.
   Identify **one** life experience and explain how it could hold a sense of mystery for a person.

B. a. Sometimes people give expression to the experience of mystery through worship.
   Describe **one** example of worship in which people express their experience of mystery in life.

b. Explain how this act of worship helps people to express their experience of mystery in life.

4. *Some experiences in life can make people wonder about the meaning of life.* .... 2012(H)

a. Examine the way in which an experience in a person's life could make him/her wonder about the mystery of life.

b. Outline **one** example of how a person's search for the meaning of life could be expressed in an act of worship.

NOTE: *This is an essay question.*

5. *I feel at home in a Hindu temple. I am aware of Presence, not personal...* .... 2005(H)
but something larger. - Yann Martel

Outline how places of worship help people to respond to the experience of mystery in life.

NOTE: *This is an essay question.*

Sign and Symbol

KEY CONCEPTS

Sign: something that communicates a brief message or a piece of information.

Symbol: something visible, i.e an object or action, representing something invisible that is difficult to put into words.

Sign

◆ A **sign** is something that communicates a brief message or a piece of information.

◆ The sole purpose of a sign is to pass on a short, clear message that is easily understood by everyone.

Symbol

◆ Symbols are more powerful than signs and touch people at a deeper level. A **symbol** is something visible, i.e an object or action, that represents something invisible that is difficult to put into words.

◆ When a person dies, for example, it can be hard to find the right words to say how one feels. The depth of one's grief is expressed in an embrace, in shared moments of silence, in the lighting of candles, and in laying down offerings of flowers.

◆ The purpose of symbols is to give people a way of communicating feelings and ideas when words alone are not enough.

Religious Symbols

◆ Religious symbols bring together:
  ▸ something visible – that can be seen, *and*
  ▸ something invisible – that cannot be seen, but that is real.

◆ God is invisible but very real for people of faith. Religion uses symbol to communicate with God when ordinary language cannot fully express everything that needs to be said.

◆ Natural elements such as:
  ⊙ Water ⊙ Fire/Light ⊙ Food
  are used as religious symbols in the rituals of many of the great world religions.

◆ Take **water** for example:
  ▸ All life depends on water for its very existence. The life-giving properties of water make it a powerful religious symbol. In Christianity, water is used at the sacrament of Baptism.

◆ The **sacraments** are the most important symbols of the Catholic Church.

◆ The **Cross** is the principal symbol of Christianity. The Cross symbolises the death and resurrection of Jesus, the central event in the Christian faith.

◆ The **Pascal Candle** is the great Christian symbol of Easter. It is a special candle representing the risen Jesus, the Light of the World. It is lit at the Easter Vigil to celebrate the resurrection of Jesus Christ.

The Power and Meaning of Religious Symbols

♦ The power and meaning of religious symbols is evident, for example in the Christian ceremony of the **Easter Vigil** on Holy Saturday night.

♦ Natural elements such as water, fire/light, and food take on religious significance at the Easter Vigil.

♦ Symbolic words and actions express a deep spiritual reality at the heart of the Christian faith. It is the Pascal Mystery that Jesus died, rose from the dead, and will come again at the end of time.

♦ The Easter Vigil in Roman Catholic, Anglican, and Orthodox Churches takes place after dark on Holy Saturday night.

♦ Important features of the Easter Vigil in the Catholic Church include:

◉ Lighting the Easter **fire** -	representing the moment of resurrection.
◉ Lighting the Pascal **candle** -	a symbol of the risen Christ, the light of the world.
◉ Pouring the **water** of Baptism -	symbolising the beginning of a new life in Jesus, as baptismal promises are renewed.
◉ The gifts of **bread and wine** in the Eucharist -	symbols that become the body and blood of Jesus Christ in Holy Communion.

♦ For details of:
  ▶ Sign and symbol in **Judaism** see pages 109-112.
  ▶ The use of symbol is less common in **Islam**.

Test Yourself

1. Explain the difference between signs and symbols.

_____

_____

_____

2. What is the purpose of religious symbols?

_____

_____

_____

_____

3. Describe how symbolic objects and actions express religious belief in one Christian ceremony.

_____

_____

_____

_____

_____

_____

Icons

KEY CONCEPT

Icon: a sacred image used as an aid to prayer mainly in the Orthodox Churches.

Icon

◆ **Icons** are sacred images of Jesus, Mary and the saints. They have an important place in worship in Orthodox churches.

◆ Orthodox Christians pray in front of icons. When people enter an Orthodox church, they take a candle, light it before an icon, and kiss the icon with respect. They then stand and gaze at the icon in prayerful silence. The image helps the person to focus their mind and heart on the presence of God.

◆ Icons are religious symbols that help people to communicate with the world of the sacred.

◆ Icons are painted on wood in a distinctive style. While the figures are recognisable, they do not look real or very life-like.

▶ The figure is perfectly still, totally at peace.

▶ The eyes are bigger and wider than normal, and look out in a gentle, timeless sort of way.

▶ The hands may be holding something, pointing towards something, or raised in a blessing.

▶ Everything about an icon has a special, religious meaning, including the use of certain colours.

◆ An **iconographer** is an artist who creates icons. Iconographers believe the inspiration for their work comes from God.

◆ An **iconostasis** is a solid screen in front of the altar in an Orthodox Church. The screen is decorated with icons of Jesus, Mary, and the church's patron saint.

Test Yourself

1. What is an icon?

_____

_____

_____

2. How are icons used in worship in Orthodox Churches?

_____

_____

_____

_____

3. *An icon is a religious symbol.* Explain what this means.

_____

_____

_____

_____

_____

Sacraments

KEY CONCEPT

Sacrament: a sacred ritual that is a visible sign of God's presence with people at key moments in their lives.

Sacrament

◆ Christians believe in the invisible and mysterious presence of God in their lives. Their sense of the sacred is expressed in symbols and celebrated in sacred rituals.

◆ Sacraments are sacred rituals. They are a visible sign of God's loving, invisible presence with people at key moments in their lives. Important moments such as: ● the birth of a child, ● religious maturity, ● getting married, ● preparing for death.

◆ **The Orthodox Churches** celebrate seven sacraments, namely:

▶ Baptism.
▶ Confirmation.
▶ Eucharist.
▶ Reconciliation.
▶ Marriage.
▶ Holy Orders.
▶ Anointing the Sick.

The first three sacraments are administered together in infancy. An eight day old baby is baptised by total immersion in water, then confirmed (it is called Chrismation) and then receives Holy Eucharist.

◆ The **Protestant Churches**, Anglicans for example, believe that a sacrament is an outward visible sign of an inward invisible grace.

Anglicans believe Jesus instituted only two sacraments namely:

▶ Baptism.
▶ Holy Communion.

The others (Confirmation, Ordination, Holy Matrimony, the Ministry of Absolution (Penance) and the Ministry of Healing (Extreme Unction)) emerged later in the Christian Church; these are 'sacramentals' or special occasions.

◆ In the **Roman Catholic Church**, the word 'sacrament' is understood in three ways.

1. Jesus as Sacrament.
2. Church as Sacrament.
3. The Seven Sacraments.

◆ In the Catholic Church the seven sacraments are divided into:

Sacraments of Initiation	◉ Baptism
	◉ Confirmation
	◉ Eucharist
Sacraments of Healing	◉ Reconciliation
	◉ Anointing the Sick
Sacraments of Vocation	◉ Marriage
	◉ Holy Orders

◆ In the sacraments of **initiation**, Jesus calls people to be full members of the Christian community:
- they are Baptised in infancy,
- receive Holy Communion at eight years of age,
- and Confirmation at twelve years of age.

◆ In the sacraments of **healing**, Jesus brings forgiveness to people in the sacrament of Reconciliation, and comfort to the ill and dying in the sacrament of the Anointing of the Sick.

◆ In the sacraments of **vocation**, Jesus calls Christians to love and serve each other and the Christian community in the sacraments of Marriage and Holy Orders.

Each sacrament has its own set of:
- ▶ Significant words.
- ▶ Significant actions.
- ▶ Key symbols.

Catholics believe that it is through these things that God reaches out and touches them at key moments in their lives.

◆ The sacraments are communal celebrations. All who attend benefit from the loving presence of God.

◆ For details of:
- ▶ Rites of passage in **Judaism** see page 113.
- ▶ Rites of passage in **Islam** see page 144.

Test Yourself

1. What is the Christian understanding of Sacrament?

_____

_____

_____

_____

2. What sacraments are celebrated in the Orthodox Churches?

_____

_____

_____

3. How are sacraments understood in the Anglican community?

_____

_____

_____

_____

_____

4. What is the meaning of sacrament in the Roman Catholic Church?

_____

_____

_____

_____

_____

_____

Sacrament of Baptism

KEY CONCEPTS

Identity: the distinct characteristics by which a person or group is recognised.

Communicating experience: experiencing an invisible reality and expressing it clearly in symbolic words and actions.

Sacrament: a sacred ritual that is a visible sign of God's presence with people at key moments in their lives.

Identity

◆ Identity is the distinct characteristics by which a person is recognised as belonging to a community of faith.

◆ Baptism is a ceremony of initiation at which a person officially becomes a Christian. Baptism establishes a person's identity as a follower of Jesus and a member of a particular Church.

Communicating Experience

◆ Christians believe in the invisible presence of God.

◆ In the Roman Catholic Church, the invisible presence of God is expressed in the symbolic words and actions of the sacraments. Sacraments communicate the experience of God's presence.

◆ In the sacrament of **Baptism**, symbols that communicate the experience of God's presence are:
  ▶ The pouring of water.
  ▶ The anointing with oil.
  ▶ Lighting of a candle.
  ▶ Clothing in a white garment.

◆ **Water** is vital for life, pouring the baptismal water symbolises and brings about the end of 'sin' and the start of a new life as a follower of Jesus.

◆ **Oil** of two kinds is used. Anointing with the *oil of Catechumens* symbolises God strengthening the child against sin and temptation. Anointing with *oil of Chrism* symbolises that the child is specially chosen to serve God.

◆ **Candle**: lighting the baptismal candle symbolises the new life of Christ present in the heart of the child.

◆ **White garment**: draping a white shawl around the child is a symbol of being clothed in Christ. The child begins a new life as a follower of Jesus, and a member of the Church.

Sacrament

Infant baptism in the Catholic Church

◆ Infant baptism in the Catholic Church is a sacred ritual. The sacrament is a visible sign of God's loving, invisible presence with the child as he/she joins the Christian community.

The Ceremony

◉ The family gather at the church and present the child for Baptism. The priest blesses the child with the sign of the cross.

◉ The Word of God is read from the Bible, the priest explains the reading and the meaning of Baptism.

◉ The priest anoints the child with oil of Catechumens.

◉ Parents and godparents renew their baptismal promises.

◉ Water from the baptismal font is poured over the baby's head. The priest says "I baptise you in the name of the Father, and of the Son, and of the Holy Spirit." This is the moment of Baptism.

◉ The child is anointed with the oil of Chrism.

◉ A white shawl is wrapped around the child. The parents hold a candle lit from the Pascal Candle.

◉ Everyone says the Lord's Prayer. The priest blesses the parents and all who attend the baptismal ceremony.

Believers Baptism in Baptist churches

◆ Some Christian Churches only baptise adults. Believers Baptism takes place when a person is ready to make a commitment to become a Christian and asks to be baptised. The Baptism is by total immersion.

◆ Believers Baptism is practiced in Baptist churches. Baptists follow the example of the New Testament, in which:

▶ Jesus was an adult when he was baptised.

▶ Jesus was baptised by total immersion in the waters of the river Jordan.

◆ Baptism is an outward sign that the person believes in Jesus and has chosen to be a Christian.

At a Believer's Baptism

◉ The congregation sing hymns, say prayers and listen to a reading from the Bible and a sermon on Baptism.

◉ Candidates wearing white robes express sorrow for their sins. They say why they wish to be baptised.

◉ The minister and each candidate step down into the baptismal pool. The person is baptised in the name of the Father, Son and Holy Spirit, and is immersed in the baptismal water.

◉ The congregation sing a hymn as the person emerges from the water.

◉ At Baptism, the believer is admitted to full membership of the church.

Test Yourself

1. What part of a person's identity is established at Baptism?

_____

2. Identify four symbols used in the Baptismal Ceremony of the Catholic Church and explain the meaning of **any two**.

_____

_____

_____

_____

3. What symbolic words and actions communicate the experience of God's presence at the moment of Baptism in a Catholic church.

_____

_____

_____

_____

4. What happens at the sacrament of Baptism in a Baptist church, and what is it's meaning for the persons involved?

_____

_____

_____

_____

Section E - Sign and Symbol

1.

This is a photograph of a religious symbol. .... 2003(O), 2010(O)

A. Pick **one** thing from this photograph which suggests that this is a religious symbol.

B. With which **one** of the following world religions is this symbol most associated? (Tick ✓ the correct box)

Buddhism ☐   Christianity ☐   Hinduism ☐   Islam ☐   Judaism ☐

C. State **one** reason why people use symbols when they are praying.

Saint Mary's Press

2. a. Read the list of religious objects and the list of world religions given below. .... 2012(O)

Match **one** religious object to the world religion with which it is most associated.

Religious Objects	World Religions
Arti Lamp	Buddhism
Menorah	Christianity
Kathina Robe	Hinduism
Crucifix	Islam
Mihrab	Judaism

Answer:

Religious Object	World Religion

b. A candle is one example of a religious object used in prayer.

Outline how **another** religious object is used in prayer by the members of a major world religion.

3. a. Buddhism ☐   Christianity ☐   Hinduism ☐   Islam ☐   Judaism ☐   .... 2009(H)

Tick ✓ **one** of the world religions above that you have studied.

Name **one** symbol associated with the world religion you have ticked above.

b. Describe the meaning of the symbol you have named above for members of the world religion with which it is associated.

c. Explain **two** reasons why people use a symbol to express religious faith.

4. a. Give **one** example of a symbol people use when they are praying. .... 2007(H)

b. Explain why people use the symbol you have given above when they are praying.

5. A. World religions have different places of worship. .... 2005(O)

Tick ✓ **one** of the following places of worship and name the world religion associated with it.

Church ☐   Mosque ☐   Shrine ☐   Synagogue ☐   Temple ☐

B. a. Name **one** religious symbol that can be seen in the place of worship you have ticked above.

b. Explain the meaning of this religious symbol.

C. Describe a religious ceremony for which people gather in the place of worship you have ticked above.

6. This is a photograph of a religious icon. ....2011(O)

    A. Pick **one** thing from this photograph which suggests that this is a religious icon.

    B. The icon in this photograph is one example of a religious symbol.
    Name **another** example of a religious symbol.

    C. State **one** reason why a religious symbol is important for members of
    a community of faith.

Adapted from www.istok.net

---

7. Examine the role a religious icon plays in worship for the members of a ....2013(H)
major world religion.

    NOTE: *This is an essay question.*

---

8.  This is a photograph of a religious ceremony. ....2013(O)

    A. Pick **one** thing from this photograph which suggests that this is
    a religious ceremony.

    B. Name **another** ceremony where the members of a world religion celebrate
    a religious occasion in a person's life.

    C. State **one** reason why the members of a world religion have a religious ceremony
    to celebrate an occasion of religious importance in a person's life.

(Source: blogspot.com)

---

9. a. Outline **one** example of how people use a religious symbolic action to express ....2014(H)
either the meaning of life *or* the mystery of life.

    b. Explain **two** reasons why people use religious symbolic actions to express *either* the meaning of life
or the mystery of life.

Vocal Prayer

OBJECTIVES
Explain the importance of prayer in the life of Jesus and in the lives of Christians today.
Differentiate between different types of prayer.

KEY CONCEPTS

Communication with God: a prayerful exchange between God and human beings.

Personal prayer: praying to God by oneself.

Communal prayer: praying to God with others as a community.

Praise and thanksgiving: prayer to praise and thank God for blessings already received.

Petition: prayer asking God for help with one's own needs or the needs of others.

Penitence: prayer admitting to wrongdoing and asking God for forgiveness.

Communication with God

- People communicate with God through prayer. Praying regularly strengthens a person's relationship with God.

- Reasons why people pray:
  - To express joy at the wonder of creation and the mystery of life.
  - To give thanks when things turn out well.
  - To ask for help or guidance in times of need.
  - To say sorry when they know they have done something wrong.

Different ways of Praying

Personal Prayer

- Personal prayer is private. Catholics, for example, sometimes pray alone.
  - Their prayer can be formal – using the fixed prayers of the Church such as the 'Lord's Prayer' and the 'Hail Mary'.
  - Their prayer can be informal – using a prayer that they have made up or composed themselves.

Communal Prayer

- Communal prayer is public. Christians gather together in a church and pray to God as a community saying the formal prayers of the Church.
  - This is evident at Mass for example, when Catholics gather to pray and worship God, not as individuals but as a community.

Jesus and Prayer

- Prayer had a central place in the life of **Jesus**, the founder of Christianity. Jesus was a person of prayer. He prayed often, alone and with others.

- Jesus prayed at important moments in his life; at his Baptism, at the beginning of his teaching ministry, before choosing his twelve disciples, before working miracles, in the Garden of Gethsemane and before his death on the cross.

Jesus at prayer.

- Jesus taught his followers how to pray by:
  - Telling parables about prayer.
  - Teaching them an actual prayer; **'The Lord's Prayer'**.

- Jesus taught his followers to:
  - Call God 'Father'.
  - Pray using words of praise, thanksgiving, petition and penitence.
  - Set time aside for prayer.
  - Pray often, alone and with others.

Different types of Prayer

Praise and Thanksgiving

◆ This prayer focuses on giving praise and thanks to God for the gift of life and all the blessings one has received.

◆ In the Mass, this prayer would be:
  ▶ The Responsorial Psalm – to praise God.
  ▶ The Eucharistic Prayer – to thank God.

Petition

◆ This prayer focuses on asking God for help for oneself or for other people.

◆ In the Mass, this prayer would be:
  ▶ The Prayers of the Faithful – for the needs of all.

Penitence

◆ This prayer focuses on saying sorry to God for any wrongdoing.

◆ In the Mass, this prayer would be:
  ▶ The Penitential Rite – for the forgiveness of sin.

Difficulties with prayer

◆ It can be difficult to pray at times because:
  ▶ we're too busy.
  ▶ we cannot see God.
  ▶ we think God isn't listening to us.

◆ Christians believe God is present and always answers their prayers, but often in ways they least expect.

◆ For details of:
  ▶ Prayer in **Judaism** see page 104.
  ▶ Prayer in **Islam** see page 139.

Test Yourself

1. Why do people need to communicate with God?

_____

_____

2. What are the main features of personal and communal prayer in the Christian tradition?

_____

_____

_____

_____

3. How important was prayer in the life of Jesus? What did Jesus teach about prayer?

_____

_____

_____

_____

4. When do people use the different types of prayer?

_____

_____

_____

_____

Silent Prayer

OBJECTIVE:

To examine meditation and contemplation and look at the life of an important person in the Christian spiritual tradition.

KEY CONCEPTS

Meditation: a form of silent prayer based on the use of an icon, a repeated word or a passage from scripture.

Contemplation: a form of deep silent prayer that does not use words or thoughts.

◆ Prayer is time spent communicating with God. Most Christian prayer relies on words. Meditation is a form of prayer that uses very few words. Contemplation is a form of prayer that uses no words at all.

◆ Meditation and contemplation enable people to experience the presence of God at the centre of their being.

Meditation

◆ Christian meditation is silent prayer of the mind.

◆ The first step involves calming the body and the mind:
  ▶ Finding a quiet place.
  ▶ Sitting in a prayerful position.
  ▶ Relaxing the body.
  ▶ Breathing deeply.

◆ The next step involves focusing on something that will draw the person's mind closer to God.
  ▶ An icon, or religious symbol.
  ▶ A passage from scripture.

◆ In meditation, the person calmly thinks about Jesus as he/she gazes at an icon, or imagines the scene in a passage from scripture.

Contemplation

◆ Contemplation is deep prayer of the heart. It is a higher, more advanced form of silent prayer.

◆ Contemplation is communication with God without the use of words or thoughts of any kind.

◆ Contemplation is a sense of being quiet and still in the presence of God.

  The person:
  ▶ Finds a quiet place.
  ▶ Quietens the body, is calm and silent.
  ▶ Quietens the mind, sheds all thoughts, all feelings, all imaginings.
  ▶ Journeys inward to the centre, to silence.
  ▶ Waits and listens.
  God does the rest.

◆ Contemplative prayer, traditionally associated with monks and nuns is for any ordinary, happy person who is content to spend time alone with God.

St. Teresa of Avila *(1515-1582)*

◆ St. Teresa of Avila is an important person in the spiritual tradition of Christianity.

◆ St. Teresa discovered the practice of contemplative prayer. She founded a new religious order (the Discaled Carmelites) dedicated to contemplative prayer and a simple way of life.

◆ Her books, especially the 'Interior Castle', describe the way a person can learn and progress in the method of contemplative prayer. Her writing greatly influenced the practice of Christian contemplative prayer up to the present day.

Test Yourself

1. What do we mean by "silent prayer"?

2. What is the main difference between meditation and contemplation?

3. How do Christians prepare for meditative or contemplative prayer?

4. How do people communicate with God in Christian meditation <u>or</u> contemplation?

5. What is the evidence that prayer was important in the life of St. Teresa of Avila?

1. Read the list of prayers and the list of world religions given below. ....2009(O)
Match **one** prayer to the world religion with which it is most associated.

Prayers	World Religions
The Our Father/The Lord's Prayer	Buddhism
The Shahada/Shahadah	Christianity
The Shema	Hinduism
The Paritta	Islam
The Rig Veda	Judaism

	Prayer	World Religion
Answer:		

2. Communal Prayer ☐ Personal Prayer ☐ ....2009(H)

Tick ✓ **one** of the above and outline what is involved in this type of prayer.

3. ....2006(H)

"Silence plays a big role for me in prayer, because if you listen hard enough you will hear God speak back to you."

When I worry I pray… I feel guilty praying because I'm always asking for something…"

Source: Veritas

Why is prayer important in the life of a person who has religious belief?

4. A. Below are pictures of gestures and positions people sometimes use in prayer. ....2004(O)
Tick ✓ **one** gesture or position and explain what it symbolises when used in prayer.

☐ Bowing   ☐ Joining hands   ☐ Kneeling   ☐ Sitting   ☐ Standing

B. People often mark important moments in life with a special celebration.
   a. Name **one** religious celebration of an important moment in life.
   b. What important moment in life is being marked by the religious celebration named above?
   c. Name **one** type of prayer that would be suitable for use in the religious celebration named above.
   d. Explain why this type of prayer would be suitable for this religious celebration.

5. Major world religions have different times of prayer each day or week ....2011(H)

Describe what happens during a regular time of prayer associated with a major world religion
that you have studied.

6. ◆ BUDDHISM ◆ CHRISTIANITY ◆ HINDUISM ◆ ISLAM ◆ JUDAISM ....2010(H)

Discuss the importance of communal prayer for members of **one** of the above major world religions using the following headings:

i. Place of Prayer.

ii. Time of Prayer.

---

7. Name an important person in the spiritual tradition of Christianity and describe ....2004(H) how he/she contributed to the Christian understanding of prayer.

NOTE: *This is an essay question.*

---

8. Profile the contribution made to the understanding of prayer by ....2011(H) **one** person associated with the spiritual tradition of a major world religion that you have studied.

NOTE: *This is an essay question.*

9.

| *Angel of God,* *my guardian dear,* *to whom God's love* *commits me here,* *ever this day,* *be at my side* *to light and guard* *to rule and guide.* |

This is a picture of a child's prayer card..2014(O)

A. Pick **one** thing from the picture which suggests that this is a prayer of petition.

B. The 'Shema' is most associated with which **one** of the following world religions?

(Tick ✓ the correct box)

BUDDHISM ☐   ISLAM ☐   JUDAISM ☐

C. State **one** thing that a prayer of petition shows about a person's belief in God.

---

10. a. ● Contemplation ● Penitence ● Petition ....2009(O)

Choose **two** of the types of prayer listed above and describe what each involves for members of a world religion.

b. Explain **one** reason why a religious person could find it difficult to pray.

---

11. **A.** CONTEMPLATION ☐   PETITION ☐ ....2011(H)

Tick ✓ **one** of the above types of prayer.

Outline what is involved in the type of prayer that you have ticked above.

B. Examine **two** ways in which the type of prayer that you have ticked above is important for members of a world religion.

C. Explain **two** reasons why people can find it difficult to pray.

---

12. **A.** Meditation is one type of prayer. Name **another** type of prayer. ....2011(O)

B. Describe **one** example of what is involved in the type of prayer that you have named above.

C. Explain **two** reasons why the type of prayer that you have named above is important for members of a community of faith.

---

13. ☐ Meditation.   ☐ Penitence. ....2007(H)

A. Tick ✓ **one** of the above types of prayer that you have studied.
Outline what is involved in the type of prayer you have ticked above.

B. Outline **two** reasons why prayer is important for members of a world religion that you have studied.

14. a. Describe **one** example of what is involved in using meditation as a type of prayer. .... 2012(H)

b. Explain **two** reasons why people use meditation as a type of prayer.

15. a. ● CONTEMPLATION ● MEDITATION .... 2014(H)

Describe an example of what is involved in **one** of the above types of prayer.

b. *People of faith express their religious beliefs in different types of prayer.*

Explain why people use *either* contemplation *or* meditation as a type of prayer to express their faith.

16. Outline the importance of prayer for Christians. .... 2003(H)

In your answer describe **two** different types of prayer that are important in the Christian tradition, and explain why they are important.

NOTE: *This is an essay question.*

17. This is a photograph of people using meditation during prayer. .... 2008(O)

www.minnesota.publicradio.org

A. Pick **one** thing from this photograph which shows that these people are using meditation to pray.

B. In a religious tradition what does the term 'meditation, mean?

C. State **one** reason why a person would use meditation to pray.

Section F - The Moral Challenge

The *Syllabus Aims* in this section are:

◆ To explore the need to order relationships at the personal, communal and global levels.

◆ To explore how this need can be expressed in a variety of ways.

◆ To identify how this need is expressed in civil and other legal codes.

◆ To show how religious belief is expressed in particular moral visions.

◆ To explore the moral visions of two major world religions, one of which should be Christianity.

◆ To analyse the impact of these visions on the lives of believers and non-believers in considering some current moral issues.

Key Concepts in the Moral Challenge *(Section F)*

Morality

OBJECTIVES:

Be aware of different descriptions of what it means to be moral.

Identify key influences on moral behaviour.

KEY CONCEPTS

Morality: a set of principles or rules to help us know the difference between right and wrong behaviour.

Influence: something that shapes or affects a person's behaviour.

Morality

◆ **Morality** is a set of principles, or rules, to help people know the difference between right and wrong behaviour. It is the basis on which moral choices are made.

◆ Morality:

▶ Helps people to judge the difference between right and wrong.

▶ Helps people to act on that judgement and do what is right and avoid what is wrong.

◆ In **'The Golden Rule'**, the great world religions appear to agree on one common guideline for human behaviour:

▶ We should treat other people the way we ourselves would like to be treated.

Influence

◆ **Influence** is something that shapes or affects a person's behaviour. A person's morality, their sense of what is right and wrong, is influenced by factors such as:

▶ their **family** (the way they are brought up).

▶ their **peers** (what matters to them).

▶ the **society** in which they live.

▶ the **education** they receive.

▶ the **religion** to which they belong.

▶ the **media** in its many forms.

◆ These influences can be positive or negative. The family has a big influence on a person's moral behaviour in childhood. Friends and peers have a considerable impact on a person's moral behaviour in adolescence.

Test Yourself

1. What is morality?

_____

_____

2. What is the 'Golden Rule'?

_____

_____

3. What can be the biggest influence on a person's moral behaviour in childhood, in adolescence and why?

_____

_____

_____

_____

_____

Action and Consequence

Show that freedom and choice are aspects of morality.

Show how our moral choices have consequences for ourselves and others.

KEY CONCEPTS

Choice: looking at different options in a situation and selecting one.

Freedom: the liberty to say, do, or think what one wants.

Action and consequence: what people do and the effect it can have on themselves and others.

Choice

◆ Choice means looking at the different options in a situation and selecting one. People make choices about all sorts of things every day. Choices about right and wrong are called **moral choices**.

◆ When making a moral choice it is advisable to stop and think about the different options in a situation before deciding what to do.

Freedom

◆ Freedom is the liberty we have to say, do, or think what we want. No one is completely free in this sense. Our society could not function if everybody just did what they wanted and ignored the effect of their actions on other people.

◆ Personal freedom and **responsibility** toward others go together. Freedom means that we can do what we choose, but only within certain limits.

Our freedom is limited by such factors as:

▶ the laws of the country.
▶ the rules of the school.
▶ the guidelines of our religion.
▶ the expectations of our parents.
▶ the attitude of our friends and peers.
▶ our own abilities.

Action and Consequence

◆ When we make a moral choice and act on it, there are consequences. We know that what we say or do is going to affect us in some way, and may also affect others.

◆ Our moral choices can have good or bad consequences for ourselves and others.

◆ When a person makes a moral choice, he/she is choosing between right and wrong. A moral person knows the difference between right and wrong and chooses to do what is right.

Test Yourself

1. What are moral choices? _____

_____

2. What things limit our personal freedom?

_____

_____

_____

3. Explain how a person's moral choice in any situation has consequences for:
   a. themselves.   **b.** others around them.

_____

_____

_____

_____

_____

Relationships

OBJECTIVE:
Explain how our moral
choices affect our
relationships at every level.

KEY CONCEPTS

Relationships: ways in which people are connected to one another.

Society: the entire web of relationships that binds communities together.

Relationships

◆ Our **relationships** are the different ways in which we, as human beings, are connected to other people.

◆ Our relationships are not all the same. We have:

  ▶ **Interpersonal** relationships - at an individual level with family and friends.

  ▶ **Communal** relationships - at a group or community level with a class, a team, a school, a parish or a neighbourhood.

  ▶ **Global** relationships - at a worldwide level, with the rest of humanity.

◆ The moral choices we make have consequences for everyone. The right choice will strengthen our relationships, but wrong choices will weaken and damage those relationships.

◆ When we make a moral choice, we need to think of the impact it will have on others - people close to us and those further away.

Society

◆ As human beings, we are members of small family groups and larger communities.

◆ Good relationships must exist for a group of any size, big or small, to function properly.

◆ **Society** is the entire web of relationships that binds communities together. It is the way people manage to live together as a group.

◆ The family, the school and the Church are units of society. Each has an important role in preparing children to be responsible members of society by teaching them good moral behaviour.

Test Yourself

1. Identify three types of human relationships and give an example of each.

_____

_____

_____

2. **a.** How can a person's moral choice to be honest, for example, strengthen his/her relationships?
   b. How can dishonesty weaken our relationships?

_____

_____

_____

_____

3. Explain how a moral choice can affect our relationship with people at every level.

_____

_____

_____

Exam Questions

1.

(Source adapted from http://dailyenglish11.blogspot.ie)

This is a picture from the cover of a school religion book. ....**2014(O)**

A. Pick **one** thing from the picture which suggests that this book is about morality.

B. In religious traditions 'morality' refers to a person's understanding of right and wrong.
(Tick ✓ the correct box)
TRUE ☐   FALSE ☐

C. State **one** way in which religion could influence a person's understanding of what it means to be moral.

---

2.   ● FAMILY   ● FRIENDS   ● SCHOOL   ....**2011(H)**

Choose **two** of the above and outline how each could influence a person's idea of what is right and wrong.

---

3. a. Below you will find different statements from people about what it means to be moral....... **2003(H), 2013(O)**

In which of the statements below is the person's idea of what is moral based on the consequences of an action? (Tick ✓ **one** box only)

☐ *"I can't take that because I might get caught and sent to prison."*

☐ *"I did that because everyone's doing it."*

b.   i. CONSIDERING THE CONSEQUENCES   ii. FREEDOM

Explain why **each** of the above is important when a person is deciding what is the right thing to do in a situation.

---

4. This is a photograph of a newspaper headline describing a road accident in which ....**2004(O)** the driver of a car killed a person and drove away.

Evening Herald

A. State **one** way in which the situation described in this headline shows the need for respect.

B. State **one** way in which the driver could be affected by his/her decision to drive away.

C. State **one** way in which society could be affected by the driver's decision to drive away.

Sources of Morality

> **KEY CONCEPT**
>
> **Moral vision:** an awareness of what is right and wrong.

Moral Vision

◆ Our **moral vision** is our awareness of what is right and wrong, fair and unfair. It's the way we see life and how we think it should be lived.

Sources of morality

◆ When we talk about sources of morality, we are asking where our moral vision, our ideas about right and wrong, actually come from. The main sources of morality are: the family, the peer group, the school, religion and the state.

◆ The **family**. Parents regard it as their duty to teach their children good moral behaviour. They want their children to know that it is good to share, to tell the truth, and to treat others with respect.

◆ The **peer group**. Friends have a big influence on what a young person says and does. This can have a positive or negative effect on the person's outlook and behaviour.

◆ The **school** can influence a person's sense of right and wrong through the words and action of teachers, the content of lessons, the code of discipline, school wide activities, and the general interaction of students and staff.

◆ **Religion**. Moral teaching on what is right and wrong is found in the sacred texts of the great world religions. For example the teaching of Jesus in the Bible is the fundamental source of morality for Christians.

◆ **The state** can influence a person's moral behaviour. The State makes laws to protect the rights of individuals and their property. The laws are enforced and must be obeyed; this ensures that citizens behave in a responsible manner.

Test Yourself

1. What is a moral vision?

_____

_____

2. What are the main influences on our moral vision?

_____

_____

_____

_____

3. How can the family **or** the school be a source of morality for young people?

_____

_____

_____

_____

Codes of Behaviour

KEY CONCEPT

Laws: codes of behaviour enforced by the state.

Moral vision: an awareness of what is right and wrong.

◆ In society most groups to which we belong i.e. the family, the school, the state, have a code of behaviour. A code is a set of rules that point out acceptable ways to behave.

◆ There are formal and informal codes of behaviour.

▶ A **formal** code is *written*. It is an official rule that must be accepted by everyone.

▶ An **informal** code is *unwritten*. It is an unofficial rule that is nontheless accepted by everyone.

◆ Codes develop gradually over time in response to people's experience of a situation.

Laws

◆ **Laws** are codes of behavior enforced by the state. Citizens are expected to obey state laws.

◆ Codes of conduct to ensure orderly behaviour go back to ancient times. No society ever allowed its members unlimited freedom of action. Codes of behaviour developed over the years to become the **state laws** we have today.

◆ The Code of Hammurabi, King of Babylon, is almost 4,000 years old. It is the first written account of a ruler making laws to govern his people. Strict punishments ensured the strong would not oppress the weak.

◆ The Brehon Laws, a system of ancient Irish Law, was in continuous use in Ireland until the 16th century. The Laws upheld the values of equality and fairness central to Irish society.

◆ The Magna Carta, introduced in England in 1215CE established the individual's right to freedom and equality under the law of the land.

◆ The principles of the Magna Carta form the basis of the constitution and state laws of many countries throughout the world today.

Moral Vision

◆ State laws are laws made by governments. The **moral vision** behind many state laws is the idea of the "common good".

◆ Laws are introduced to keep order, protect the rights of citizens, and to benefit society as a whole.

Test Yourself

1. What is the difference between formal and informal rules and codes of behaviour?

_____

_____

2. Why is it necessary for a country to have laws?

_____

_____

3. Historically, what developments contributed to the evolution of state law that we have today?

_____

_____

4. What moral view do you see behind any one of the codes or laws above?

_____

_____

Religious Moral Vision

> ## KEY CONCEPT
>
> **Religious moral vision:** an awareness of what is right and wrong shaped by religious beliefs.

◆ A moral vision is a person's awareness of what is right and wrong. A moral vision may be:

▶ *religious* - shaped by a religion such as Judaism or Christianity, for example.

▶ *non-religious* - shaped by a belief system such as Humanism, for example.

Religious Moral Vision

◆ A religious moral vision is a person's awareness of what is right and wrong shaped by their religious beliefs. Jews have a moral vision shaped by the Jewish faith. Christians have a moral vision shaped by the Christian faith.

◆ People of faith look to their religion for guidance when faced with moral issues.

◆ Both Christians and Jews follow a **moral code**, the ten commandments. (Exodus 20:2-17)

The Ten Commandments

(as written by some Christian Churches today)

1. I am the Lord your God, you shall not have other gods before me.

2. You shall not take the name of the Lord, your God, in vain.

3. Remember to keep holy the Sabbath day.

4. Honour your father and your mother.

5. You shall not kill.

6. You shall not commit adultery.

7. You shall not steal.

8. You shall not bear false witness against your neighbour.

9. You shall not covet your neighbour's wife.

10. You shall not covet your neighbour's goods.

Jewish Moral Vision

◆ The **Tenakh** is the sacred text containing the religious beliefs and moral vision of Judaism.

◆ A key feature of the Jewish moral vision is the **Covenant** or sacred agreement between God and the Jewish people.

Star of David

◆ On Mount Sinai, God gave Moses the **Torah** which is the Law and the ten commandments. The Torah outlines how Jews must live if they are to be faithful to the Covenant.

◆ The **Ten Commandments**.

▶ The first three commandments show the importance of having love and respect for God.

▶ The next seven commandments show the importance of having respect for other people.

◆ The moral vision of Jewish people, their view of right and wrong, is shaped by:

▶ The *Covenant*.
  (The sacred agreement between God and the Jewish people.)

▶ The *Torah*.
  (The Law and Ten Commandments.)

▶ The *Talmud*.
  (Teachings of Jewish rabbis down the centuries.)

Christian Moral Vision

- The **Bible** is the sacred text containing the religious beliefs and moral vision of Christianity.

- A key feature of the Christian moral vision is:
  - ▶ The teaching of Jesus.
  - ▶ The life of Jesus.

The Cross

The Commandment of Love

- Jesus said that the ten commandments and all the laws of the Jewish tradition could be summed up in one great commandment of love:

  "Love the Lord your God…and love your neighbour as yourself." (Mark 12:28-34)

  Love of God and love of neighbour is central to the Christian moral vision.

- Jesus' main teaching on morality is found in the **Sermon on the Mount** in the New Testament (Matthew, chapters 5 and 6).

- Jesus, through his teaching and the example of his own life, showed people how to love as God loves.

- The Christian ideal is for people to have the same moral vision - the same sense of right and wrong as Jesus.

Test Yourself

1. What is a religious moral vision?

   _____

   _____

   _____

2. In what way do the Law and the Ten Commandments shape the moral vision of Jewish people?

   _____

   _____

   _____

   _____

   _____

3. How does the life and teaching of Jesus shape the moral vision of Christian people?

   _____

   _____

   _____

   _____

   _____

   _____

   _____

Wisdom of Others

KEY CONCEPTS

Authority: the power of sacred texts and religious leaders to guide people on moral issues.

Tradition: religious belief and practice handed down from generation to generation.

Sources of moral guidance in the major world religions

	Religion	Sacred Text	Leaders	
✡	● Judaism	- Tenakh - Talmud	- Rabbi	
✝	● Christianity	- Bible	- Minister - Priest - Bishop	- Pope
☪	● Islam	- Qur'an - Hadith	- Imam	
ॐ	● Hinduism	- Vedas	- Priest	
☸	● Buddhism	- Tipitaka	- Monk	- Dalai Lama

Authority

◆ **Authority** is the power of sacred texts and religious leaders to guide people on moral issues. People of faith believe that this authority, where it exists, comes from God.

◆ When Christians, for example, need guidance on moral issues, they believe it is important to find out what God wants them to do.

They can learn what God wants by:

▶ Reading the Bible.

▶ Following Church teaching.

◆ Christians, especially in the **Protestant Churches**, believe the Bible is the only authority and the main source of guidance on moral issues. It alone shows people how to follow Jesus and do God's will in the world.

◆ **Roman Catholics** believe that the Bible and the religious leaders of their Church both have the authority to guide people on moral issues. Church leaders interpret the message of the Bible, especially the teaching and example of Jesus in the New Testament, and help people to apply it to their daily lives.

Tradition

- In the Roman Catholic Church, when people need guidance on moral issues, they turn to:
  - ▶ the teaching of Jesus in the Bible.
  - ▶ the teaching of the Church.

- When the Pope and the bishops teach about moral issues, they are passing on the tradition of the Church.

- Tradition is Christian belief and practice that has been handed down from one generation to the next since the time of Christ. It is the collective wisdom or teaching of the Catholic Church of the past 2,000 years.

- The **Magisterium**, consisting of the Pope and the bishops, is the official teaching authority of the Catholic Church. Its teaching is passed on to Catholics through:
  - ▶ *Encyclical Letters* - written by the Pope.
  - ▶ *Pastoral Letters* - written by bishops.
  - ▶ *Teaching Documents*
    - the Catechism of the Catholic Church.
    - the Documents of Vatican Council 2.

- The Church's teaching in these letters and documents guides Catholics in making moral decisions. Catholics get to learn about these teachings from the priest during sermons at Mass.

Test Yourself

1. How do people of faith find out how to live a good moral life?

_____

_____

_____

_____

_____

2. What is the source of authority on moral issues:

    a. in many Protestant Churches?

_____

_____

_____

    b. in the Roman Catholic Church?

_____

_____

_____

3. Explain what the term 'Tradition' means in the Roman Catholic Church.

_____

_____

_____

_____

_____

Exam Questions

---

1. A. A person's understanding of right and wrong is influenced by many factors. ....2006(O)

Family ☐   Friends ☐   School ☐   State ☐

Tick ✓ **one** of the above and give an example of how it could have an effect on a person's understanding of right and wrong.

B. Tick ✓ **one** of the statements listed below that is associated with a world religion you have studied.

Buddhism	Christianity	Hinduism	Islam	Judaism
Act towards others exactly as you would act towards yourself.	Treat others as you would like them to treat you.	Do nothing to others which, if done to you, could cause you pain.	None of you truly believe, until you wish for others what you wish for yourself.	What is harmful to yourself do not do to others.
☐	☐	☐	☐	☐

Describe how the idea expressed in the statement ticked above can have an effect on the behaviour of members of this world religion today.

C. Give **one** example of how the idea expressed in the statement ticked above can be seen in the life of the founder / earliest followers of the world religion with which it is associated.

---

2. a. Read the list of moral codes and the list of world religions given below. ....2013(O)

Match **one** moral code to the world religion with which it is most associated.

Moral Codes	World Religions
The Beatitudes	Buddhism
The Dharma Sutras	Christianity
The Decalogue	Hinduism
The Eightfold Path	Islam
The Five Pillars	Judaism

	Moral Code	World Religion
Answer:		

b. Outline **two** ways in which a religious moral code influences the lifestyle of members in the world religion with which it is most associated.

---

3. Select a creed or moral code from those listed below. ....2004(H)

■ The Ten Commandments   ■ The Five Pillars   ■ The Law of Karma   ■ The Eightfold Path

a. Outline **three** rules/guidelines from the creed or moral code you have ticked.

b. Describe **two** ways in which the way of life of a follower is influenced by the creed or moral code of this world religion.

---

4. This drawing shows a moral code. ....2006(O)

1. I am the Lord your God: You shall have no other gods before me.

2. You shall not make wrongful use of the name of the Lord your God.

3. Remember the Sabbath day and keep it holy.

4. Honour your father and your mother.

5. You shall not murder.

6. You shall not commit adultery.

7. You shall not steal.

8. You shall not bear false witness against your neighbour.

9. You shall not covet your neighbour's house.

10. You shall not covet your neighbour's wife.

Ex. 20:3, 7, 8, 12, 13-17.   *Adapted from Softkey Multimedia Inc.*

A. Explain why this is an example of a moral code.

B. Name **one** religious moral code.

C. Give **one** reason why a moral code is important in a community of faith.

---

5. a. The Ten Commandments are one example of a religious moral code. ....2011(O)
Name **another** religious moral code.

b. Describe **two** ways in which a moral code can be of assistance to the members of a community of faith.

---

6. a. Name **one** moral code that could guide a person in deciding ....2008(O)
what is the right thing to do in a situation.

b. Explain **one** reason why a moral code could help a person decide
what is the right thing to do in a situation.

---

7. *Moral codes express the rights people are entitled to, as well as the responsibilities* ....2005(H)
they have towards others.

a. Name **one** moral code you have studied.

b. State **one** right it expresses.

c. State **one** responsibility it expresses.

d. Explain how the moral code you have named above could help a person in making a moral decision.

---

8. Analyse the ways in which a religious moral code expresses the beliefs ....2009(H)
of a world religion you have studied.

NOTE: *This is an essay question.*

---

9.   ● AUTHORITY   ● TRADITION   ....2012(H)

Outline how **each** of the above could guide the judgement of members
in a community of faith about what is right and wrong on an issue.

NOTE: *This is an essay question.*

Developing Morality

KEY CONCEPTS

Moral growth: the process by which people learn to distinguish right from wrong, and then do what is right.

Moral maturity: the stage beyond self interest where people take the needs of others into account when making moral decisions.

Moral Growth

◆ **Moral growth** is the process by which people learn to distinguish right from wrong, and then do what is right. We learn about right and wrong from experience and the guidance of others.

◆ Moral growth is age related and takes place gradually over time.

Young Children are self-centred and learn quickly that good behaviour leads to praise and reward while bad behaviour leads to punishment. Reward and fear of punishment influence moral choice in childhood.

Pre-teens start to apply reason to moral situations and begin to understand the idea of consequences. However, moral choices continue to be made in the expectation of reward, or the avoidance of punishment.

Teenagers apply the use of reason to most moral issues. A greater awareness of all the consequences of moral choice is now developing. Moral choices, however, tend to be influenced by the desire to seek approval from others at home or at school, but especially from friends and peers.

◆ The transition to a stage of moral maturity can take place for some people during adolescence.

Moral Maturity

◆ **Moral maturity** is the stage beyond self-interest, where people take the needs of others into account when making moral decisions.

◆ It is a mark of moral maturity when a person moves on from being selfish to being altruistic, and is willing to put the interests of others first, above their own.

◆ Many people remain at a level of moral immaturity all their lives, while others go on to become morally mature individuals.

*The morally **immature** person:*

▶ Acts out of a desire for reward, or the fear of punishment.

▶ Is selfish, considers only his/her own needs.

▶ Ignores the consequences of his/her behaviour on others.

*The morally **mature** person:*

▶ Acts out of a deep personal conviction about what is right, and what is good.

▶ Is altruistic; considers the needs of others.

▶ Will stop to think of the consequences of his/her actions before deciding to act.

▶ Has the courage of his/her convictions; will actually do what he/she believes to be right.

Test Yourself

1. What is the meaning of moral growth?

_____

_____

_____

_____

2. At what stage of moral development:
   a. does the use of reason begin?

   _____ _____

   _____

   b. is there a real awareness that moral choices have consequences for the self and others?

   _____

   _____

3. What is moral maturity?

_____

_____

_____

_____

_____

_____

4. Provide an example of a situation that shows the difference between the behaviour of a morally immature person and a morally mature person.

_____

_____

_____

_____

_____

_____

_____

_____

_____

_____

Conscience

KEY CONCEPT

Conscience: the ability to know and judge what is right and wrong in a particular situation.

Conscience

◆ Conscience is the ability to know and judge what is right and wrong in a particular situation. We rely on our conscience to guide us when we have to make a moral decision. Our conscience helps us in two ways:

▶ To judge what is right and wrong.

▶ To act on that judgement and do what is right.

◆ My conscience is not simply a little 'voice' in my head, or a guilty feeling I might have, it is my judgement of what is the best thing to do in a particular situation.

Developing a Conscience

◆ Conscience does not grow or develop by itself, it needs the help and example of parents, teachers, priests and ministers. The home, the school, and the church have a vital role in helping people to develop a healthy and informed conscience.

◆ Developing our conscience is an important part of our growth in moral maturity.

An Informed Conscience

◆ The Catholic Church teaches that:

▶ people should follow their conscience and do what is right.

▶ people have a duty to inform their conscience and find out the right thing to do.

◆ Informing one's conscience involves gathering the necessary facts and information about a moral issue, and using that information to make a moral decision.

◆ Roman Catholics, for example, are guided by:

▶ The teaching of Jesus in the Bible.

▶ The teaching of their Church.

▶ Prayer.

▶ Trustworthy people who give good advice.

◆ People of faith turn to God and to others outside themselves for help and guidance in making moral decisions.

Test Yourself

1. What is meant by conscience?

_____

_____

2. How can parents help their children to develop a healthy conscience?

_____

_____

3. How does a person develop an informed conscience on a moral issue?

_____

_____

_____

Exam Questions

---

1. a. Moral immaturity can be seen when..... .... 2005(O), 2012(O)

   b. Outline **two** examples of what is involved in a person's growth towards moral maturity.

---

2. Profile the way in which a person's judgement of right and wrong can ....2010(H)
develop as he/she grows from moral immaturity to moral maturity.

---

3. a. A person's conscience helps him/her to _____ ....2012(H)

   b. Discuss how a person's conscience can develop as he/she grows to moral maturity.

---

4. **A.** Outline what the term conscience means. ....2008(H)

   B. Explain how a person's religious faith could influence his/her conscience.

   C. Apart from religious faith, explain how **one** other factor could influence a person's conscience.

   D. Describe **one** way in which a person's conscience can develop as he/she grows older.

---

5.   ● INFORMED CONSCIENCE   ● INTEGRITY   ....2014(H)

Evaluate the importance of **each** of the above for a person in deciding what is right and wrong
on a moral issue.

NOTE: *This is an essay question.*

Moral Decision-making

KEY CONCEPTS

Decision making: the process of making up one's mind about moral issues.

Truth: being honest with oneself, others and God.

Integrity: being upright and honest and sticking to one's moral principles.

Decision Making

◆ Learning how to make moral decisions is an important part of growing up and becoming morally mature.

◆ Moral **decision making** is a complex activity. When the process is analysed, we can see that it involves a number of different steps. Christians, when faced with a moral decision, are encouraged to take the following steps:

Steps in moral decision making

1. Stop, look at the **facts** of the situation.

2. List the **options**, work out the **consequences** of each option for oneself and others.

3. Get good **advice**.

4. Be aware of one's **values**.

5. **Pray** for guidance.

6. Follow one's **conscience**. Make a **decision**.

Truth

◆ **Truth** and honesty are important values for many people, and especially for Christians. To tell the truth is the eighth commandment of God.

◆ Truth and honesty are the basis for all social relationships in the family, among friends and in the wider community of business, politics, and the professions.

◆ Honest people tell the truth, are trustworthy and always keep their word. Everyone can rely on them.

Integrity

◆ Being honest and truthful is not always easy, it often costs us something. A person of **integrity** is one who is upright and honest and sticks to their moral principles, even when it costs.

◆ People of integrity have a high level of moral maturity. They follow their conscience and do what is right, even if it is at some cost to themselves.

Test Yourself

1. What are the steps in the moral decision making process?

_____

_____

_____

2. Why is it important to be truthful?

_____

_____

3. What is the meaning of integrity?

_____

_____

_____

Social Justice

KEY CONCEPTS

Justice: to treat all people fairly and respect their rights.

Peace: harmony between people instead of disorder or conflict.

Justice/Peace

- A religious moral vision is a person's view of right and wrong, shaped by their religious beliefs.

- Justice is an important part of the religious moral vision of both Christianity and Judaism.

- Justice is about treating all people fairly and respecting their rights. The U.N. Universal Declaration of Human Rights outlines thirty basic rights to which all people are entitled.

- Yet injustice persists, the world is divided between the rich and poor, the 'have's' and the 'have nots'.

Poverty in the developing world.

Christian Moral Vision

- Christians believe that a person has rights, not simply because a human law says so, but because he/she is created in the image of God. It is for this reason that their dignity must be respected, and their rights protected.

- Christians learn about Jesus' teaching on love and justice in the **New Testament**. To act justly is good, but Christians must do more. They have to go beyond what is just, and act in the same caring, compassionate way Jesus did. In the Gospels this is seen:
  - In the parable of the Good Samaritan.
  - In the way Jesus behaved toward the poor, the sick, and to social outcasts.

Jewish Moral Vision

- Jewish rabbis have taught that:
  - To help the poor is a duty required by God.
  - People should be helped in a sensitive way that allows them to keep their dignity and self-respect.

- Jews learn about justice in the **Tenakh**. Jewish scripture, suggests practical things that can be done to ensure that everyone's needs are met.

- The prophets were people called by God to speak out against injustice in Jewish society. The prophet Amos, for example, spoke on behalf of the poor who were being exploited and badly treated. He demanded that the rich and the powerful change their ways and act justly toward the less well-off.

Justice in action

◆ When a Christian or a Jew makes a decision to
act justly and help people in need, they are likely
to be influenced by the moral vision of their
religious tradition.

◆ There are many ways to help people in need at
home and abroad. For example:

  ▶ Buying ethically produced goods, from
    Fair Trade for example.

  ▶ Supporting voluntary organisations such as:
    - the *Saint Vincent de Paul Society*.
    - *Trocaire*.
    - *Christian Aid*.
    - *Tzedek* (a Jewish aid agency).

Test Yourself

1. What is meant by justice?

_____

_____

_____

2. What religious teachings encourage Christians to act justly and help people in need?

_____

_____

_____

_____

_____

3. What religious teachings encourage Jews to act justly and help people in need?

_____

_____

_____

_____

_____

Respect for Life

KEY CONCEPTS

Respect: to have a high regard for someone or something, and to treat each with great care.

Life: the state, or quality, of being alive.

Respect for Life

◆ Respect for life is important in the moral vision of Christianity and Judaism because human life:
  ▶ is a gift from God.
  ▶ is sacred and deserves to be treated with care and respect.

◆ Some people believe that human life begins at conception, others believe that human life begins at birth, or when a baby can survive outside the womb. Exactly when life begins is a crucial factor in the issue of abortion.

◆ **Abortion** is an operation to end a pregnancy by removing a foetus, an unborn child from the womb. Although abortion is now legal in many countries, most religions teach that abortion is morally wrong.

◆ Some Christian Churches accept that abortion is wrong but that it could be allowed under certain circumstances. The decision would not be taken lightly but would be seen as the lesser of two evils.

The Catholic Moral Vision

◆ The Catholic Church teaches that abortion is morally wrong in all circumstances. Catholics believe:
  ▶ Human life is sacred and should be treated with respect as it is a gift from God.
  ▶ Human life begins at conception.
  ▶ The unborn child is a separate human being and has a right to life.
  ▶ God creates life; only God can take it away.

The Jewish Moral Vision

◆ Judaism teaches that abortion is morally wrong but is allowed in certain circumstances. Jews believe:
  ▶ All life is sacred, as it is a gift from God.
  ▶ The teaching of some rabbis that life does not begin until the moment of birth.
  ▶ Abortion is wrong as the taking of life is against the law of God.
  ▶ Although it is sad and regrettable, abortion is allowed under certain circumstances.

Test Yourself

1. What religious belief influences Christians and Jews to respect human life?

_____

_____

2. What religious teaching encourages Catholics to oppose abortion?

_____

_____

_____

_____

3. What is the Jewish position on abortion?

_____

_____

_____

Care for the Earth

OBJECTIVE:
Show how a religious moral vision can influence decisions on the environment.

KEY CONCEPTS

Respect: to have a high regard for someone or something, and to treat each with great care.

Stewardship: the way people care for the Earth on behalf of God.

Respect

◆ Today there is a lack of respect for the Earth.
  ▶ The Earth's atmosphere is badly damaged.
  ▶ Rainforests are destroyed.
  ▶ Rivers and seas are polluted.
  ▶ The quality of the land and the welfare of animals are casualties in modern methods of food production.

◆ To respect the Earth means to have a high regard for it and to treat it with care. An attitude of deep respect is the starting point of any action to protect the Earth.

◆ Christians and Jews believe the Earth is worthy of respect because it is a gift from God.

Stewardship

◆ A steward is like a caretaker who looks after someone else's property. Stewardship in a religious sense is about caring for the Earth on behalf of God.

◆ Christians and Jews believe God created the Earth and put humans in charge to look after it.

◆ People do not own the Earth, but are its caretakers. It is everyone's responsibility to pass it on in perfect condition to the next generation.

◆ In 1995, the leaders of the world's major religions issued a joint statement on the environment. They made the point that it is a person's religious duty and responsibility to care for the Earth.

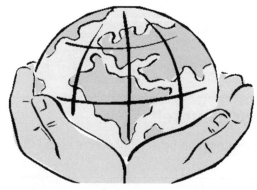

The Christian Moral Vision

◆ The **Bible** teaches that:
  ▶ God created the Earth.
  ▶ God put humans in charge to look after it.

◆ The Christian attitude to the environment should be one of good stewardship.

◆ Leaders of the Christian Churches have each spoken out about environmental issues in recent times.

◆ To respect and care for the environment is an important part of the moral vision of Christianity.

The Jewish Moral Vision

◆ The **Tenakh** teaches that:
  ▶ God created the Earth.
  ▶ God put humans in charge to look after it.

◆ The Jewish attitude to the environment is one of good stewardship. This means looking after it in very practical ways.

◆ Jewish respect for nature, especially for land and for trees, goes back to the time of Abraham. Tree planting often marks important occasions such as weddings and bar-mitzvahs.

◆ To respect and care for the environment is an important part of the moral vision of Judaism.

What to do about the environment

◆ A person's religious moral vision is likely to influence his/her decision to do something positive to help the environment.

◆ Stewardship involves:
  ▶ having respect for the environment.
  ▶ doing something to care for the environment on a daily basis.

  'Reduce, re-use, recycle' is a good place to begin.

Test Yourself

1. What religious belief influences Jews and Christians to have a deep respect for the environment?

_____

_____

_____

2. What is the religious meaning of good stewardship?

_____

_____

_____

_____

3. How could a person's religious moral vision influence their behaviour toward the environment?

_____

_____

_____

_____

_____

_____

Moral Failure

OBJECTIVE:
Outline the Christian vision
of moral failure and its
consequences.

KEY CONCEPTS

Sin: any deliberate thought, word or action that damages a person's relationship with God and other people.

Judgement: the belief that in the end God will judge each person on their moral behaviour.

Sin

◆ Moral failure means failing to act as a moral person. In the Christian tradition, the word for moral failure is 'sin'. Sin always causes harm.

◆ **Sin** is any deliberate thought, word, or action that damages a person's relationship with God and other people. Relationships are very important within the Christian moral vision, sin damages relationships.

◆ In the Bible the story of Adam and Eve in the book of Genesis is a symbolic story that sets out to explain the origin of sin and to show how sin damages relationships.

◆ The Catholic Church teaches that there is mortal and venial sin.

  ▶ **Mortal sin** is the most serious type of sin, it *breaks* one's relationship with God.

  ▶ **Venial sin** is the less serious type of sin, it *weakens* one's relationship with God.

◆ For Christians, sin means turning away from God. Sin is a failure to love God and one's neighbour in the way that Jesus taught.

◆ People need help to make the right choices and avoid sin. Christians believe the strength to do what is right comes from Jesus and the sacraments.

Judgement

◆ Judaism, Christianity and Islam, teach that people will be held responsible for the moral choices they make in life.

◆ **Judgement** is the religious belief that in the end, God will judge each person on their moral behaviour. The good will go to **heaven**. The wicked will be sent to **hell**.

◆ Catholics believe that heaven is a state of perfect happiness in the presence of God. Hell is a state of total unhappiness in the absence of God, and purgatory is an in-between state of preparation for eventual union with God.

Test Yourself

1. What is the Christian understanding of moral failure?

_____

_____

_____

2. Explain the difference between mortal and venial sin in Catholic moral teaching.

_____

_____

_____

3. What is the meaning of Judgement after death?

_____

_____

Restoring Relationships

> **KEY CONCEPTS**
>
> Forgiveness: to have pity and be willing to excuse someone's mistake or wrongdoing.
>
> Reconciliation: making the effort to heal and restore a broken relationship.

Forgiveness

◆ Christians believe they must follow the teaching of Jesus and forgive those who hurt or offend them. Forgiveness means to have pity on someone and be willing to excuse their mistake or wrongdoing.

◆ **Jesus taught forgiveness** through:
  ▶ Parables.
  ▶ Miracles.
  ▶ Table fellowship.

◆ Jesus told his followers that God is forgiving. Christians believe therefore, that since God forgives them, they must forgive others.

◆ Forgiveness rules out revenge. Revenge has no place in the Christian moral vision. Forgiveness begins when the person turns to God in prayer, asking that God take away the hatred and bitterness in their heart.

Reconciliation

◆ Sin damages the relationships people have with each other. It also damages their relationship with God because their behaviour means they have turned away from God.

◆ Relationships are important and when they break down, they need to be mended. People need to work things out and be reconciled with each other and with God.

◆ When people make an effort to heal and restore a broken relationship, this effort is called reconciliation.

Christianity

Restoring relationships: The Sacrament of Reconciliation

◆ In the Roman Catholic tradition, the Sacrament of Reconciliation heals and restores broken relationships bringing people back to God, and to one another.

◆ Catholics confess their sins to a priest, believing that Jesus gives the priest power to forgive sins.

◆ Through the words and actions of the sacrament, the priest offers forgiveness on behalf of God and the Christian Community.

◆ The parts of the Sacrament of Reconciliation are:
  ▶ *Confession*
    - the person tells his/her sins to the priest.
  ▶ *Penance*
    - the priest gives a penance to fit the sin.
  ▶ *Sorrow*
    - the person expresses sorrow for his/her sins.
  ▶ *Forgiveness*
    - the priest offers the person God's forgiveness.

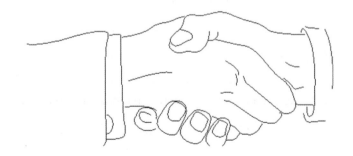

Judaism

Restoring Relationships: Yom Kippur

◆ Yom Kippur is the holiest day in the Jewish year. It is a day when Jews make amends to God for what they have done wrong.

◆ Jews fast all day on Yom Kippur. They attend a service in the synagogue, and pray to God expressing sorrow for their sins and asking for forgiveness.

◆ Everything in the synagogue is covered in white. The rabbi leading the synagogue service wears white too. The colour is a symbol, it shows that when people are sorry God will forgive their sins.

◆ The Shofar, a ram's horn, is blown loudly at the end of the service. It is to remind everyone to keep their promises and do God's will in the year ahead.

Test Yourself

1. What is the Christian teaching on forgiveness?

_____

_____

_____

_____

_____

2. What is the meaning of reconciliation?

_____

_____

_____

_____

3. Describe the method of healing and restoring broken relationships in either:
   a. Christianity - the Roman Catholic Church.   *or*   **b.** Judaism.

_____

_____

_____

_____

_____

_____

_____

_____

_____

_____

1. This is a photograph of people showing concern about a moral issue. ....2008(O)

A. Pick **one** thing from this photograph which shows that these people are concerned about a moral issue.

B. Give **one** reason why religion could influence a person's view of right and wrong on a moral issue.

C. Describe **one** stage in the process a person goes through in deciding if something is right or wrong.

Mrzine.monthlyreview.org/okeefe200306.html

2. a. ....2013(H)

I have responsibilities, as my actions have an effect on others.

(Source: SoftKey Multimedia)

Examine the role that the idea expressed above plays in how a morally mature person decides what is right and wrong.

b. Considering the consequences is one stage in the process of making a moral decision.

Describe what is involved in **another** stage of the process a person goes through in deciding what is the right thing to do in a situation.

3. Tick ✓ **one** of the following major world religions that you have studied: ....2011(H)

BUDDHISM ☐   CHRISTIANITY ☐   HINDUISM ☐   ISLAM ☐   JUDAISM ☐

a. Name **one** moral code associated with the world religion that you have ticked above.

b. Describe the way in which a moral code could guide a person when making a moral decision.

c. Outline what is involved in another **two** stages of the process a person would go through in making a moral decision.

4. a. Outline a situation in which a person has to make a moral decision. ....2005(H)

b. Explain how a person's religion could influence his / her moral decision-making in the situation you have outlined above.

5. This is a photograph of people working for justice. ....2012(O)

A. Pick **one** thing from this photograph which suggests that these people are working for justice.

B. Give **another** example of a way in which the members of a community of faith can work for justice.

C. State **one** reason why the members of a community of faith work for justice.

Adapted from www.peaceeagle.org

6. a. Describe **one** example of the work being done by the members of .... 2007(O), 2014(H)
   a major world religion to promote justice in the world today.

   b. Explain **two** reasons why the members of a major world religion work for justice in the world today.

---

7. a. A religious moral vision can inspire people to work for justice. ....2004(O)

   a. Outline **one** religious moral vision you have studied.

   b. Explain how this religious moral vision could inspire people to work for justice.

   b. Explain how this religious moral vision can be seen in the work for justice of a member, or members, of any religious organisation you have studied.

---

8. a. Religion can influence a person's view of what is right and wrong in a situation. ....2009(H)
   Name **one** other influence on a person's view of what is right and wrong.

   b.   Buddhism ❏   Christianity ❏   Hinduism ❏   Islam ❏   Judaism ❏
   Tick ✓ **one** of the world religions above that you have studied.

   Describe **one** example of the work for *either* justice *or* peace being done by members of the world religion you have ticked above.

   c. Explain **two** reasons why members of a world religion would work for *either* justice *or* peace.

---

9. This photograph shows an example of stewardship. .... 2003(H), 2007(O)

www.conservancy.bc.ca

   A. Pick **one** thing from the photograph which shows that this is an example of stewardship.

   B. What is stewardship?

   C. Describe **another** example of stewardship.

---

10. a. In religious traditions the term 'stewardship' means... ....2009(H)

   b. Outline **one** example of stewardship in a community of faith that you have studied.

   c. Explain **two** reasons why stewardship is important for a community of faith.

---

11. a. In religious traditions stewardship involves a person's responsibility to... .... 2004(H), 2013(H)

   b. Describe **two** examples of how stewardship is encouraged by the teaching of a major world religion.

---

12. a. JUSTICE ❏   STEWARDSHIP ❏   ....2010(O)
   Tick ✓ **one** of the words listed above and outline what it means in a religious tradition.

   b. Explain **one** reason why working for *either* justice *or* stewardship is important for the members of a community of faith today.

---

13. a. In religious traditions the term 'sin' refers to _____ ....2012(O)

   b. Describe **two** consequences which sin can have for the members of a community of faith.

---

14. a. In religious traditions the term 'forgiveness' refers to_____ ....2014(O)

    b. Describe **two** examples of how the teaching of a major world religion encourages its members to show forgiveness.

---

15. a. Outline **one** example of the teaching on forgiveness found in ....2012(H)
a major world religion that you have studied.

    b. Profile how the members of a major world religion express their need for forgiveness in an act of worship.

---

16. **A.** Outline the understanding of forgiveness found in the teaching of . ...2010(H)
a major world religion that you have studied.

    B. a. Explain **two** reasons why reconciliation is seen as important by members of a world religion.

       b. Describe **one** way in which a world religion offers its members an opportunity for reconciliation.

---

17. a. In religious traditions reconciliation involves the renewing of relationships . ...2008(O)
that have been broken.

    (Tick ✓ the correct box)　❏ True　❏ False

    b. Outline **one** way in which members of a community of faith try to bring about reconciliation between people today.

    c. Explain **two** reasons why members of a community of faith try to bring about reconciliation between people today.

Law and Morality

KEY CONCEPTS

Civil law: the laws of a state that regulate the behaviour of people within the state.

Constitution: a document outlining the fundamental political principles by which a state is governed.

Pluralism: the view that all groups in society must have equal representation.

Religious fundamentalism: the view that the laws of a state should be based on the moral laws of its dominant religion.

Libertarianism: the view that people should be free to behave as they choose, without undue interference from the state.

Civil Law

◆ A state is a country with its own system of government. The state has a duty to:
  ▶ protect the rights of citizens.
  ▶ maintain law and order.

This is achieved by the government passing laws to regulate the behaviour of people within the state. Laws are enforced by the police and courts of law.

Constitution

◆ Laws are made for 'the common good'. A government makes laws according to its vision of what is best for the country as a whole.

◆ A government's vision of what is best for the country is expressed in it's constitution.

◆ A constitution is a document outlining the fundamental political principles by which a state is governed. The Irish Constitution contains a set of guidelines the government must follow when introducing new laws.

◆ A constitution is important because:
  ▶ it prevents the abuse of power.
  ▶ it protects the rights of citizens.

Law and Morality

◆ State laws influence our moral actions as everyone in the country must obey the law. However law and morality are not one and the same.

◆ In any country, what is legal may not necessarily be good or even moral. This can lead to a conflict between personal morality and state law. For example:
  ▶ In some countries, state law demands military conscription. This raises a moral problem for the Society of Friends (Quakers), who are pacifists and opposed to all forms of violence.
  ▶ Some countries have introduced laws to legalise abortion. This raises a problem for Roman Catholics who oppose abortion because of their belief that all human life is sacred.
  ▶ Then there are some states that are basically unjust and many of their laws are immoral, for example:
    - The Nazi system in Germany, where the government imposed laws that discriminated against Jews and led to their genocide.
    - The Apartheid system in South Africa, where the government imposed laws that divided people along racial lines.

- Christians accept:
  - ▶ That people should respect and obey just laws that are clearly for the common good.

  Christians do not accept:
  - ▶ That the law of the state contains the final word on what is right and wrong.

- Christians say that there is a higher standard than the law of the state, and they believe this is the law of God. The Catholic Church, for example, teaches: *"God's law continues to bind no matter what the civil (state) law says."* (Pastoral letter of the Irish Bishops.)

- If there is conflict or a clash between the Law of God and the Law of the State, people of faith follow their conscience and do what is right, even if it means breaking the law.

- A morally mature person, therefore, is one whose behaviour is influenced more by their personal moral vision than by the laws of the state.

Law and Religious Morality

- How far should religious morality influence the law of the state? There are three different views:
  - ▶ Pluralism.
  - ▶ Religious Fundamentalism.
  - ▶ Libertarianism.

Pluralism

- **Pluralism** is the view that all groups in society must have equal representation, and that state laws cannot be based on the moral outlook of any one religious tradition.

- The state has the task of trying to balance the rights of all groups, including minorities, without favouring any group in particular.

- In a pluralist society, law and religious morality are ideally separate from one another, e.g. in Ireland.

Religious Fundamentalism

- **Religious fundamentalism** is the view that the laws of a state should be based on the moral laws of its dominant religion.

- Religious fundamentalists get their inspiration from the sacred texts of their religion, where every word is accepted as the literal truth.

- Fundamentalists believe so strongly in the fixed nature of their faith that they want its religious laws to be made the laws of the state, e.g. in Iran.

Libertarianism

- **Libertarianism** is the view that people should be free to behave as they choose, without undue interference from the state.

- The individual's right to freedom takes priority over all other rights.

- Morality is seen mainly as a private matter. The way people choose to think and to act should not be restricted by outside influences such as the Church or the State, e.g. in Holland.

Test Yourself

1. Explain the following terms.   **a.** the state.   **b.** state law.

_____

_____

_____

_____

2. What is the constitution of a country?

_____

_____

3. When might state law and personal morality come into conflict?

_____

_____

_____

_____

_____

_____

_____

_____

4. Should the law of the state be the only standard by which people decide what is right and wrong?

_____

_____

_____

_____

5. What is Pluralism?

_____

_____

6. What is Fundamentalism?

_____

_____

7. What is Libertarianism?

_____

_____

---

1. **"Priest objects to government laws on Church design."** ....2004(H)

The headline above refers to a situation where a conflict arose between government law and the views of a religious leader.

a. Outline a situation where there could be a conflict between a country's law and a religion.

b. Explain how **two** of the following could influence a person's judgement of right and wrong in the situation you have described above.

■ Family   ■ Peer group   ■ Civil law   ■ Religion

c. Explain how a morally mature person would judge between right and wrong in the situation you have described above.

---

2. a. Give one example of a situation where there could be conflict ....2007(H)
between a country's law and a religion.

b. Pluralism ☐   Religious Fundamentalism ☐

Tick ✓ **one** of the above and outline how it sees the relationship between a country's law and a religion.

---

3. a. Outline what libertarianism sees as the relationship between ....2008(H)
personal morality and a country's law.

b. Examine how there might be conflict between the libertarian point of view and a country's law on **one** moral issue you have studied.

NOTE: *This is an essay question.*

---

4. ● RELIGIOUS FUNDAMENTALISM   ● LIBERTARIANISM   ....2013(H)

Profile an example of how there could be conflict on a moral issue between a country's law and one of the points of view listed above.

NOTE: *This is an essay question.*

---

5. ● LIBERTARIANISM   ● RELIGIOUS FUNDAMENTALISM ....2011(H)

Compare how the relationship between a country's law and religion is seen from **each** of the above points of view.

NOTE: *This is an essay question.*

Junior Certificate
Religious Education Examination

The Examination Paper - *an overview*

> ❖ The **Higher Level** paper - has **FIVE** sections to be answered.
> - is two hours long.
>
> ❖ The **Ordinary Level** paper - has **FOUR** sections to be answered.
> - is two hours long.

❖ The examination paper is laid out in sections.

It is important to know:

- what is expected in each section.

- what marks can be obtained.

- how much time to spend on each section overall.

Higher level paper	Type of question	Marks (Total = 400)	Time to spend on it.
⚪ Section 1	Short questions.	50	15 minutes
⚪ Section 2	Picture questions.	30	15 minutes
⚪ Section 3	Comprehension.	50	15 minutes
⚪ Section 4	Six questions.	200	55 minutes
⚪ Section 5	Essay question.	70	20 minutes

Ordinary level paper	Type of question	Marks (Total = 400)	Time to spend on it.
⚪ Section 1	Short questions.	80	20 minutes
⚪ Section 2	Picture questions.	60	20 minutes
⚪ Section 3	Comprehension.	60	20 minutes
⚪ Section 4	Six questions.	200	60 minutes

Section 1 - *Short Questions*

❖ This section contains twenty questions.
You must answer **ten** of them.

❖ At **higher level** spend <u>15 minutes</u> on this section.
At **ordinary level** spend <u>20 minutes</u> on this section.

❖ The questions cover **every** part of the course.

<u>TIP</u> Read through all the questions first. Pick the ten questions you know best and answer those.

Keep written answers short - a few words will do.

Only attempt the remaining questions if you have time to spare.

❖ Practice the short questions.
The *Short Questions* from the 2014 (Higher Level) examination paper are presented next.

Section 1 (50 marks)

YOU SHOULD SPEND ABOUT 15 MINUTES ANSWERING QUESTIONS IN THIS SECTION.

YOU MUST ANSWER **TEN** OF THE FOLLOWING TWENTY QUESTIONS.

IN QUESTIONS WHERE YOU ARE REQUIRED TO TICK ✓ THE CORRECT BOX, TICK **ONE** BOX ONLY.

(All questions carry 5 marks each)

1. The Roman Catholic Church is a Christian denomination in Ireland today.
Name **another** Christian denomination in Ireland today.

_____

2. Jesus of Nazareth was born in Bethlehem. (Tick ✓ the correct box)

True ☐ False ☐

3. In religious traditions the term 'peace' refers to _____

_____

4. A 'saffron robe' is a religious garment most associated with which **one** of the following world religions?

(Tick ✓ the correct box)

BUDDHISM ☐   ISLAM ☐   JUDAISM ☐

5. Confirmation is one example of a Christian sacrament.
Name **another** example of a Christian sacrament.

_____

6. The sea where Jesus called his first disciples was named: (Tick ✓ the correct box)

THE DEAD SEA ☐   THE MEDITERRANEAN SEA ☐   THE SEA OF GALILEE ☐

7. In religious traditions the term 'ministry' refers to _____

_____

8. Read the list of people of faith and the list of major world religions given below. One person has been matched to the major world religion with which he/she is most associated as an example for you. Make **one** other match.

People of Faith	World Religions
Gandhi	Buddhism
Khadijah	Christianity
Mary Magdalene	Hinduism
Moses	Islam
Siddhartha Gautama	Judaism

	People of Faith	World Religion
Example:	Mary Magdalene	Christianity

Answer:

9. The celebration of a Bar Mitzvah is most associated with which **one** of the following world religions?

(Tick ✓ the correct box)

CHRISTIANITY ☐   ISLAM ☐   JUDAISM ☐

10. The Hindu religion is associated with polytheism.   (Tick ✓ the correct box)

          True ☐   False ☐

11. In religious traditions the term 'peace' refers to _____

_____

12. 'Halal' food is most associated with which one of the following world religions?   (Tick ✓ the correct box)

    BUDDHISM ☐   CHRISTIANITY ☐   ISLAM ☐

13. Josephus is one example of an historical source of information about Jesus of Nazareth.
Name **another** example of an historical source of information about Jesus of Nazareth.

_____

14. Humanism holds the view that when looking for the meaning of life a person should turn to the supernatural or belief in God.   (Tick ✓ the correct box)

          True ☐   False ☐

15. In religious traditions the term 'tolerance' refers to _____

_____

16. Pluralism is associated with the idea that everyone has the right to express religious or non-religious views.
               (Tick ✓ the correct box)

          True ☐   False ☐

17. In religious traditions the term 'sin' refers to _____

_____

18. Belief in reincarnation is most associated with which **one** of the following world religions?

               (Tick ✓ the correct box)

    HINDUISM ☐   ISLAM ☐   JUDAISM ☐

19. Religious fundamentalism holds the view that _____

_____

20. A morally mature person thinks of others when making decisions about right and wrong.

               (Tick ✓ the correct box)

          True ☐   False ☐

Section 2 - *Picture Questions*

❖ This section contains four photographs and a set of questions.
You must select **three** photographs and answer the questions on each.

❖ At **higher level** spend <u>15 minutes</u> on this section.
At **ordinary level** spend <u>20 minutes</u> on this section.

❖ The pictures relate to different parts of the course.

TIP Look closely at the pictures. They may contain clues to help you answer the questions.
Answers in full sentences work best.

❖ Practice the picture questions.
The *Picture Questions* from the 2014 (Higher Level) examination paper are presented next.

Section 2 (30 marks)

YOU SHOULD SPEND ABOUT 15 MINUTES ANSWERING QUESTIONS IN THIS SECTION.

CHOOSE **THREE** OF THE FOLLOWING PHOTOGRAPHS AND ANSWER THE QUESTIONS ON EACH.

(All questions carry 10 marks each)

Question 1. This picture is based on a Gospel account of Jesus celebrating the Last Supper.

(Source: www.theliterates.ca)

A. Pick one thing from this picture which suggests that it is based on Jesus' celebration of the Last Supper.

_____

_____

(2 marks)

B. According to the Gospels which one of the following people was present at the Last Supper with Jesus?   (Tick ✓ the correct box.)

PAUL ☐   PETER ☐   PRISCILLA ☐

(2 marks)

C. State **two** reasons why Jesus celebrated the Last Supper.

(i) _____

_____

(ii) _____

_____

(6 marks)

Question 2. This is a photograph of a person who is a religious leader.

(Source:http://news.yahoo.com)

A. Pick one thing from the photograph which suggests that this person is a religious leader.

_____

_____

(2 marks)

B. Pope Francis is the name of a religious leader associated with a Christian denomination.   (Tick ✓ the correct box.)

TRUE ☐   FALSE ☐

(2 marks)

C. State **two** reasons why the term 'authority' can be associated with the role of a leader in a community of faith.

(i) _____

_____

(ii) _____

_____

(6 marks)

Question 3. This is a picture from the cover of a school religion book.

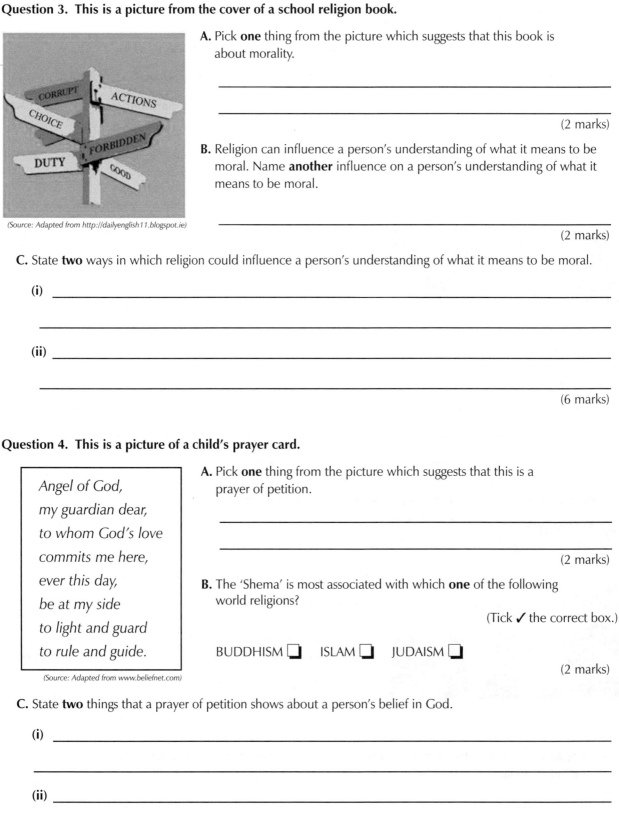

A. Pick **one** thing from the picture which suggests that this book is about morality.

_____

_____

(2 marks)

B. Religion can influence a person's understanding of what it means to be moral. Name **another** influence on a person's understanding of what it means to be moral.

_____

(2 marks)

(Source: Adapted from http://dailyenglish11.blogspot.ie)

C. State **two** ways in which religion could influence a person's understanding of what it means to be moral.

(i) _____

_____

(ii) _____

_____

(6 marks)

Question 4. This is a picture of a child's prayer card.

Angel of God,
my guardian dear,
to whom God's love
commits me here,
ever this day,
be at my side
to light and guard
to rule and guide.

(Source: Adapted from www.beliefnet.com)

A. Pick **one** thing from the picture which suggests that this is a prayer of petition.

_____

_____

(2 marks)

B. The 'Shema' is most associated with which **one** of the following world religions?

(Tick ✓ the correct box.)

BUDDHISM ☐   ISLAM ☐   JUDAISM ☐

(2 marks)

C. State **two** things that a prayer of petition shows about a person's belief in God.

(i) _____

_____

(ii) _____

_____

(6 marks)

Section 3 - *Comprehension*

❖ This section contains a passage to be read.
You must answer **all** the questions on it.

❖ At **higher level** spend <u>15 minutes</u> on this section.
At **ordinary level** spend <u>20 minutes</u> on this section.

❖ The passage can refer to any part of the course.

> TIP Read the passage and all the questions through once.
>
> Carefully re-read the passage underlining words and points that might answer the questions.
>
> Near the end you will be asked to write a statement explaining the meaning of certain concepts. Do this by:
>
> a. Referring to the passage.
>
> b. Referring to an example outside the passage.

❖ Practice the comprehension questions.
The *Comprehension* passage from the 2014 (Higher Level) examination paper is presented next.

Section 3 (50 marks)

YOU SHOULD SPEND ABOUT 15 MINUTES ANSWERING QUESTIONS IN THIS SECTION.

READ THE BLOG BELOW AND ANSWER ALL THE QUESTIONS THAT FOLLOW.

PEOPLE OF FAITH TODAY

The Irish boxer Katie Taylor recently took time out from her busy schedule to thank God and all the people who supported her in winning a gold medal at the Olympics. "I'd like to thank everyone for their prayers... because I couldn't have done this without them. God has been so great to me these last few years in my career and I'd be nothing without Him... I wouldn't be standing here as a champion if it wasn't for God in my life.. I just want to honour Him in everything I do..."

(Adapted from www.f3.thejournal.ie & rsvpmagazine.ie)

The Newcastle United football club have established an area for Islamic players to worship before matches. Players have been using various rooms at the grounds to worship before games. A club member explained: "prayer has become an important part of the build up to big games." It is important to look after the players and now they will get a proper prayer room.

Footballers celebrate their goal scoring during a match by touching their foreheads on the ground in prayer.

(Adapted from www.mirror.co.uk & myheartbeatsfootball.wordpress.com)

---

1. Describe one example of how the religious faith of people can be seen in the articles on the above notice board.

_____

_____

_____

_____

_____

_____

_____

_____

_____

_____

_____

_____

(10 marks)

2. MATERIALISM ☐   SECULARISM ☐

Tick ✓ **one** of the above and outline how the way of looking at the world that you have ticked could pose a challenge to the religious faith of a person.

_____

_____

_____

_____

_____

_____

_____

_____

_____

(14 marks)

3.   ● CONTEMPLATION   ● MEDITATION

Describe an example of what is involved in **one** of the above types of prayer.

_____   _____

TYPE OF PRAYER   _____

_____

_____

_____

_____

_____

(12 marks)

4. _People of faith express their religious beliefs in different types of prayer._

Explain why people use either contemplation or meditation as a type of prayer to express their faith.

_____   _____

TYPE OF PRAYER   _____

_____

_____

_____

_____

_____

_____

(14 marks)

Section 4 - *Six Questions*

❖ This section contains six questions.

❖ At **higher level** - you answer **four** questions.
- spend <u>55 minutes</u> on this section.

At **ordinary level** - you answer **five** questions.
- spend <u>60 minutes</u> on this section.

❖ The questions follow the structure of the religious education course.

A - Communities of Faith.

B - Foundations of Religion: Christianity.

C - Foundations of Religion: Major World Religions.

D - The Question of Faith.

E - The Celebration of Faith.

F - The Moral Challenge.

<u>TIP</u> Each question has a heading. It tells you which section of the course is being examined.

Read all six questions before selecting the ones you will answer.

Good answers will show a clear understanding and accurate knowledge of the concepts in each section of the course.

This part of the exam paper is worth 200 marks - half the total marks.

❖ Practice the six questions.

The *Six Questions* from the 2014 (Higher Level) examination paper are presented next.

Section 4 (200 marks)

YOU SHOULD SPEND ABOUT 55 MINUTES ANSWERING QUESTIONS IN THIS SECTION.

YOU MUST ANSWER **FOUR** OF THE FOLLOWING SIX QUESTIONS.

(All questions carry 50 marks each)

Question 1. COMMUNITIES OF FAITH

A. a.   ● COMMITMENT   ● COMMUNICATION   ● SHARING

Choose **two** of the above and describe how each can be seen in a community of faith today.

(i) _____   _____

_____

_____

_____

_____

(ii) _____   _____

_____

_____

_____

_____

(12 marks)

b. COMMUNITY BREAKDOWN ☐   LACK OF CO-OPERATION ☐

Tick ✓ **one** of the above and explain why this would be a challenge for the members of a community of faith.

_____

_____

_____

_____

_____

_____

_____

_____

(15 marks)

B. a. 'The Pope' is one example of a title that is given to a leader in a community of faith in Ireland today.
Name **another** title that is given to a leader in a community of faith in Ireland today.

_____

(5 marks)

b.　　　● COMMUNITY BREAKDOWN　　　● LACK OF CO-OPERATION

Suggest how the leader of a community of faith could address the challenge posed by **one** of the above.

●　_____　_____

_____

_____

_____

_____

_____

_____

_____

_____

_____

_____

_____

_____

_____

(18 marks)

Question 2. FOUNDATIONS OF RELIGION - CHRISTIANITY

A. a.　Name **one** example of a parable told by Jesus. _____

_____

(5 marks)

b.　Describe the story Jesus told in the parable that you have named above.

_____

_____

_____

_____

_____

_____

_____

_____

_____

_____

_____

_____

(12 marks)

B. a. Outline **one** characteristic of the Kingdom of God that Jesus preached in the parable which you have named in part Aa) above.

_____

_____

_____

_____

_____

_____

_____

_____

_____

_____

_____

_____

(15 marks)

b. Explain **two** reasons why Jesus used parables to teach people about the Kingdom of God.

(i) _____

_____

_____

_____

_____

_____

_____

_____

(ii) _____

_____

_____

_____

_____

_____

_____

_____

(18 marks)

Question 3. FOUNDATIONS OF RELIGION - MAJOR WORLD RELIGIONS

A. Tick ✓ **one** of the following major world religions that you have studied:

Buddhism ❑   Hinduism ❑   Islam ❑   Judaism ❑

a. Name **one** place of pilgrimage that is most associated with the world religion which you have ticked above.

_____

(5 marks)

b. Explain **two** reasons why the members of the world religion that you have ticked go on pilgrimage to the place which you have named in part Aa) above.

(i) _____

_____

_____

_____

_____

_____

(ii) _____

_____

_____

_____

_____

(12 marks)

B. a.   ◆ Buddhism   ◆ Hinduism   ◆ Islam   ◆ Judaism

Name a sacred text that is associated with one of the above world religions and explain **two** reasons why it can be described as a document of faith.

SACRED TEXT: _____   WORLD RELIGION: _____

(i) _____

_____

_____

_____

_____

_____

(ii) _____

_____

_____

_____

_____

(18 marks)

b. Describe what happened from the oral to the written stages in the development of the sacred text that you have named in *part B a.* above.

_____

_____

_____

_____

_____

_____

_____

_____

_____

_____

_____

_____

_____

_____

(15 marks)

Question 4. THE QUESTION OF FAITH

A. a. Name **one** major world religion that is associated with monotheism.

_____

(5 marks)

b. Explain **one** reason why monotheism is associated with the major world religion that you have named in *part Aa)* above.

_____

_____

_____

_____

_____

_____

_____

_____

_____

_____

_____

_____

(15 marks)

B. a. Describe **one** example of how religion and science have similar views of creation.

_____

_____

_____

_____

_____

_____

_____

_____

_____

_____

_____

_____

_____

_____

_____

_____

_____

_____

_____

_____

(15 marks)

b. Explain **one** reason why there has been tension between the religious and scientific views of creation.

_____

_____

_____

_____

_____

_____

_____

_____

_____

_____

_____

_____

_____

_____

_____

(15 marks)

Question 5. THE CELEBRATION OF FAITH

A. a. Tick ✓ **one** of the following major world religions that you have studied:

Buddhism ❑   Christianity ❑   Hinduism ❑   Islam ❑   Judaism ❑

Name **one** religious building that is most associated with the world religion which you have ticked above.

_____

(5 marks)

b. Describe **two** examples of how the building that you have named above is used for worship.

(i) _____

_____

_____

_____

_____

_____

(ii) _____

_____

_____

_____

_____

_____

(14 marks)

B. a. Outline **one** example of how people use a religious symbolic action to express *either* the meaning of life *or* the mystery of life.

_____

_____

_____

_____

_____

_____

_____

_____

_____

_____

_____

_____

(15 marks)

b. Explain **two** reasons why people use religious symbolic actions to express *either* the meaning of life *or* the mystery of life.

(i) _____

_____

_____

_____

_____

_____

_____

(ii) _____

_____

_____

_____

_____

_____

(16 marks)

Question 6. THE MORAL CHALLENGE

A. a. Describe **one** example of the work being done by the members of a major world religion to promote justice in the world today.

_____

_____

_____

_____

_____

_____

_____

_____

_____

_____

_____

_____

_____

_____

(15 marks)

b. Explain **two** reasons why the members of a major world religion work for justice in the world today.

(i) _____

_____

_____

_____

_____

_____

_____

(ii) _____

_____

_____

_____

_____

_____

_____

(14 marks)

B. a. In religious traditions the term 'reconciliation' refers to _____

_____

(5 marks)

b. Outline **two** methods by which a major world religion offers its members an opportunity for reconciliation.

(i) _____

_____

_____

_____

_____

_____

_____

(ii) _____

_____

_____

_____

_____

_____

_____

(16 marks)

Section 5 - *The Essay Question*

❖ This section contains six questions.

❖ **Higher level only** - answer **one** question.

- spend <u>20 minutes</u> on this section.

❖ The questions follow the structure of the Religious Education course.

A - Communities of Faith.

B - Foundations of Religion: Christianity.

C - Foundations of Religion: Major World Religions.

D - The Question of Faith.

E - The Celebration of Faith.

F - The Moral Challenge.

<u>TIP</u> Each question relates to a section of the course.

Read all the questions carefully.

Select a question for which you can identify at least six good points of information relevant to the title.

A good answer will:

- Make links between two different sections of the course.

- Contain a number of key concepts, not just one developed in detail.

❖ Practice the essay question.

The *Essay Questions* from the 2014 (Higher Level) examination paper are presented next.

Section 5 (70 marks)

YOU SHOULD SPEND ABOUT 20 MINUTES ANSWERING QUESTIONS IN THIS SECTION.

YOU MUST ANSWER **ONE** OF THE FOLLOWING SIX QUESTIONS.

(All questions carry 70 marks each)

Question 1. Examine the work being done by a community of faith found in Ireland today to promote dialogue between different major world religions using each of the following headings:

    i. The inspiration for the work.

    ii. The impact of the work.

Question 2. Profile what life in Palestine was like for people living at the time of Jesus using **each** of the following headings:

    i. Geography.

    ii. Religion.

Question 3.   ✦ Buddhism   ✦ Hinduism   ✦ Islam   ✦ Judaism

Imagine you are preparing a presentation about a religious festival that is associated with one of the above world religions. Outline the points you would make in your presentation about the religious festival in answer to **each** of the following questions:

i. What happens during the celebration of the religious festival?

ii. Why do members of the world religion celebrate the religious festival today?

Question 4. Imagine you have been asked to write an article for a local magazine about religious practice in Ireland over the last hundred years. Outline what you would write in your article making reference to each of the following:

i. Changes in religious practice.

ii. Influences on religious practice.

Question 5. Profile **two** benefits that communal prayer can have for the members of a community of faith.

Question 6.   ● INFORMED CONSCIENCE   ● INTEGRITY

Evaluate the importance of **each** of the above for a person in deciding what is right and wrong on a moral issue.

PLEASE MAKE SURE YOU GIVE THE NUMBER OF THE QUESTION YOU ARE ANSWERING
IN THE SPACE BELOW.

Section 5. Question _____

(70 marks)

BLANK PAGE

Coimisiún na Scrúduithe Stáit
State Examinations Commission

JUNIOR CERTIFICATE EXAMINATION, 2015
RELIGIOUS EDUCATION - HIGHER LEVEL

Total Marks: 400

THURSDAY, 11 JUNE - AFTERNOON, 2.00 to 4.00

General Directions for Candidates

1. Write your EXAMINATION NUMBER in this box:

2. WRITE ALL ANSWERS INTO THIS ANSWER BOOK.

3. YOU MUST ATTEMPT ALL 5 SECTIONS ON THIS PAPER.

For the Superintendent only

Centre Stamp

For the Examiner only

Question	Mark
SECTION 1	
SECTION 2	
SECTION 3	
SECTION 4 Question 1	
SECTION 4 Question 2	
SECTION 4 Question 3	
SECTION 4 Question 4	
SECTION 4 Question 5	
SECTION 4 Question 6	
SECTION 5	
Mark for Paper	
Mark for Journal	
Total	

1. Total of end of page totals	
2. Aggregate total of all disallowed question(s)	
3. Total mark awarded (1 minus 2)	
Note: The mark in row 3 above must equal the mark in the 'Mark for Paper' box across.	

(50 marks)

YOU SHOULD SPEND ABOUT 15 MINUTES ANSWERING QUESTIONS IN THIS SECTION.

YOU MUST ANSWER **TEN** OF THE FOLLOWING TWENTY QUESTIONS.

IN QUESTIONS WHERE YOU ARE REQUIRED TO TICK ✓ THE CORRECT BOX, TICK **ONE** BOX ONLY.

(All questions carry 5 marks each)

1. The term 'inter-faith dialogue' refers to _____

_____

2. Tacitus provided historical information about Jesus of Nazareth.   (Tick ✓ the correct box)

   True ☐   False ☐

3. Materialism promotes the view that _____

_____

4. During his childhood in Palestine Jesus lived in the Province of Galilee.   (Tick ✓ the correct box)

   True ☐   False ☐

5. In religious traditions the term 'mission' refers to _____

_____

6. One reason for community breakdown is _____

_____

7. Atheism holds the view that God exists.   (Tick ✓ the correct box)

   True ☐   False ☐

8. Read the list of religious objects and the list of world religions given below. One religious object has been
   matched to the world religion with which it is most associated as an example for you. Make **one** other match.

Religious Objects	World Religions		Religious Object	World Religion
Bindi	Buddhism	*Example:*	Cross	Christianity
Cross	Christianity			
Mandala	Hinduism	*Answer:*		
Menorah	Islam			
Prayer mat	Judaism			

9. The name Allah is most associated with which **one** of the following world religions?   (Tick ✓ the correct box)

   CHRISTIANITY ☐   ISLAM ☐   JUDAISM ☐

10. The 'Feeding of the Five Thousand' is one example of a miracle performed by Jesus.
    Give **another** example of a miracle performed by Jesus.

_____

11. In religious traditions the term 'peace' refers to _____

_____

12. The Israelites were led out of slavery in Egypt by: (Tick ✓ the correct box)

    MALACHI ☐   MARK ☐   MOSES ☐

13. Religion can be described as a source of morality in a person's life.
State **another** source of morality in a person's life.

_____

14. A sign is an action, image or word that communicates one clear message.   (Tick ✓ the correct box)

        True ☐   False ☐

15. Agnosticism holds the view that _____

_____

16. In the Christian tradition Jesus' celebration of the Last Supper is associated with which **one** of the following days of Holy Week?   (Tick ✓ the correct box)

    WEDNESDAY ☐   THURSDAY ☐   FRIDAY ☐

17. To pardon or show mercy is an example of forgiveness.   (Tick ✓ the correct box)

        True ☐   False ☐

18. Read the list of religious festivals and the list of world religions given below. One religious festival has been matched to the world religion with which it is most associated as an example for you. Make **one** other match.

Religious Festivals	World Religion
Diwali	Buddhism
Easter	Christianity
Ramadan	Hinduism
Rosh Hashanah	Islam
Vesak/Wesak	Judaism

Example:

Religious Festival	World Religion
Easter	Christianity

Answer:

19. One title given to Jesus was 'Messiah'. Name **another** title that was given to Jesus.

_____

20. The celebration of seven sacraments is most associated with which **one** of the following Christian denominations?   (Tick ✓ the correct box)

    METHODIST ☐   PRESBYTERIAN ☐   FRIDAY ☐

(30 marks)

YOU SHOULD SPEND ABOUT 15 MINUTES ANSWERING QUESTIONS IN THIS SECTION.

CHOOSE **THREE** OF THE FOLLOWING PHOTOGRAPHS AND ANSWER THE QUESTIONS ON EACH.

(All questions carry 10 marks each)

Question 1. This is a photograph of a person reading from a sacred text.

(Source: www.conservapedia.com)

A. Pick **one** thing from the photograph which suggests that this person is reading from a sacred text.

_____

_____

_____

(2 marks)

B. Tick ✓ one of the following world religions and name a sacred text associated with it:

BUDDHISM ❏   CHRISTIANITY ❏   HINDUISM ❏

ISLAM ❏   JUDAISM ❏

Name of sacred text: _____

(2 marks)

C. Give **two** reasons why a text is regarded as sacred by the members of a world religion.

(i) _____

(ii) _____

(6 marks)

Question 2. This is a photograph of a community of faith.

(Source: Ken O' Halloran - Irish Independent)

A. Pick **one** thing from the photograph which suggests that these people are members of a community of faith.

_____

_____

_____

(2 marks)

B. Being the leader is one role that a person can have in a community of faith. Name **another** role that a person can have within a community of faith.

_____

(2 marks)

C. Give **two** reasons why people have different roles in a community of faith.

(i) _____

_____

(ii) _____

_____

(6 marks)

Question 3. This is a photograph of a building that is a place of worship for the members of a community of faith.

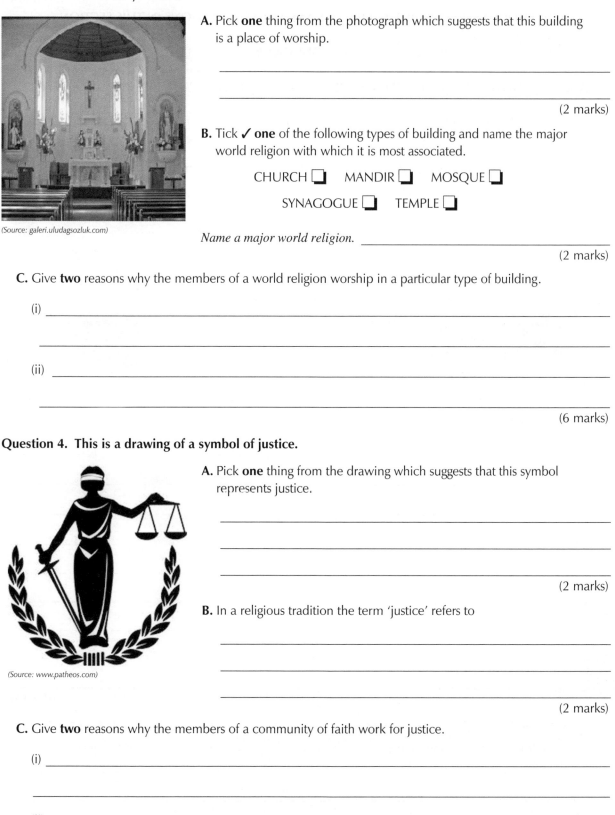

(Source: galeri.uludagsozluk.com)

A. Pick **one** thing from the photograph which suggests that this building is a place of worship.

_____

_____

(2 marks)

B. Tick ✓ **one** of the following types of building and name the major world religion with which it is most associated.

CHURCH ☐   MANDIR ☐   MOSQUE ☐

SYNAGOGUE ☐   TEMPLE ☐

Name a major world religion. _____

(2 marks)

C. Give **two** reasons why the members of a world religion worship in a particular type of building.

(i) _____

_____

(ii) _____

_____

(6 marks)

Question 4. This is a drawing of a symbol of justice.

(Source: www.patheos.com)

A. Pick **one** thing from the drawing which suggests that this symbol represents justice.

_____

_____

_____

(2 marks)

B. In a religious tradition the term 'justice' refers to

_____

_____

_____

(2 marks)

C. Give **two** reasons why the members of a community of faith work for justice.

(i) _____

_____

(ii) _____

_____

(6 marks)

YOU SHOULD SPEND ABOUT 15 MINUTES ANSWERING QUESTIONS IN THIS SECTION.

READ THE BLOG BELOW AND ANSWER ALL THE QUESTIONS THAT FOLLOW.

HOME   ABOUT   RECENT BLOGS   BLOGGING GUIDELINES   CONTACT

TIME TO THINK - *Do we give enough time to thinking about the meaning of life?*

Last week when I was walking home from school, the wind grew so strong that it forced me to stop where I was standing and notice the leaves falling from the trees. The colours and sounds of nature made me think about the beauty of the world and my place in it.

Sometimes I like to listen to music and sit on the beach looking out to sea, thinking about my life. I find talking to God and praying about the things that matter in life helps me to make sense of my life.

✎ P.J.   (Source: http://www.kabbalahblog.info;ibtimes.co.uk;pixshark.com)

1. Explain how an experience described in the blog above gave PJ a sense of awe and wonder about the meaning of life.

_____

_____

_____

_____

_____

_____

_____

_____

_____

(10 marks)

2. *Recognising the beauty of nature is one example of how a person could experience awe and wonder in life.*
   Outline **another** example of how an experience in life could make a person wonder and ask questions about the meaning of life.

_____

_____

_____

_____

_____

_____

_____

_____

_____

_____

_____

(12 marks)

3. Explain **two** reasons why taking time for reflection can help people in their search for the meaning of life.

(i) _____

_____

_____

_____

_____

(ii) _____

_____

_____

_____

_____

(12 marks)

4. _People sometimes turn to religion when searching for the meaning of life._

Outline how the teaching of **one** of the following world religions could help believers in their search for the meaning of life.

◆ BUDDHISM   ◆ CHRISTIANITY   ◆ HINDUISM   ◆ ISLAM   ◆ JUDAISM

_____   _____

(WORLD RELIGION)   _____

_____

_____

_____

_____

_____

_____

(16 marks)

(200 marks)

YOU SHOULD SPEND ABOUT 55 MINUTES ANSWERING QUESTIONS IN THIS SECTION.

YOU MUST ANSWER **FOUR** OF THE FOLLOWING SIX QUESTIONS.

(All questions carry 50 marks each)

Question 1. COMMUNITIES OF FAITH

A. a. Describe **two** examples of how religious commitment can be seen among the members of a community of faith in Ireland today.

(i) _____

_____

_____

_____

_____

(ii) _____

_____

_____

_____

_____

(12 marks)

b. Explain what inspires religious commitment among the members of a community of faith in Ireland today.

_____

_____

_____

_____

_____

_____

(12 marks)

B. a. BUDDHISM ☐   CHRISTIANITY ☐   HINDUISM ☐   ISLAM ☐   JUDAISM ☐

Tick ✓ **one** of the above world religions and describe an example of what the term 'revelation' refers to in the world religion that you have ticked.

_____

_____

_____

_____

_____

_____

_____

_____

(12 marks)

b. Outline **one** way that the understanding of revelation influences the religious practice of members in the world religion that you have ticked in *part B a.* above.

_____

_____

_____

_____

_____

_____

_____

_____

_____

_____

_____

_____

(14 marks)

Question 2. FOUNDATIONS OF RELIGION - CHRISTIANITY

A. a. According to the Gospels the name of **one** disciple of Jesus of Nazareth was:

_____

(5 marks)

b. Describe what happened in **one** incident from the life of Jesus when he called a person to become his disciple.

_____

_____

_____

_____

_____

_____

_____

_____

_____

_____

_____

(14 marks)

B. a. Outline **two** examples of the sacrifices that were involved for the first Christians in being disciples of Jesus.

(i) _____

_____

_____

_____

_____

_____

_____

_____

_____

(ii) _____

_____

_____

_____

_____

_____

_____

_____

_____

(16 marks)

b. Explain **one** challenge that Christians today face in being disciples of Jesus.

_____

_____

_____

_____

_____

_____

_____

_____

_____

_____

_____

_____

_____

(15 marks)

Question 3. FOUNDATIONS OF RELIGION - MAJOR WORLD RELIGIONS

A. Tick ✓ **one** of the world religions below that you have studied.

Buddhism ☐   Hinduism ☐   Islam ☐   Judaism ☐

a. Describe a religious ceremony that marks **one** of the following events in the life of a member of the world religion that you have ticked above:

● BIRTH   ● MARRIAGE   ● DEATH

_____ _____

(EVENT) _____

_____

_____

_____

_____

_____

_____

_____

(14 marks)

b. Compare what is involved in the religious ceremony that you have described above with the way in which the event is marked in **another** major world religion.

_____

_____

_____

_____

_____

_____

_____

_____

_____

_____

_____

_____

_____

_____

_____

_____

(18 marks)

B. Explain **two** reasons why the members of the world religion that you have ticked in *part A.* above perform a religious ceremony to mark *either* birth *or* marriage or death.

(i) _____

_____

_____

_____

_____

_____

_____

(ii) _____

_____

_____

_____

_____

_____

_____

(18 marks)

Question 4. THE QUESTION OF FAITH

A. a. ● CHILDHOOD FAITH ● MATURE FAITH

Describe the main characteristics of **one** of the above stages of faith.

_____   _____

(STAGE OF FAITH) _____

_____

_____

_____

_____

_____

_____

_____

_____

_____

_____

_____

(12 marks)

b. Examine the role that trust can play in the development of a person's faith.

_____

_____

_____

_____

_____

_____

_____

_____

_____

(12 marks)

B. a. *People can look at the question of faith from different points of view.*
   Describe what is involved in **each** of the following points of view:

   ● FUNDAMENTALISM   ● INDIVIDUALISM

   ● _____   _____

_____

_____

_____

_____

   ● _____   _____

_____

_____

_____

_____

(12 marks)

b. *People can express faith in different ways:*   ● MONOTHEISM   ● POLYTHEISM
   Outline an example of how **one** of the above can be seen in a major world religion that you have studied.e

_____

_____

_____

_____

_____

_____

_____

_____

_____

(14 marks)

Question 5. THE CELEBRATION OF FAITH

A. a. Read the list of prayers and the list of major world religions given below.

Match **one** prayer to the major world religion with which it is most associated.

Prayers	World Religions
The Apostles' Creed	Buddhism
The Paritta	Christianity
The Shahadah	Hinduism
The Shema	Islam
The Rig Veda	Judaism

Answer:

Prayer	World Religions

(5 marks)

b. Outline **two** difficulties with prayer that may be experienced by the members of a major world religion today.

(i) _____

_____

_____

_____

_____

(ii) _____

_____

_____

_____

_____

(12 marks)

B. a *In religious traditions certain individuals stand out as people of prayer.*

Tick ✓ **one** of the following major world religions and name a person associated with prayer in the religion that you have ticked.

Buddhism ☐   Christianity ☐   Hinduism ☐   Islam ☐   Judaism ☐

Person of prayer. _____

(5 marks)

b. Explain why prayer was important in the life of the person that you have named in *part B a.* above.

_____

_____

_____

_____

_____

_____

_____

_____

(12 marks)

c. Outline how the person that you have named in *part B a.* above has influenced the understanding of prayer among the members of his/her world religion today.

_____

_____

_____

_____

_____

_____

_____

_____

_____

_____

_____

_____

_____

_____

_____

_____

_____

(16 marks)

Question 6. THE MORAL CHALLENGE

A. a. For a religious person to behave morally involves _____

_____

(5 marks)

b. Explain **two** ways that a failure to behave morally can have consequences for the members of a major world religion.

(i) _____

_____

_____

_____

_____

_____

_____

_____

(ii) _____

_____

_____
_____
_____
_____
_____
_____
_____
_____
_____
_____

(20 marks)

B. a. Pluralism holds the view that all groups within a society have a right to carry out their
religious and cultural practices.   (Tick ✓ the correct box)

TRUE ❏   FALSE ❏

(5 marks)

b. Explain how **each** of the following could guide a person in deciding what is right or wrong in a situation:

● AUTHORITY   ● TRADITION

● _____   _____
_____
_____
_____
_____
_____
_____
_____
_____
_____

● _____   _____
_____
_____
_____
_____
_____
_____
_____
_____

(20 marks)

YOU SHOULD SPEND ABOUT 20 MINUTES ANSWERING QUESTIONS IN THIS SECTION.

YOU MUST ATTEMPT **ONE** OF THE FOLLOWING SIX QUESTIONS.

(All questions carry 70 marks each)

Question 1. Profile the way that **two** Christian denominations today are promoting respect for their own beliefs and the beliefs of others.

Question 2. ● POLITICAL LEADERS ● RELIGIOUS LEADERS

Assess the extent to which **each** of the above played a role in the events that led to the death of Jesus.

Question 3. ✦ Buddhism ✦ Hinduism ✦ Islam ✦ Judaism

Compare the religious practice of the earliest followers of **one** of the world religions listed above with the religious practice of its members today.

Question 4. Compare the pattern of religious belief in Europe with that found in another part of the world today.

Question 5. ✦ Buddhism ✦ Christianity ✦ Hinduism ✦ Islam ✦ Judaism

Analyse the nature and function of **two** different types of prayer for the members of a world religion listed above.

Question 6. Examine what is involved in **two** stages in the development of a person's conscience and discuss the role each stage plays in his/her growth to moral maturity.

PLEASE MAKE SURE YOU GIVE THE NUMBER OF THE QUESTION YOU ARE ANSWERING
IN THE SPACE BELOW.

Section 5. Question _____

(70 marks)

BLANK PAGE

The Journal - *an Overview*

> **An important aim of journal work is to encounter religion as a living reality in one's own community.**

❖ The Religious Education Journal:

- Is part of the Junior Certificate examination at Higher and Ordinary level.

- Is worth 100 marks: 20% of the total marks for the exam.

- Is an account of the work you have done on **one** official journal title.

- Is undertaken by you and a class group under the guidance of a teacher.

❖ Each student must fill out an **official journal** booklet.
It will be sent to the Department of Education on your behalf.

❖ It may be helpful to fill out a **draft journal** before writing up the official journal.
You will find a draft copy of the Journal Booklet beginning on page 309.

> **The Journal - is divided into five sections.**
>   **- you must complete each section.**

Section 1 - *Introduction* (12 marks)

This section is about the title of your journal work, and what you hope to achieve.

There are five separate tasks as follows:

1. Tick (✓) the box

Did you do the journal work:
- On your own? ❏
- Or as part of a group? ❏

2. Write down the **official** title of the journal work.

Your answer will begin like this:
The title I chose for journal work is ….

3. Write a **personal** title for the journal.

TIP - Make up a title for the journal in your own words. Use plain language.

- This title must be clearly linked to the official title.

Your answer will begin like this:
The personal title of my journal work is…

4. State why you chose this topic for your journal work.

TIP - How is this topic relevant to you?

- Give at least three reasons why the topic is of personal interest and relevance to you.

Your answer will begin like this:
I chose this title because…

5. State what you hoped to learn by doing journal work on this topic.

TIP - Be specific. List three or four things you wanted to find out.

- Make sure all your points link back to the title.

Your answer will begin like this:
By doing journal work on this title I hoped to…

Section 2 - *Getting Started* (12 marks)

This section is about the preparations you made before you began your journal work.

Now that you had chosen a topic for your journal, what did you intend to do in order to find out more about it?

❖ What sources of information could you use?

❑ research material on the internet.

❑ consult library books and published articles.

❑ conduct a survey.

❑ arrange to interview a particular person or persons.

❑ visit a place relevant to the title and complete a worksheet on it.

❑ invite guest speakers to the class.

❑ watch a relevant film clip or a documentary and discuss it afterwards.

TIP - Select at least **three** options from the suggestions above.

❖ Write a detailed description of what you planned to do.

TIP - State what sources of information you were going to use.

- Explain why each one was selected.

- Show a clear link between the journal title and each thing you planned to do.

Your answer for this section can begin like this:
To prepare for doing my journal work I…

Section 3 - *Work* (24 marks)

This section is about describing the actual work carried out by you and the group.

It involves three separate tasks as follows:

1. Mention the activities that were planned in Section 2, and whether they actually happened.

TIP - Say what the group did.

- Give a detailed description of everything that **you** did.

- If you used books or websites, note each title or address and the kind of information found there.

- Make sure you link all your comments back to the title.

Your answer can begin like this:
To do my journal work I…

2. Pick at least **one** activity from all the work you have done.
Explain why you decided to include this particular activity in your journal work.

TIP - Say why it was good to do this instead of doing something else.

Your answer can begin like this:
I included this in my journal work because…

3. Your **reaction** to the work you did on the title.

TIP - Write your thoughts on what you learned about the topic.
No need to describe how you gathered this information.

- What did you find out that was interesting?
Elaborate on two or three things.

- Were you disappointed about anything you discovered?
If so, explain what you mean by this.

- Mention the reaction of the group. Is their response the same as yours, or different?

Your answer can begin like this:
My reaction to doing this work was…

Section 4 - *Discoveries* (42 marks)

This section is about what you learned from doing your journal work.

NOTE: Most marks are awarded to this section.

The answer is in three parts: - learning.
- skills.
- links.

1. Learning

a. What have you learned since you started work on this title?

   TIP - Identify three or four new points of information that you have acquired.

   - Explain each point in detail.

   Your answer can begin like this:
   I learned…

b. How did working on this topic affect you personally?

   TIP - Have your opinions or attitudes changed in any way?

   - Do you have a different opinion or attitude about this topic now?

   - In your answer use phrases such as:
      ▼ From now on I will…
      ▼ I will be more aware of…
      ▼ I will be more open to…
      ▼ I will no longer…
      ▼ I will appreciate…

   Your answer can begin like this:
   As a result of what I have learned I will…

2. Skills

a. What skills have you used in your journal work? Tick **two** (✓).

The skills listed are:

❏ Enquiry skills — asking questions seeking information about people, organisations, issues.

❏ Observational skills — noticing or observing someone or something, and carefully recording what you have seen.

❏ Problem solving skills — being able to find a solution to problems that might arise.

❏ Research skills — finding out new facts, analysing the facts and then using the information.

❏ Reflective skills — thinking about what you have observed and found out.

❏ Organisational skills — planning and carrying out all aspects of the work and completing it on time.

❏ Evaluation skills — judging how much was learned through the observations and findings of your journal work.

b. Write the name of the two skills selected.

TIP - Explain in detail how each skill was used.

Your answers can begin like this:

i. I used _____ skills
when I………………
ii. I used _____ skills
when I………………

3. Links

What links can you see between your journal work and other parts of the Religious Education course that you have studied?

Is there a link between your work and something in:

- Section A - Communities of Faith.
- Section B - Foundations of Religion: Christianity.
- Section C - Foundations of Religion: Major World Religions.
- Section D - The Question of Faith.
- Section E - The Celebration of Faith.
- Section F - The Moral Challenge.

TIP - Clearly identify two links.

- Explain the connection between your journal work and the sections of the course you identified.

Your answers can begin like this:

i. My journal work reminded me of studying…   because…
ii. My journal work reminded me of studying…   because…

306

Section 5 - *Looking back* (10 marks)

This section is about being able to reflect on the experience of doing journal work.

Reflecting

When you look back on your journal work try to answer the following questions.

a. What went well?

   TIP - Comment on your strengths and the use of particular skills.

   - Identify the best or the most interesting part of the work, and explain why it is so.

b. What would you do differently if you were to do it all again?

   TIP - Comment on what didn't go according to plan.

   - What changes would you make if you were to attempt the title again.

c. If another student was about to start work on the same title, and wanted some advice, what would you say to him or her?

   TIP - Make at least two recommendations on the basis of your own insight and experience.

Your answer for this section can begin like this:

Looking back at my experience of doing journal work on this title…

Coimisiún na Scrúduithe Stáit

JUNIOR CERTIFICATE EXAMINATION

Religious Education Journal Booklet

Total Marks: 100

General Directions for Candidates

1. Write your EXAMINATION NUMBER in this box:

2. WRITE ALL ANSWERS IN THIS BOOKLET

3. YOU MUST ATTEMPT ALL 5 SECTIONS IN THIS BOOKLET.

For the Superintendent only

Centre Stamp

Please indicate the level at which the candidate took the examination.

Please tick ✓ the correct box.

Ordinary level ❑   Higher level ❑

For the Examiner only

Note: Transfer Mark for Journal to grid of examination answer booklet.

Question	Mark
SECTION 1	
SECTION 2	
SECTION 3	
SECTION 4	
SECTION 5	
Mark for Journal	

SECTION 1
INTRODUCTION

GROUP / INDIVIDUAL

Did you do journal work on your own or as part of a group? (Tick ✓ the correct answer)

Journal work on my own ❏   *Journal work as part of a group* ❏

TITLE

The title I chose for the journal work is... _____

_____

The personal title of my journal work is... _____

_____

(2 marks)

I chose this title because... _____

_____

_____

_____

_____

(4 marks)

BEGINNING

What did you
hope to achieve
by doing journal
work on this title?

By doing journal work on this title I hoped to... _____

_____

_____

_____

_____

_____

_____

_____

_____

_____

_____

_____

(6 marks)

SECTION 2
GETTING STARTED

PREPARING

Consider for example:

What problems did you face in planning to do journal work on this title?

What assignments did you plan to carry out?

What research did you plan to conduct?

What people did you plan to contact/ interview?

What arrangements/ plans did you make for visits or events?

Etc.

To prepare for doing my journal work I ... _____

_____

_____

_____

_____

_____

_____

_____

_____

_____

_____

_____

_____

_____

_____

_____

_____

_____

_____

_____

_____

_____

_____

_____

(12 marks)

SECTION 3
WORK

DESCRIBING

What work did you actually do to complete your journal on this title?

If you did your journal work as part of a group, remember to also outline the work done by the rest of the group.

What assignments were completed, events attended or activities organised, as part of your journal work?

To do my journal work I ... _____

_____

_____

_____

_____

_____

_____

_____

_____

_____

_____

_____

_____

_____

_____

_____

_____

_____

_____

_____

_____

_____

_____

(12 marks)

SECTION 3

WORK *(continued)*

Why were these assignments/ events/ activities included as part of your journal work?

I included this in my journal work because ... _____

_____

_____

_____

_____

_____

_____

_____

(6 marks)

YOUR REACTION

What was your first reaction to these assignments/ events/ activities?

My reaction to doing this work was ... _____

_____

_____

What part did you find most interesting? Why?

_____

_____

What part did you find hardest? Why?

_____

_____

If you were working as part of a group what was your group's first reaction to these assignments/ events/ activities?

_____

_____

_____

How was this similar to or different from your own reaction?

_____

_____

Etc.

_____

_____

(6 marks)

SECTION 4
DISCOVERIES

LEARNING

What did you learn from working on this title for your journal?

I learned ... _____

_____

_____

_____

_____

_____

_____

_____

_____

_____

_____

(10 marks)

How have you been affected by doing journal work on this title?

Do you have a different attitude?

Do you have a different opinion?

Etc.

As a result of what I have learned I will ... _____

_____

_____

_____

_____

_____

_____

_____

_____

_____

(10 marks)

SECTION 4
DISCOVERIES *(continued)*

SKILLS

Tick ✓ **two** of the following skills used in your journal work and explain how you used these skills.

Enquiry skills ❑   Observational skills ❑   Problem-solving skills ❑   Research skills ❑

Reflective skills ❑   Organisational skills ❑   Evaluation skills ❑

i. *I used* _____ *skills*

   when I ... _____

   _____

   _____

   _____

   _____

   _____

   _____

   _____

                                                                   (5marks)

ii. *I used* _____ *skills*

   when I ... _____

   _____

   _____

   _____

   _____

   _____

   _____

   _____

                                                                   (5 marks)

LINKING

What topics/ themes studied in your Religious Education course over the last three years relate to what you discovered in journal work?

i. My journal work reminded me of studying ... _____

_____

_____

*because ...*_____

_____

_____

_____

_____

_____

_____

_____

_____

(6 marks)

ii. My journal work reminded me of studying ... _____

_____

_____

*because ...*_____

_____

_____

_____

_____

_____

_____

_____

(6 marks)

SECTION 5
LOOKING BACK

REFLECTING

What do you think went well in your journal work?

If you were starting again, would you do journal work on this title differently?

Imagine someone in your school is starting out on journal work and has chosen the same title as you.

What advice would you give?

Etc.

Looking back at my experience of doing journal work on this title ... _____

_____

_____

_____

_____

_____

_____

_____

_____

_____

_____

_____

_____

_____

_____

_____

_____

_____

_____

_____

_____

(10 marks)